THE RULER WHO SERVES

Also by Ray C. Stedman

Adventuring Through the Bible
Authentic Christianity
Body Life
God's Final Word
God's Loving Word
Is This All There Is to Life?
Our Riches in Christ
Spiritual Warfare
Talking with My Father
Waiting for the Second Coming

Discovery House Publishers

Books, music, and videos that feed the soul with the Word of God

Box 3566 Grand Rapids, MI 49501

THE
RULER
WHO SERVES

RAY STEDMAN

EDITED BY JAMES DENNEY

The Ruler Who Serves
© 2002 by Elaine Stedman

Discovery House Publishers is affiliated with RBC Ministries, Grand
Rapids, Michigan 49512.

Discovery House books are distributed to the trade exclusively by
Barbour Publishing, Inc., Uhrichsville, Ohio 44683.

Book Design: Sherri L. Hoffman

Unless otherwise indicated, Scripture references are from the New
International Version, © 1973, 1978, 1984 by International Bible
Society. Used by permission.

Library of Congress Cataloging-in-Publication Data

Stedman, Ray C.
    [Ruler who serves]
    The ruler who serves : exploring the gospel of Mark / by Ray C. Sted-
man.
        p. cm.
    Originally published: The ruler who serves. Waco, Tex.: Word
Books, c1976.
        ISBN 1-57293-073-X
    1. Bible. N.T. Mark VIII-XVI—Commentaries. I. Title.

BS2585.3 .S74 2002
226.3'07—dc21
                                                        2001053896

Printed in the United States of America
03 04 05 06 07 08 09 /DP/ 9 8 7 6 5 4 3 2

Contents

Foreword

An author I read many years ago drew a distinction between those who manufacture servanthood and those who distribute it.

"Manufacturers" derive their motivation to serve from within themselves. They serve because they pity the needy or because they believe they have a duty to give something back to the world (noblesse oblige). Some have a compulsive need to be needed; others serve out of guilt and fear. In any case, "manufacturers" soon find their efforts dreary and empty, and they lose interest; for, as Ray Stedman continues to remind us, "the flesh [human endeavor] counts for nothing" (John 6:63).

"Distributors," on the other hand, serve out of an intimate connection to Jesus. They sit at His feet, listen to His words, learn from His great heart, respond to Him in prayer, drink in His love, draw on His power, and distribute His compassion to others. That's what keeps Jesus' servants going for the long haul. They give away all that He has given to them, a concept Ray weaves through the warp and woof of these studies.

It was my privilege to gather weekly with staff members at Peninsula Bible Church when Ray was first thinking his way through the gospel of Mark in preparation for preaching this material, and then I heard each text taught on subsequent Sundays. More importantly, I saw the texts lived out in Ray's life, for he was truly a leader who served over the long haul. He was my friend and teacher for many years, and I sorely miss him. But like Abel, though now in God's presence, he "still speaks."

David Roper
Boise, Idaho

fifteen

The Way of the Cross

➤ **Mark 8:34–38**

Some years ago, a Christian businessman and friend of mine, Howard Butt, wrote an article entitled "The Art of Being a Big Shot." One statement he made particularly impressed me as a powerful truth about the Christian life:

It is my pride that makes me independent of God. It's appealing to me to feel that I am the master of my fate, that I run my own life, call my own shots, go it alone. But, that feeling is my basic dishonesty. I can't go it alone. I have to get help from other people, and I can't ultimately rely on myself. I'm dependent on God for my very next breath. It is dishonest of me to pretend that I'm anything but a man—small, weak, and limited. So, living independent of God is self-delusion. It is not just a matter of pride being an unfortunate little trait, and humility being an attractive little virtue; it's my inner psychological integrity that's at stake. When I am conceited, I am lying to myself about what I am. I am pretending to be God, and not man. My pride is the

9

idolatrous worship of myself. And that is the national
religion of hell!

That is a profound restatement of what I call the way of the
cross. It is an eloquent interpretation of what Jesus means when
He says, "If anyone would come after me, he must deny himself
and take up his cross and follow me." To follow the way of the
cross means to give up all rights to run our lives, to submit ourselves to His leadership and His lordship.

To take the way of the cross is to follow in the footsteps of
Jesus, for He was the first to walk that path. In this study, we will
watch Him as He turns His footsteps toward that bloody instrument of terror and torture, and we will discover what it means to
take up one's cross and follow Him.

Turning His Steps Toward the Cross

We now enter the second half of Mark's gospel. In the first half,
we watched as Jesus, the Servant, came healing the sick, helping
the hurting, comforting the brokenhearted, restoring shattered
lives. His power and authority could be glimpsed as undercur-
rents of His ministry, but for the most part that power and authority remained cloaked by His role as a servant.

Now, however, the disciples know who Jesus is. This Servant
is none other than the Christ, the Anointed One of God. He is the
Servant who rules in all the far-flung creation of God.

And yet, no sooner have the disciples discovered who Jesus
is than He begins to predict His suffering and death. This startling
revelation of the approaching death of the Christ is disturbing for
these disciples. They greet it with denial.

But this revelation represents the turning point in the gospel
of Mark. From this point, Jesus is on His way to Jerusalem, trudg-

ing inexorably into the darkness of Gethsemane's garden, then toward the judgment hall of Pilate, then to the intolerable torture of the bloody whipping post, and finally to the grisly cross. Yet, all along the way, we see that He is still ministering to people, still healing, still comforting, and still bringing blessing to needy men and women.

His role has been transformed. From this point on, we see Him not as the Servant who rules but as the Ruler who serves.

Let's look at an outline of the second half of Mark's gospel. This second half falls into two major divisions. From Mark 8:34 through the end of Mark 13, we have the section I call "The Way of the Cross." This section deals with our Lord's preparation of His disciples for the terrible events that await Him in Jerusalem. Mark 14–16 make up the section I call "The Cross and the Empty Tomb," the events of the crucifixion and resurrection of Jesus.

In the first division, "The Way of the Cross," there are also two subdivisions. In the first our Lord prepares the disciples at Caesarea and at Capernaum and proceeds down the Jordan River valley. In the second we read about the events at Jericho, on the Mount of Olives, and in Jerusalem. In this study, we will look only at that portion of His preparation of the disciples that took place at Caesarea Philippi in the north of Galilee at the foot of Mount Hermon.

As we begin this first division of the second half of Mark's gospel, we must recall the context of events. Jesus has just announced the cross to His disciples. In response, Peter rebukes Jesus, for which Jesus rebukes Peter. At this point Mark records Jesus' next words:

> *Then he called the crowd to him along with his disciples and said: "If anyone would come after me, he must deny himself and take up his cross and follow me."* (MARK 8:34)

Here Jesus tells us what it means to be a disciple. Notice that Jesus does something that raises questions in people's minds. He calls together not only His disciples but also the crowd. Some commentators have wondered what this means. Was Jesus seeking to make disciples? That is, was He evangelizing the crowd? Or was He primarily addressing His disciples and telling them what the cost of discipleship would be?

Many people read this passage and wonder, "Can I be a Christian and not be a disciple? Is discipleship the same as being a Christian, or is it a second and much more intense stage of Christianity? Are there many Christians but only relatively few disciples?" These are important questions. In this study, we will go to the Lord's words for the answers.

The Three Steps of Discipleship

As we look at Mark 8:34, the first thing we learn about Christian discipleship is that it is a three-step process. In the first step, "If anyone would come after me, he must deny himself." Notice that Jesus does not say, "He must hate himself." Jesus does not ask us to despise ourselves or destroy ourselves or neglect our basic needs. The word "deny" has a specific meaning, which we need to understand in order to grasp this first step of discipleship.

To deny means to "disavow a person or thing; to state that one has no connection whatsoever with someone or something." Interestingly, this is the very word used to refer to Peter's denial of Jesus a little later on in Mark's gospel. As Peter was standing in the courtyard of the high priest, warming himself at a fire, a servant girl said to Peter, "You also were with that Nazarene, Jesus." Mark records, "But he denied it." When the servant girl again accused him, Mark records, "Again he denied it." Later

Peter again denies knowing Christ, sealing his denial with a curse on himself (see Mark 14:66–72).

It is important to understand that Jesus does not mean what we usually mean by the term "self-denial." By this we usually mean that we are giving up something. One example of self-denial is when people give up something they enjoy, such as eating meat or sweets or watching television, during the season of Lent. But Jesus is not talking about self-denial in this sense. He is never concerned so much about what we do as about who we are. To deny oneself in the sense that Jesus means is a different concept.

Denying self means that we repudiate our natural feelings about ourselves, our ownership of ourselves, and even our right to run our lives. We abdicate the right to decide what we are going to do or where we are going to go. At this point, Jesus is saying something fundamental and even shocking. It strikes at the heart of our existence, because the one thing that we, as human beings, value and defend above all else is our right to make our own decisions. We demand to be the captains of our fate, and we will fight to the death any outside attempt to overrule our wills.

Now, perhaps, it becomes clear that Jesus is not asking us to give up this habit or that privilege. He is demanding that we give up our selves. A statement from the New Testament sums up the first step of discipleship, and it is so profound a statement that it is carved on the wall of the sanctuary at Peninsula Bible Church: "You are not your own; you were bought at a price" (1 Corinthians 6:19–20). If you are going to follow Jesus, you no longer own yourself. You give up all rights to yourself, and you yield those rights to Jesus. That is why we call Him Lord. A lord is a sovereign king, whose merest word is absolute law.

If Jesus is the Lord of your life, you are no longer the lord over your self. Jesus has all rights. You have none. You willingly surrendered those rights when you chose to follow Christ and walk the way of the cross. "If anyone would come after me," said Jesus, "he must deny himself." That is the first step of discipleship.

The second step immediately follows: "and take up his cross." What does "take up his cross" mean? I am sure that those words were almost incomprehensible to the disciples when Jesus first spoke them. They didn't understand why Jesus was talking about the cross, that instrument of Roman execution. They did not understand where Jesus was heading. But He knew. And He knew that after the awful events that were to come in Jerusalem, after the torture and anguish of the cross was answered by the joy and glory of resurrection, the disciples would remember those words. And they would understand.

Many people think that a cross is any kind of trial or hardship we have to endure: a harsh and despotic boss at the office, a spiteful mother-in-law, a disagreeable neighbor, a cantankerous car that refuses to start on cold mornings. "Well," we say, "I guess that's just my cross to bear." But that is not what Jesus means. In fact, such a view trivializes what the cross means. Jesus had obstacles, trials, setbacks, and opposition, but He had only one cross. That cross represented much more than mere problems or annoyances. The cross stood for shame, humiliation, torture, and death.

So what does it mean for us to take up our cross? It means that if any shame, pain, humiliation, or even death comes our way for the sake of following Christ, then we are to welcome it. Whatever happens to us for the sake of the gospel, we are to accept it, glory in it, and cling to it, because that is our cross. God will give us the grace to endure it. He will use that terrible circumstance in our lives to make us more like Christ, and the ultimate result will be resurrection and glory, just as the cross led to resurrection and glory in the life of Jesus. That is why the cross is so valuable to us.

Now, perhaps, you begin to see what a radical approach to life this is, and how different it is from the way the world tells us we should think and act. The world says, "If pain comes your way, escape it, avoid it, numb it with alcohol or drugs. If someone hurts you, get even. If someone humiliates you, strike back. Stand up for your rights. Assert yourself. Look out for number one." But the message of Jesus is, "Take up your cross." That is the second step of discipleship.

The third step is "follow me." What does it mean to follow Jesus? Quite simply, it means to obey Him. Before we were Christians, our lives were characterized by disobedience; it is only logical that our lives as Christians must move in the opposite direction, toward complete obedience to Christ.

I have been saddened and amazed, over the years, at the number of people I have met who call themselves Christians yet blatantly, even proudly, declare that they do not follow or obey Him. We all struggle in the area of obedience. I fail in this area on a continuing basis; this is the struggle we all contend with in our fallen humanity. But the Lord is not saying He expects perfection of His disciples. He is telling us what discipleship means, what it involves—and discipleship involves following Him. It means that we commit ourselves to carrying out His commands and looking to Him as our example and source of strength. When we fail, we repent and recommit ourselves to a new resolve to follow in obedience.

We see how obedience works in the lives of the Twelve. Jesus entrusted them with much of His ministry, and they obeyed Him. For example, when Jesus fed the multitudes, He gave them the bread and fish to distribute to the people, and in obedience, they did so. But the disciples could not supply the food. That was for Jesus to do. God supplies the resources, and disciples (like you and me) supply the willingness and obedience. That is what Christianity is all about.

What has Jesus commanded us to do? What commands are we to obey? He has told us to love one another (John 13:34–35), to love even our enemies (Matthew 5:44), to pray for those who hurt us (Matthew 5:44), to forgive those who offend us (Matthew 6:14–15), to show kindness even to the ungrateful and selfish (Luke 6:35), and to give as freely as we have received (Matthew 10:8). When we obey these commands of Christ, we are not only doing what He said, but also we are doing what He did, for Jesus exemplified all of these commands again and again in His life.

We won't always feel like showing love to the unloving and forgiveness to the unforgiving, but obedience is not about following our feelings; it is about following Christ. We are to obey even when obedience cuts across the grain of our feelings. Obeying Christ is not a natural thing to do; it is a supernatural act. "Follow me" means we live in obedience to these commands of Christ and to all the other exhortations found in Scripture. Jesus said, "Follow me." That is the third step of discipleship.

In the Greek, these three steps are stated in the present, continuous tense. That means, "Keep on denying yourself, keep on taking up your cross, keep on following me." This is not the decision of a moment but a program for a lifetime. These three steps, carried out simultaneously and continuously, present to us what it truly means to be a disciple or follower of Jesus Christ.

Jesus does not paint an attractive picture of discipleship, does He? His words surely struck the disciples and the crowd like a ton of falling bricks. In fact, John tells us that many who had followed

Christ suddenly turned away and followed Him no more, because these words seemed too harsh and demanding (John 6:66). Jesus never invites people to follow Him without first telling them what it will cost. He does not seek followers under false pretenses. He wants us to understand that true discipleship will shatter us, change us, and make us into a different kind of people. It must. If it has any meaning in our lives, following Christ is going to shake us to the core of our being.

Living by Losing: The Great Paradox of Discipleship
Next Jesus gives us the right motive for authentic Christian discipleship. As Mark records, Jesus says:

> *"Whoever wants to save his life will lose it, but whoever loses his life for me and for the gospel will save it."* (MARK 8:35)

That is motive enough! Who is not interested in saving his or her life? In other words, who is not interested in making life worthwhile, making it rich and complete and worth the living? We all want that. God designed us with that hunger for life. "If life is what you want," Jesus says, "I'll tell you how to acquire it."

Here is a paradox. The only way you can save your life, says Jesus, is by losing it. In this paradox, Jesus underscores that there are only two possible attitudes toward life, and they are mutually exclusive. Everyone, without exception, lives by one or the other.

The first attitude toward life is that of the world: save your life in the here and now! Take care of yourself first. Focus on fulfilling yourself, on satisfying yourself, on gratifying yourself. In every situation, your first concern is what's in it for me. That is the attitude of the world. And if you live by this attitude, you will ultimately lose your life and all that is of eternal importance.

The other attitude toward life is that of Jesus: think nothing of your life, your self, your wants, your desire for pleasure and comfort and security. Fling all of that away and move out in obedience to God, in utter dependence on God, entrusting your temporal and eternal future to Him.

This is the attitude expressed by Paul, who said, "I consider my life worth nothing to me, if only I may finish the race and complete the task the Lord Jesus has given me" (Acts 20:24). This is to be a way of life, Jesus says. Trust God, obey Him, and put the responsibility for what happens on His infinitely broad shoulders. That is the life of a true disciple and follower of Jesus Christ.

There are only two attitudes toward life, and each attitude produces its own distinct and different result. If you choose to focus on clutching your life in the here and now, you will ultimately lose your life. That is not a mere platitude; Jesus is stating a fundamental, unbreakable law of life. Those who focus on saving and gratifying the self will end up with nothing but a handful of cobwebs and ashes. We see this tragic principle at work in the dying words of some of the most famous people in history.

As he was dying, the French philosopher Voltaire said to his physician, Dr. Fochin, "I will give you half of what I am worth if you will give me six months of life." The doctor replied that it could not be done. "Then I shall die," Voltaire moaned, "and go to hell!"

Thomas Hobbes, the seventeenth-century philosopher and skeptic, lay on his deathbed, pondering the loss of his soul. "If I had the whole world at my disposal," he said, "I would give it to live one day. I am about to take a leap into the dark."

Honoré Gabriel Mirabeau, the French revolutionary and unbeliever, asked his doctor for an opiate as he lay dying in 1791. "Give me laudanum," he begged, "that I may not think of eternity."

"Nothing matters. Nothing matters," were the last words of film producer Louis B. Mayer, who died in 1957.

"I must end it. There's no hope left," read the suicide note of comedian Freddie Prinze, who shot himself while at the height of his fame and success in 1977.

But compare those words of loss, hopelessness, and despair with the dying words of Christians.

"I die hard but am not afraid to go," said George Washington, the first American president and a man of deep Christian faith, who died in 1799.

"See in what peace a Christian can die" was the final statement of writer Joseph Addison, who died in 1719.

John Hus, the great Reformer, calmly prayed as he was bound to a stake to be burned alive: "Father, into thy hands I commit my spirit."

Evangelist Dwight L. Moody's dying words were "Earth is receding, heaven is opening, and this is my coronation day."

David Brainerd, missionary to American Indians, lay dying of tuberculosis in 1747. "I am going into eternity," he said, "and it is sweet to me to think of eternity."

Augustus Toplady, theologian and composer of the hymn "Rock of Ages," died of tuberculosis in 1778, when he was thirty-eight years old. Moments before his death, he said, "I enjoy heaven already in my soul."

Adoniram Judson, the great American hymn writer and missionary to India and Burma, fell sick and died during an ocean voyage. Before his death, he said, "I go with the gladness of a boy bounding away from school. I feel so strong in Christ."

And another American missionary, Jim Elliot, wrote these words in his diary at the age of twenty-two: "He is no fool who gives what he cannot keep to gain what he cannot lose." A few years later, he was killed by South American Indians as he tried to take the gospel to them.

Jesus did not come to call us to a lifetime of misery, barrenness, darkness, and death. He called us to life, to richness, to enjoyment, to fulfillment. But He has told us that the path to all of these wonderful things leads through the cross. True Christian discipleship leads us to eternal life and fulfillment beyond anything we can imagine, but the only way we can find that infinite quality of life is by means of the cross.

That is the great and wonderful paradox of the Christian life.

True Discipleship: Deeds, Not Words

The final issue is set forth in our Lord's words in the closing verses of Mark 8:

> *"What good is it for a man to gain the whole world, yet forfeit his soul? Or what can a man give in exchange for his soul?"* (MARK 8:36–37)

These questions of Jesus are the most searching, penetrating questions of all. They pierce to the core of our humanity. What good is it to get all the things you want, only to lose your life and soul in the process? Is it not the essence of wisdom, if you are going to invest your time and energy in something, to make sure you will be able to enjoy the fruit of that investment? You can spend all you have on pleasure and possessions, but once your life is gone, what do you have left to barter with?

Many years ago, archaeologists discovered the tomb of Charlemagne, emperor of France (742–814). During his lifetime, Charlemagne's goal had been to Christianize all of Europe. When his tomb was opened, the men who entered it found something amazing. The tomb was filled with treasures, and in the center of one large vault the men found a throne. Seated on the throne were the skeletal remains of Charlemagne. A Bible lay open on the lap of the skeleton, a bony finger pointing at the words of Jesus, "What good is it for a man to gain the whole world, yet forfeit his soul? Or what can a man give in exchange for his soul?" What a tremendous lesson for us from history!

There is no way we can cheat or fake the life of discipleship. Either we are genuine disciples, or we will lose everything in the final analysis. Jesus says:

> *"If anyone is ashamed of me and my words in this adulterous and sinful generation, the Son of Man will be ashamed of him when he comes in his Father's glory with the holy angels."* (Mark 8:38)

Deeds, not words, will tell the story. It is not what we say we believe that matters. It is how we show our belief by the way we live. A true disciple boldly acknowledges Jesus as Lord by the way he or she lives on a daily basis.

I once heard of a boy who was concerned about being teased by his classmates for being a Christian. He devised a way of praying over his lunch in the cafeteria without anyone knowing he was praying: he would bend over and pretend to be tying his shoe. Is that what Jesus means when He says, "If anyone is ashamed of me, I will be ashamed of him"? Yes, in a way, but I think little incidents like this are only peripheral to what our Lord is talking about. There are much bigger ways in which we show ourselves to be ashamed of Christ.

Most of us are nervous about making an open profession of faith in Christ. We wonder what people will think of us or how they will respond to us. We worry about appearing to be religious fanatics. But being nervous about witnessing is not sin; it is merely temptation. What our Lord is talking about here is a continuous, habitual way of life that outwardly calls itself Christian but inwardly adopts the values of the world. This, Jesus says, is what will be revealed in the Day of Judgment. At the close of the Sermon on the Mount, Jesus said:

> *"Many will say to me on that day, 'Lord, Lord, did we not prophesy in your name, and in your name drive out demons and perform many miracles?' Then I will tell them plainly, 'I never knew you. Away from me, you evildoers!' "*
> (MATTHEW 7:22–23)

Here, then, is the answer to the question we asked at the beginning: Can I be a Christian and not be a disciple? You can come to Christ, and all who come to Christ are given life, if they come to Christ in honesty and sincerity. But unless you take up the work of discipleship, this life is given in vain. Paul calls this "[receiving] God's grace in vain" (see 2 Corinthians 6:1). Only true disciples enter into the abundant life.

We are not all good disciples at all times. We are fallen human beings, and we will fail. But our Lord has made provision for failure in our lives. The test of true disciples is not whether or not they occasionally fail but whether or not the aim of their lives is to take up their cross and follow Christ. If that is truly the aim of your life, regardless of your occasional failures, then you are a disciple of Jesus Christ, and He is your Lord.

In *Mere Christianity,* C. S. Lewis suggests that we in the Christian church are a kind of invasion force, secretly and stealthily moving into an "enemy-occupied world," and the enemy, of course, is the devil. We are, Lewis says, "a sort of secret society to undermine the devil." Then he poses the question that many people ask: Why does God use a secret society in His war against the devil? Why doesn't He land in force and toss the devil out on his ear? We can't know for sure, says Lewis, but we can guess. God wants to give us the chance of freely, willingly joining His side, of becoming His disciples. We must choose to deny ourselves, take up our crosses, and follow Him—and we must choose now. Tomorrow may be too late. Lewis explains why:

> God is going to invade, all right. But what is the good of saying you are on His side then, when you see the whole natural universe melting away like a dream, and something else—something it never entered your head to conceive—comes crashing in; something so beautiful to some of us, and so terrible to others, that none of us will have any choice left? . . . It will be too late then to choose your side. There is no use saying you choose to lie down when it has become impossible to stand up. That will not be the time for choosing; it will be the time when we discover which side we have really chosen, whether we realised it before or not. Now, today, this moment, is our chance to choose the right side. God is holding back, to give us that chance. It will not last forever. We must take it or leave it.[1]

This is the same message Jesus gave to the people of His day. Becoming a Christian is not easy. It is radical. It demands nothing less of us than that we deny ourselves, take up our cross, and follow Jesus.

The way of the cross is a hard way, a narrow way. But it is the only pathway to life.

sixteen

Glory on the Mountaintop

➤ **Mark 8:38–9:29**

It was the last and most ambitious of all of the works of the great High Renaissance painter Raphael. It is called *The Transfiguration.*

Commissioned in 1517 by Cardinal Giulio de Medici for the Cathedral of Narbonne in France, *The Transfiguration* now hangs in the Vatican. The painting is divided into an upper level and a lower level. Dominating the upper half is a depiction of Jesus floating above the Mount of Transfiguration in an aura of brilliant clouds, accompanied on either side by Moses and Elijah. On the ground at His feet are Peter, James, and John, all shielding their faces from the Lord's brilliance.

The lower half of the painting presents the foreground of the scene. The other disciples at the foot of the mountain point upward, directing our attention to the transfigured Christ. To the right of the disciples, a demonized boy writhes, wide-eyed and contorted, waiting for the Lord to descend from the mountain and release him from his spiritual torment. The boy is held by his distraught father. The mother kneels nearby, begging for help from the disciples. It is the perfect juxtaposition of the people's misery and the Lord's majesty, of the Mount of Transfiguration rising above the valley of human despair.

Raphael died before he could put the final touches on *The Transfiguration*. The painting is technically unfinished, yet it seems perfect and complete. The last detail Raphael completed before his death was the face of Jesus. The features are serene yet strong, bold, masculine, and unforgettable. Raphael seems to have summoned every ounce of his creative strength to paint that memorable face.

And yet, for all its magnificent color and light, its powerful composition, and its emotional force, we know that Raphael's *The Transfiguration* is a pale and inadequate representation of this dramatic historical event. No artist could ever capture the blinding brilliance of the light that poured forth from the Mount of Transfiguration. No image summoned from a human mind could adequately express the awe and amazement that Peter, James, and John experienced in the presence of the transfigured Christ.

A painting like Raphael's, as beautiful as it is, presents a problem. The problem is that it takes an event from history and enshrines it in pigment and canvas, giving it the appearance of a scene out of mythology or folklore. It is important that we remember that the transfiguration of Jesus was a real, historic event that occurred atop a mountain in the land of Palestine some two thousand years ago. Although Raphael's painting conveys an ethereal, almost fantasylike quality, I hope we will begin to see this historical event with a tangible, three-dimensional realism.

So let's climb that mountain along with Jesus, Peter, James, and John. Let's look at this event through their eyes. Together, let's rediscover the meaning, the reality, and the wonder of the transfiguration of our Lord Jesus Christ.

Jesus Predicts His Transfiguration

The Transfiguration is one of the most dramatic events in Scripture, ranking only after the crucifixion and resurrection of our Lord. This event follows His announcement of the cross and of the way of discipleship. It is clear from Mark's account that Jesus knew the Transfiguration was approaching. He announced it at least six full days before it took place. Jesus had led the Twelve to the foot of Mount Hermon so they could prepare for this event, and I believe that the Transfiguration occurred on Mount Hermon, that beautiful snow-covered mountain north of the Sea of Galilee.

The account begins in the closing verse of Mark 8 and continues through the first thirteen verses in Mark 9. The chapter and verse divisions in Scripture, remember, were added long after the Bible was written and should not be considered inspired by God. As often happens throughout Scripture, these divisions in the gospel story serve to interrupt rather than enhance and organize the storyline.

As we begin reading, we are immediately struck by the fact that the Lord explains the reason for the Transfiguration before it ever happens. Mark records:

> *He said to them, "I tell you the truth, some who are standing here will not taste death before they see the kingdom of God come with power."* (MARK 9:1)

Some liberal commentators have misunderstood this passage. They claim that Jesus was predicting the time of His second coming, saying that He expected His return to occur within the lifetime of people who were alive at that moment. Obviously this has not taken place, and many people have been troubled by this interpretation. Some have even gone so far as to say that Jesus was mistaken as to the time of His return.

But if you link this statement with what immediately follows, Jesus' meaning becomes clear. He is referring to the Transfiguration, saying that some who were there at that moment would not taste death until they saw this manifestation of the kingdom of God and the glory of His coming. This then provides a clue as to what the event meant. It is a preview that Jesus gives of the coming glory. He states that it will manifest His coming into His kingdom with power. On subsequent occasions, as He is teaching the disciples on the Mount of Olives and other places, He speaks of that coming with power: "At that time the sign of the Son of Man will appear in the sky, and all the nations of the earth will mourn. They will see the Son of Man coming on the clouds of the sky, with power and great glory" (Matthew 24:30).

Notice that Jesus has just referred to His triumphant return at the close of Mark 8:

> *"If anyone is ashamed of me and my words in this adulterous and sinful generation, the Son of Man will be ashamed of him when he comes in his Father's glory with the holy angels."* (MARK 8:38)

That is the future event that three of the Twelve are allowed to preview. The fact that this is the case is made clear by Peter. Our Lord chose Peter and James and John to be with Him on the mountaintop. Peter later refers to this event in one of his New Testament letters:

> *We did not follow cleverly invented stories when we told you about the power and coming of our Lord Jesus Christ,*

but we were eyewitnesses of his majesty. For he received honor and glory from God the Father when the voice came to him from the Majestic Glory, saying, "This is my Son, whom I love; with him I am well pleased." We ourselves heard this voice that came from heaven when we were with him on the sacred mountain. (2 PETER 1:16–18)

Thus Peter confirms the purpose of the Transfiguration. Jesus was giving three of His closest disciples a foretaste of what it will be like when He comes again in power and glory, with all His holy angels.

Also implied in Jesus' words is the fact that this event also awaits the believer at death. Notice that Jesus says, "There are some standing here who will not taste death before they see the kingdom of God come with power." The implication is that in most cases, it is by the act of tasting death that the believer will see the kingdom of God come with power. Other passages confirm that when a believer dies, in that instant when the believer leaves time and enters eternity, he or she immediately witnesses the coming of the Lord with His angels. This is why the New Testament letter of Jude records,

Enoch, the seventh from Adam, prophesied about these men: "See, the Lord is coming with thousands upon thousands of his holy ones." (JUDE 14)

This beautiful event awaits every believer at death. Whenever a loved one dies, remember this wonderful truth, and be comforted.

But here, before the Transfiguration, our Lord predicts that some who were then present would have a foretaste of this wonderful event before the end of their earthly lives. The Transfiguration, then, was to encourage the disciples. Jesus had just announced the way of the cross and His coming death in Jerusalem. This announcement was profoundly depressing and disheartening to the disciples. So Jesus gave them this incident to strengthen their faith, to encourage them that His mission on earth would not end in darkness and disaster, but that it would ultimately triumph. And this event should also encourage us in our lives as we must take up our cross. Whatever obstacles and tragedies we face in life, we know that our lives will ultimately end in glory and triumph.

Four Aspects of the Transfiguration

Now let us look at the event itself. As you read Mark's account, place yourself in the sandals of these three disciples. What would you feel if you experienced this event?

> After six days Jesus took Peter, James and John with him and led them up a high mountain, where they were all alone. There he was transfigured before them. His clothes became dazzling white, whiter than anyone in the world could bleach them. And there appeared before them Elijah and Moses, who were talking with Jesus.
>
> Peter said to Jesus, "Rabbi, it is good for us to be here. Let us put up three shelters—one for you, one for Moses and one for Elijah." (He did not know what to say, they were so frightened.)
>
> Then a cloud appeared and enveloped them, and a voice came from the cloud: "This is my Son, whom I love. Listen to him!"
>
> Suddenly, when they looked around, they no longer saw anyone with them except Jesus. (MARK 9:2–8)

Four dramatic occurrences in this account rivet our attention.

First, there is the glorious change in the person of the Lord. The account in Matthew supplies a few additional details. Putting these two accounts together, we see that the face of Jesus began to shine with an intense light. His garments became white, and His whole being radiated glory. Some critics of the Bible interpret these details as suggesting that Jesus was praying on the mountaintop when the sun suddenly broke through the clouds and shone on Him, so that His appearance only seemed to be supernaturally changed. Assuming that is the correct explanation, how does it account for the appearance of Moses and Elijah? No, it is clear, as the gospel writers go to great lengths to underscore, that this was a supernatural event and that the change in Jesus' appearance was a supernatural change. Peter, James, and John were witnessing a brightness of light and a whiteness of white for which there was no earthly explanation.

What happened to Jesus? For a moment, a glimpse of eternity shone through the veil of His humanity. The disciples caught a glimpse of the glory that was the Son's long before He was born on earth as a human being. We catch a sense of the Son's pre-existent glory in the great prayer of Jesus that is recorded in John: "And now, Father, glorify me in your presence with the glory I had with you before the world began" (John 17:5). This glory, which belonged to God the Son before the moment of creation, was suddenly revealed to the three disciples on that mountaintop.

One implication that flows from this event is the fact that our Lord did not have to die. That is one of the meanings of the Transfiguration. He had no reason to pass through death. He could step back across the boundary of time into eternity without passing through death. You and I are bound by time. We must die, but He did not have to. When He laid down His life, He did so willingly and deliberately.

I am sure that this is what John refers to in his gospel when he writes, "The Word became flesh and made his dwelling among us. We have seen his glory" (John 1:14). Although John was an eyewitness to the Transfiguration, he does not record the event in his gospel. Yet this statement, "We have seen his glory," leaves no doubt in my mind that John is referring to his vivid recollection of that astounding moment on the mountain.

The second dramatic occurrence in this account is the appearance of Moses and Elijah, who return from heaven and begin to talk with Jesus. It is interesting that the disciples have no difficulty recognizing these men. Jesus does not pause to make introductions: "Peter, James, and John, I'd like you to meet Moses and Elijah." The disciples knew instantly who they were. In glory there will be no need for introductions; we will know each other instantly. This account gives us a glimpse into heaven.

Many people have wondered why Moses and Elijah were chosen to be there. Why not Isaiah, Jeremiah, David, Abraham, or Noah? I believe it is because these two men were preeminently the representatives of the Law and the Prophets, the two great Old Testament sections that pointed to the coming of the Messiah. Moses was the great lawgiver. Elijah was the first and greatest of the prophets.

These two men represent the two ways by which people have entered heaven and will enter heaven. Moses left this life through the normal, natural process of death. No one was present when Moses died, but God buried him, the Old Testament says. Although the body of Moses still lies in some unmarked grave on a mountaintop beyond the Jordan River, Moses, in a resurrected body, was present on the mountain with Jesus.

Elijah, by contrast, was one of two men who were privileged to be caught up into heaven without experiencing death (the other was Enoch; see Genesis 5:24). We have the dramatic story in the Old Testament of Elijah's ascension into glory, caught up in a fiery chariot, without passing through the normal process of death (see 2 Kings 2:11).

We have a prediction of this same phenomenon in the New Testament. Believers today normally enter into glory through death, as Moses did. But Paul tells us that the generation of Christians who are living on the day of the Lord's return shall not taste of death.

> *Listen, I tell you a mystery: We will not all sleep, but we will all be changed—in a flash, in the twinkling of an eye, at the last trumpet. For the trumpet will sound, the dead will be raised imperishable, and we will be changed.*
>
> (1 CORINTHIANS 15:51–52)

> *For the Lord himself will come down from heaven, with a loud command, with the voice of the archangel and with the trumpet call of God, and the dead in Christ will rise first. After that, we who are still alive and are left will be caught up together with them in the clouds to meet the Lord in the air. And so we will be with the Lord forever.*
>
> (1 THESSALONIANS 4:16–17)

So there are two ways by which believers can enter into glory, and these two ways are represented in the Transfiguration by Moses and Elijah.

I am always intrigued by the fact that Moses is present at the Transfiguration, because it means that he finally made it into the

Promised Land. In the wilderness, God told Moses that he would not be permitted to lead the children of Israel into the Promised Land because of his disobedience. He could see the land but could not enter. That prohibition, however, was only in time. At the Transfiguration, Moses had passed from time into eternity, and so he was permitted to enter the land and stand on the mountaintop. I can imagine him looking all around and saying, "So here is the land I longed to see! I've been wanting to come here for ages, and I've finally made it!"

Luke gives us only the briefest account of the conversation among Jesus, Moses, and Elijah. He writes:

> *Two men, Moses and Elijah, appeared in glorious splendor, talking with Jesus. They spoke about his departure, which he was about to bring to fulfillment at Jerusalem.*
> (LUKE 9:30–31)

When he says that they "spoke about his departure," Luke means that they discussed Jesus' departure from earth by means of a cross and a resurrection just outside the city of Jerusalem. How I wish the disciples had thought to write down a full transcript of that heavenly discussion! Did Moses talk with the Messiah about how His sacrifice was the fulfillment of all the animal sacrifices demanded by the law? Did Elijah talk about how the death and resurrection of the Messiah would fulfill so many Old Testament prophecies? I think these matters were probably discussed, but we cannot know for sure, this side of eternity.

The third element of great interest in this account is the proposal made by Peter. After hearing these men discussing these strange events together, Peter, in his usual impulsive manner, interrupts: "Rabbi [that is, Master or Teacher], it is good for us to be here. Let us put up three shelters—one for you, one for Moses and one for Elijah." In other words, Peter says, "This is tremendous! Let's construct three buildings, one for each of you. Then let's settle down here and make this our world headquarters." Peter evidently had in mind that they would transform that mountain into the headquarters for the worldwide reformation movement that Jesus was about to begin.

Mark and Luke make an interesting commentary on Peter's proposal. Mark 9:6 records, "He [Peter] did not know what to say, they were so frightened." And Luke 9:33 observes that Peter "did not know what he was saying." So the assessment of Scripture is that Peter spoke foolishly, without any understanding of what Jesus had been trying to teach him. Mark, who undoubtedly got this account from Peter's lips, indicates that the motive that led Peter to speak was fear. And it wasn't just Peter who was afraid; Mark includes all three of the disciples when he writes, "they were so frightened." It has been said that there are two kinds of people, those who have something to say and those who have to say something. Peter was someone who had to say something. He blurted out whatever came to his mind, without stopping to think whether it made sense or not.

Immediately after Peter made his foolish proposal, the fourth dramatic event occurred. Suddenly the disciples were overshadowed by a cloud. Matthew tells us it was a bright cloud, a cloud of light. I believe that this was the same cloud mentioned in the Old Testament, which hovered over the tabernacle during the day: the glory of God, called the Shekinah. Then Peter, James, and John heard a voice speaking out of the cloud, saying, "This is my Son, whom I love. Listen to him!" There is no doubt that this statement from God the Father came as a rebuke to Peter's foolish proposal. The Father was saying, "Peter, do not put Jesus on a par with Moses and Elijah. Listen to Him. He is the one of whom Moses and Elijah spoke. He is the one who fulfilled all the predictions of the prophets and who is about to fulfill all the sacrifices of the law. Listen to Him; this is no mere man like Moses and Elijah. This is my beloved Son."

On three occasions in the New Testament the voice of God spoke directly from heaven concerning the work of Jesus. One was at His baptism, when He began His ministry. There the words were addressed to Jesus: "You are my Son, whom I love; with you I am well pleased" (Mark 1:11). It is evident that the voice of God the Father came at that time to launch the ministry of Jesus. Here, on the Mount of Transfiguration, the Father speaks again, this time to correct a mistake the disciples are making.

The third account occurs in John 12, just before Jesus goes to the cross. When Jesus speaks of having completed the work the Father gave Him to do, He says in prayer, "Father, glorify your name!" In response, a voice comes from heaven saying, "I have glorified it, and will glorify it again" (John 12:28). This is a reference to the cross and the resurrection to follow. So three times we witness the voice of the Father from heaven: to launch Jesus' ministry; to correct a mistaken idea about Him; and to complete the testimony that Jesus gave by His life and ministry.

A Verbal Quarantine and a Misunderstanding

Mark ends this account by telling us that as the voice spoke, the scene suddenly faded. The world returned to normal. With majestic simplicity Mark states the transition: "Suddenly, when they looked around, they no longer saw anyone with them except Jesus" (Mark 9:8).

In the next section we have the discussion that ensued as Jesus, Peter, James, and John came back down the mountainside.

> *As they were coming down the mountain, Jesus gave them orders not to tell anyone what they had seen until the Son of Man had risen from the dead. They kept the matter to themselves, discussing what "rising from the dead" meant.*
>
> *And they asked him, "Why do the teachers of the law say that Elijah must come first?"*
>
> *Jesus replied, "To be sure, Elijah does come first, and restores all things. Why then is it written that the Son of Man must suffer much and be rejected? But I tell you, Elijah has come, and they have done to him everything they wished, just as it is written about him."* (MARK 9:9–13)

Two features are important in this account. First, there is the verbal quarantine that Jesus imposes on these three disciples. Second, there is evidence that the disciples still do not understand what they have witnessed or what Jesus has been telling them. Let's look more closely at each of these features of the story.

First, the verbal quarantine. Once again Jesus forbade the disciples to talk of a miraculous occurrence they had seen. It seems that they were not even to discuss it with the other disciples. The obvious question is why Jesus does. Why does He show them His transfiguration and His glory, then swear the disciples to silence?

That brings us to the second feature of this account. Looking closely at this story, we can discover two reasons why Jesus commands them not to speak of what they have seen. Both reasons have to do with the fact that they do not understand what they have seen and heard.

For one thing, their information was incomplete. They could not understand what they had witnessed without the resurrection to put it into perspective. The disciples apparently ignored all Jesus had said about the resurrection. Apart from that fact, their message about the Transfiguration would be a sensational but ultimately meaningless jumble that would only mislead and misinform anyone they told.

For another thing, their understanding was incomplete. Not only was their information incomplete, but they even misunderstood the information they did have. They kept the matter to themselves but wondered what "rising from the dead" meant. Probably, like Martha (John 11), they thought that Jesus was talking about the great future resurrection, when all the dead would rise as foretold in the Old Testament. They did not understand that Jesus was speaking of His resurrection, even though He had been predicting His resurrection on the third day for some time.

This helps to explain why the disciples asked, "Why do the teachers of the law say that Elijah must come first?" It is clear that they believed that what they had seen on the mountain—Elijah and Moses speaking with Jesus—was the fulfillment of the prophecy of Malachi that Elijah must come before the great and terrible day of the Lord:

> *"Surely the day is coming; it will burn like a furnace. . . .*
> *See, I will send you the prophet Elijah before that great and*
> *dreadful day of the Lord comes."* (MALACHI 3:1, 5)

The disciples were baffled because it seemed that Elijah had come in the wrong order, *after* the appearance of the Messiah. They could not understand that, because they thought that the appearance of the Messiah was supposed to occur on "that great and dreadful day of the Lord." So they asked Jesus to explain: "Why do the teachers of the law say that Elijah must come first?" Note that the emphasis is on the word "first." They do not know how to tie the resurrection to this prophecy, and they do not know how to explain that Elijah did not come first and restore all things before Messiah appeared.

Jesus' answer to them is instructive. We must observe it carefully, because the pronouns are confusing at first glance. Jesus says to them, "To be sure, Elijah does come first, and restores all things. Why then is it written that the Son of Man [here Jesus refers to Himself, not Elijah] must suffer much and be rejected?" Notice that Jesus has changed the subject from Elijah to Himself. Then He says, "But I tell you, Elijah has come [here, Jesus shifts the subject to Himself again], and they have done to him everything they wished, just as it is written about him." Who does Jesus refer to in the rest of that sentence? Who do those pronouns refer to? If you do not read carefully, you would think they refer to Elijah. But in truth, they refer to Jesus, the Son of Man, not Elijah. This agrees with His previous statement that the Son of Man must suffer much and be rejected.

It is not written anywhere of Elijah that he would suffer and be rejected. This can only be a reference to the Messiah. So Jesus is saying, "Elijah will come; but as to Messiah, they are doing to Him whatever they please, as it is written of Him." He changes the focus of their question from Elijah to Himself. He is saying that the real issue is not that Elijah has come first but that the suffering and death of the Messiah must come first. That should be the disciples' focus. That is what Jesus continually tried to teach them in preparing them for the horror and despair of the cross.

We should also note that in Matthew's account of this event, Jesus refers to John the Baptist as having fulfilled, in metaphoric way, Malachi's promise concerning Elijah. You may recall that at the announcement of the birth of John the Baptist, an angel appeared to John's father and said that John would go before the Lord to prepare His way and that He would do so in the spirit and power of Elijah. The Bible does not tell us that John was the reincarnation of Elijah; John and Elijah were two distinct and different men. But John did come in the spirit and power of Elijah, fulfilling an Elijahlike ministry.

Our Lord makes clear that before Messiah appears in His second coming, Elijah will come first. But Jesus doesn't want the disciples to get caught up in far-future speculations about Elijah. He wants them to understand the looming issue that is fast approaching: the torture and death of the Messiah on the cross.

At the Foot of the Mountain

This account closes with the story of an event that took place at the foot of the mountain: the deliverance of the demonized boy. This is the same demonized boy who is depicted, along with his parents, in the lower portion of Raphael's painting. The painter understood that there was an important link between the transfiguration of Jesus and the healing that He performed after He came down from the mountain. Mark begins by recounting the failure of the disciples who had stayed behind at the foot of the mountain.

> When they came to the other disciples, they saw a large crowd around them and the teachers of the law arguing with them. As soon as all the people saw Jesus, they were overwhelmed with wonder and ran to greet him.
>
> "What are you arguing with them about?" he asked.
>
> A man in the crowd answered, "Teacher, I brought you my son, who is possessed by a spirit that has robbed him of speech. Whenever it seizes him, it throws him to the ground. He foams at the mouth, gnashes his teeth and becomes rigid. I asked your disciples to drive out the spirit, but they could not."

"O unbelieving generation," Jesus replied, "how long shall I stay with you? How long shall I put up with you? Bring the boy to me." (MARK 9:14–19)

We need to be understanding of these disciples. They lacked faith, just as Jesus said, but they faced a difficult problem. This boy presented an especially difficult case, as Jesus acknowledged. It was not a simple case of epilepsy, although the symptoms seem like classic symptoms of epilepsy. But the Bible records instances of epilepsy and demon possession and distinguishes between them. Here the problem was not caused by epilepsy but by demonic power. We will later see that Jesus asks the boy's father, "How long has he been like this?" The father replies, "From childhood." This was Jesus' clue that it was a difficult case. To make matters worse, while Jesus and the three disciples were up on the mountain, the disciples found themselves surrounded by unbelieving scribes ("teachers of the law") who opposed everything they did. So the disciples were asked to do a difficult task under extremely trying circumstances.

Why did they fail? The Lord put His finger on the basic reason: their lack of faith. But notice something crucial. We almost always think of faith as some kind of expectation that something is going to happen. If we can believe something is going to happen, it will happen. These disciples did believe a healing would happen, and they were surprised and dismayed when it did not. They had seen people delivered from demons before when they commanded the demons in Jesus' name. But this time it did not happen. So faith is not merely a sense of expectation that something will happen. Faith, as Jesus defines it, is something more. But what?

If you think about it, it becomes clear. The disciples had faith, but their faith was misplaced. Instead of having faith in

God, they had faith in the process they had been following. They fell into the trap of thinking that if they said the right words and followed the right ritual, the demon would have to leave. Without realizing it, they had transferred their faith from the reality of God to the ritual of a formula.

That is so often what we do. We think that if we perform this ritual, say this prayer, give this offering, recite this creed, then a certain result will take place in our lives. We forget that it is not the ritual, prayer, offering, or creed that has power. The power resides in God alone. It is He who acts.

So Jesus reproved them for shifting their faith from God, who is real, to a formula, which is powerless. Our faith must be focused in God if it is to be a fresh, vital, and powerful faith. The power of that kind of faith is exemplified by our Lord. As Mark records:

> *So they brought him. When the spirit saw Jesus, it immediately threw the boy into a convulsion. He fell to the ground and rolled around, foaming at the mouth.*
>
> *Jesus asked the boy's father, "How long has he been like this?"*
>
> *"From childhood," he answered. "It has often thrown him into fire or water to kill him. But if you can do anything, take pity on us and help us."*
>
> *" 'If you can'?" said Jesus. "Everything is possible for him who believes."*
>
> *Immediately the boy's father exclaimed, "I do believe; help me overcome my unbelief!"*
>
> *When Jesus saw that a crowd was running to the scene, he rebuked the evil spirit. "You deaf and mute spirit," he said, "I command you, come out of him and never enter him again."*

> *The spirit shrieked, convulsed him violently and came out. The boy looked so much like a corpse that many said, "He's dead." But Jesus took him by the hand and lifted him to his feet, and he stood up.* (MARK 9:20–27)

Notice the father's honest doubt as he comes to Jesus. He said, "If you can do anything, take pity on us and help us." And Jesus gently challenges the man: " 'If you can'? Everything is possible for him who believes." The question, says Jesus, is not whether He can accomplish the healing but whether the man has faith. And the man responds with heartrending honesty: "I do believe; help me overcome my unbelief!" He believes, yet he also doubts. He is honest about his weakness, and he casts himself on the Lord of mercy, asking for help to increase his struggling faith. Such faith is small, but it is like a grain of mustard seed; focused on the power and person of God, this faith is enough to move mountains. The moment this father confessed his faith and his doubts, it was enough. God was ready and willing to act. Jesus spoke the word, and the boy was delivered.

As the demon leaves the boy, the severity of the case becomes obvious. The demon comes out of him violently and reluctantly, even though commanded by the Son of God. It cries out and convulses the boy, then leaves him as if he is dead. But Jesus lifts the boy by the hand, and all is well. In the final verses of this account, we discover the secret of the power that restored the boy:

> *After Jesus had gone indoors, his disciples asked him privately, "Why couldn't we drive it out?"*
> *He replied, "This kind can come out only by prayer."*
> (MARK 9:28–29)

Jesus does not mean prayer uttered at that moment, because Jesus did not pray when He cast out this demon. He is not talking about a certain kind of prayer that you say at the moment you want to deliver someone from a demon. Jesus is talking about a lifestyle of prayer. In other words, "This kind cannot be driven out except by a heart which is kept fresh and alive and in touch with God by continual prayer." That is where Jesus' power came from. He was always in touch with the Father. He was always drawing on his Father's power. He always walked in reliance on God. He referred every event of His existence to the God who lived within Him. He prayed to the Father with such constancy and consistency that prayer to Jesus was like breathing out and breathing in.

In closing, I want to go back to the beginning of this story for a moment. Remember that in Mark 9:1, Jesus said, "I tell you the truth, some who are standing here will not taste death before they see the kingdom of God come with power."

What had these disciples just seen? They had seen the kingdom of God come with power into the life of a father and his boy. Why did it come? It came because Jesus lived in continual communion and communication with the living God. A lifestyle of prayer is the key to experiencing the kingdom of God, the power of God, in our daily lives.

seventeen

The Child in Our Midst

➤ **Mark 9:30–50**

The son of an English admiral, William Penn was born to wealth and privilege in 1644. He was aimless and unambitious in his youth. After being expelled from Oxford, he spent some time managing his father's properties in Ireland. In his early twenties, Penn heard a powerful sermon by Quaker preacher Thomas Loe, and Penn's life was transformed. He plunged into radical Christianity and became a champion of the poor and powerless. In fact, his activism landed him in prison on several occasions.

While he was imprisoned in the Tower of London at the age of twenty-four, Penn wrote a devotional book called *No Cross, No Crown,* which he called an attempt "to show the nature and discipline of the holy Cross of Christ; and that the denial of self . . . is the alone way to the Rest and Kingdom of God."

A few years later, in 1677, Penn sailed with Quaker leader George Fox to America, where he founded a city, Philadelphia, the City of Brotherly Love, and a colony, Pennsylvania, which he named after his late father. His goal in founding this city and this colony was to create a society of Christian love, brotherhood, and religious liberty, a "holy experiment," as he termed it, that he rightly predicted would become "the seed of a nation." Although

America hasn't always lived up to Penn's dream, much of what is great about America flows from his vision.

Throughout his life, William Penn remained true to the words he wrote as a new Christian: no cross, no crown. If we are to receive the crown of God's favor in eternity, we must take up our cross and follow Jesus.

That is the lesson Jesus has gently but firmly been teaching His disciples: no cross, no crown. This is the lesson we all need to grasp, because if you are like me, you do not like the cross in your life. We Christians often make much of the joy and love and the glory of Christianity while downplaying the reality of suffering and persecution, of discipline and dying. It is easy to see why the church avoids such unpleasant subjects. But Jesus makes clear to His disciples—and to us—that there is no resurrection without a crucifixion. No cross, no crown.

As we continue our study in Mark, we will see how Jesus continues to prepare His disciples for the traumatic and shattering events to come, for the cross of Calvary and the crown of the resurrection.

A Debate on the Road

Mark tells us that following the Transfiguration and the healing of the demon-controlled boy, Jesus passed through Galilee again on His way to Capernaum. Mark underscores the teaching and training ministry of the Lord toward His disciples.

> *They left that place and passed through Galilee. Jesus did not want anyone to know where they were, because he was teaching his disciples. He said to them, "The Son of Man is going to be betrayed into the hands of men. They will kill him, and after three days he will rise." But they did not*

understand what he meant and were afraid to ask him about it. (MARK 9:30–32)

It is evident that Jesus took the back roads on the way to Capernaum. He deliberately avoided the crowds so that He could spend time with His disciples. All through the gospels you see that His target was these twelve men. He was intent on conveying truth to them, above all else.

As He instructs them and prepares them for what is to come, a new element is added: "The Son of Man is going to be betrayed into the hands of men." Jesus bluntly tells His disciples that His death will come as an act of betrayal. Only a friend could betray Jesus. What this meant to Judas we are not told, but Jesus knew what would happen.

Mark records that the disciples were baffled by what Jesus said—and afraid. They wanted to understand what He was telling them, but they were afraid to ask. Why? Were they afraid of His rebuke? For it is true that Jesus had rebuked them for lack of faith, yet there is no evidence in Scripture that He ever rebuked anyone for asking Him a question. So I don't think they feared His rebuke. Rather, I think they feared His answer. They didn't ask because they were afraid to know the truth. They preferred to bury their heads in the sand rather than find out what was going to happen to Jesus and who was going to betray Him.

Jesus tries to confront them with the fact of the cross, even though they don't want to hear it, because He wants them to be prepared when the time comes. But as we will later see, when the time comes they are unprepared. They have avoided the truth, but they cannot escape it. The fact of the cross is coming at them like a steamroller.

As they follow Jesus toward Capernaum, the disciples have a discussion on the road, and the subject of their discussion shows how little they understand of what Jesus is trying to teach them. They think that Jesus cannot overhear them as they whisper to each other, but He knows what is in their hearts. Mark writes:

> *They came to Capernaum. When he was in the house, he asked them, "What were you arguing about on the road?" But they kept quiet because on the way they had argued about who was the greatest.*
>
> *Sitting down, Jesus called the Twelve and said, "If anyone wants to be first, he must be the very last, and the servant of all."*
>
> *He took a little child and had him stand among them. Taking him in his arms, he said to them, "Whoever welcomes one of these little children in my name welcomes me; and whoever welcomes me does not welcome me but the one who sent me."* (MARK 9:33–37)

Our Lord evidently knew what the disciples were discussing. Perhaps He overheard. Perhaps He merely sensed the tone of their conversation. In any case, He knew. So when they arrived at the house in Capernaum, He asked them, "What were you arguing about on the road?" It's a simple, normal question, but He is met by an embarrassed silence. When the Master asks, all their squabbling suddenly seems petty, egotistical, and immature—which it was. If only we had a continual sense of Jesus' presence with us. If only we could be aware of His eyes on us, His questioning of us: "What are you saying? What are you doing? What are you thinking?" I'm sure such an awareness would radically alter the way we live our lives.

The disciples' argument was probably occasioned by the events of the Transfiguration. James, Peter, and John had been chosen to go up on the mountain with the Lord and observe this marvelous sight. Afterwards, Jesus had warned them to tell no one what they had seen. I believe the three disciples obeyed Jesus and kept the matter to themselves. But we all know how to keep a secret in such a way as to incite the curiosity and envy of everyone around. When Peter, James, and John returned from the mountain, the others probably said, "Tell us what happened up there." And you can imagine the three disciples saying, "Oh, we're not permitted to tell anyone—not even you." And the other nine disciples would feel excluded and offended. It is not hard to imagine how, given those dynamics, a debate might arise as to which of the Twelve is the greatest.

To silence this debate, Jesus makes an astonishing statement about human ambition. He calls the disciples to Himself and shares with them a great paradox: "If anyone wants to be first, he must be the very last, and the servant of all." The embarrassed disciples did not expect this. No doubt they expected a rebuke for their egotism, but Jesus does not do that. He doesn't even tell them that their desire to be the greatest is wrong. I believe this is because God has built into every human heart the desire to succeed, and it is a good desire, not an evil one. Instead of rebuking that desire, He channels it in a righteous direction. He says, "You want to be great? Fine. Let me show you the way to true greatness, true success. If you want to succeed, then don't try to get others to serve you. True success comes as you become the servant of all."

Jesus is saying that there are two kinds of greatness, two kinds of ambition. There is the ambition to be approved and applauded by people and the ambition to be approved and commended by God. The measure of true greatness is not how many servants I have but how many I have served today.

Once again Jesus underscores for us the fact that Christianity is a radical faith. It revolutionizes our thinking. It goes against the natural instincts of the human will, and it goes against the self-centered notions of this world. This is why, as we grow and mature in the Christian faith, we learn more and more to act not according to the way we feel or according to how the people in the world around us act. We act on a different basis, because we serve a different purpose.

To drive this lesson home, Jesus called a boy to Him, wrapped His arms around the child, and said, "Whoever welcomes one of these little children in my name welcomes me; and whoever welcomes me does not welcome me but the one who sent me." He was saying, "Is it true greatness you fellows want? Then show kindness to little children. Show kindness to all who seem small, forgotten, and insignificant. Don't try to be a big shot. Just have a big heart. Any kindness you show to the least significant among you is counted as a kindness to me."

The Three Lessons of a Child

Lesson 1

Then Jesus went on to teach His disciples what could be called the three lessons of a child, the three true and righteous ambitions we should all set for our lives. Jesus wants us to know that it is right and godly to be ambitious if we are ambitious for right and godly things.

The first lesson is found in these words: "Whoever welcomes one of these little children in my name welcomes me." Note that all-important phrase "in my name." The motive for welcoming and showing kindness to others should be that it is done as unto the Lord, it is done in His name. It is not done because you will receive something of value in return. Bible commentator William Barclay offers this meaningful insight:

> Now, a child has no influence at all. A child cannot advance a man's career, nor enhance a man's prestige. A child cannot give us things; it's the other way around. A child needs things. A child must have things done for him. And so Jesus is saying, "If a man welcomes the poor, ordinary people, the people who have no influence, and no wealth, and no power, the people who need things done for them, then he's welcoming me. And more than that, he's welcoming God."

The first mark of true greatness is that you do not show respect in expectation of benefits. You welcome others in the Lord's name because they are people, and all people have value and worth in God's eyes, even the smallest, the least, the most humble and ordinary.

This principle is unwittingly illustrated in the next section by John, who interrupts Jesus:

> *"Teacher," said John, "we saw a man driving out demons in your name and we told him to stop, because he was not one of us."*
>
> *"Do not stop him," Jesus said. "No one who does a miracle in my name can in the next moment say anything bad about me, for whoever is not against us is for us."*
>
> (MARK 9:38–40)

Why did John interrupt? What had Jesus said that prompted this announcement? Perhaps it was the phrase Jesus used, "in my name." Perhaps that phrase reminded John of the man the disciples had seen who was casting out demons in Jesus' name. So John, and apparently some of the other disciples, had ordered the man to stop because he wasn't one of the Twelve.

This is a typically human reaction, even among Christians. It is the spirit of sectarianism, of division, of schism. "Well, he can't be good because he didn't go to our seminary," or, "He doesn't belong to our denomination," or, "He doesn't adhere to our doctrinal position on this or that theological fine point." So we shut him down.

Perhaps John was troubled by the success this man was having. He wasn't one of the Twelve, yet he was casting out demons. It was not a phony ministry. The man was performing as advertised, and he was accomplishing all this in the name of Jesus. Yet John had never heard of the man. So his success seemed to rankle John. And this is so typical of human nature. A rival is all the more intolerable if he is a successful rival.

Perhaps John is asking Jesus, "Did we do the right thing in stopping this man?" Or perhaps John is announcing this action, expecting to receive a commendation from Jesus. If that is the case, then John is disappointed, because the Lord's answer is, "Oh, no! Don't forbid him. For anyone who does a mighty work in my name will not soon afterward be able to speak evil of me. If he's not opposing us, treat him as one of us." What does Jesus mean by that?

Jesus is saying that if this man was casting out demons in the Lord's name, then obviously there was some faith in the man's heart. God does not respond to anything but faith. And though no one knew much about this man and what he believed—and there may have been considerable error in what he taught—the fact that demons were being cast out in the Lord's name indicated something real and authentic about the man's ministry and faith. When you see a spark of genuineness, said Jesus, don't quench it; encourage it. Don't reject people because they don't get every theological detail right. They are still on the way, they are still learning, but they are moving toward the same destination you are. So encourage them.

I recall with sadness how many churches, at the height of the Jesus Movement of the 1970s, turned their backs on the earnest, seeking young people who came to their doors. Those churches missed a beautiful opportunity for ministry because they could not look beyond the strange clothing the Jesus People wore, their long hair, their strings of beads, their tie-dyed shirts, their bare feet. The staid, respectable church people said, "We don't want this kind among us," and they failed to note the signs of true faith among these young people. How it must have broken the Lord's heart to see His church turning His children away.

I once saw an announcement of a meeting of the Gay People's Union at Stanford University. Two prominent speakers were featured, a lesbian professor at San Francisco State University and a homosexual young man ordained to the ministry in a liberal denomination. They spoke about homosexuality in the church. So I took one of the interns of our church with me, and we went to the meeting. We found about a hundred young people there, plus a few older persons, and the numbers were evenly divided between men and women. The lesbian professor spoke first, and she was angry and vitriolic. She bitterly denounced the church and called for its destruction, because she saw the Christian church as the enemy of human liberty and freedom.

The young man was gentler in his approach. He told of his desire to find a place within the church even as he had struggled for years with his sexual identity. He recounted having been mistreated by people in the church after going public with his homosexuality. I knew that much of what he said about the unloving and hurtful attitudes he had encountered in the church was tragically true.

But I noticed one thing in particular as he spoke. Several times, he referred to Jesus and His ministry with people. He spoke of Jesus with reverence and affection. And I found it was true, exactly as our Lord said to John in this passage, that no one who uses His name will soon after be able to speak evil of Him. Whenever this young man spoke of Jesus, it was with respect and admiration for His ministry among despised and outcast people.

Near the end of this meeting, I felt it was time to say something for the church. So I stood, identified myself, and said, "I can agree with much that has been said about the church, but I don't think you have come to grips with the real issue—the stance of Christianity toward homosexuality. The nearest you came was when this young man spoke of Jesus and the woman at the well." He had referred to the fact that Jesus had not castigated or scorned the woman, although she had lived an immoral life. I continued, "Nevertheless Jesus did speak to her about her condition—having lived with five husbands and now living with a man who was not her husband. He then offered her release, a way out of a pattern of living that was hurtful to herself and others. That, I believe, is the true Christian position. Homosexuality is very injurious; it destroys lives and families. Jesus understands that, but He doesn't want to denounce people or drive them away. He wants to offer to them compassion, love, and a way out."

As I looked around that room, I didn't see perverts or degenerates, as some people in the church have unfortunately labeled homosexuals. I saw hurting, fragmented, confused lives—souls

Jesus died to save, souls in search of the secret of life. Paul's words in Romans came to my mind: his statement about homosexuals "receiving in their own persons the due penalty of their error" (Romans 1:27 NASB). I thought of that passage, and I hurt for the people in that room.

The stance of the church toward those who are involved in a tragic, sinful, self-destructive pattern of living—whether homosexual sin or heterosexual sin, whether alcoholism or drug abuse or gambling addiction or whatever else it might be—should not be a stance of stigma, rejection, and disgust. Rather, we are to love others as Jesus loved. We are to accept with open arms but also with an honest evaluation of sin. Like Jesus, we must show grace and speak the truth. Grace and truth together are the only ways the church can help people find authentic release and recovery.

This is what Jesus is saying to His disciples. The mark of greatness is that you look not at a person's outward appearance or at the outward characteristics he or she manifests, or even at the things the person stands for. Instead, you must see in every person a human being, made in God's image, a soul groping after truth and life. And if the name of Jesus is respected, do not quench that spark but encourage it.

Lesson 2

The second lesson that Jesus teaches the disciples, using a child as an illustration of truth, is found in the next passage.

> "I tell you the truth, anyone who gives you a cup of water in my name because you belong to Christ will certainly not lose his reward.
>
> "And if anyone causes one of these little ones who believe in me to sin, it would be better for him to be thrown into the

sea with a large millstone tied around his neck."

(MARK 9:41–42)

Remember that Jesus speaks these words with His arms still wrapped around the little child. The mark of true greatness in the kingdom of God, He says, is that you take humanity seriously, you care for human need, and you long to see every human being grow to his or her full, God-given potential. The slightest act of service and ministry in Jesus' name will be rewarded by God.

But the flip side of the Lord's word contains a severe warning. Any moral damage or spiritual injury done to a young believer is more serious than murder. "If anyone causes one of these little ones who believe in me to sin," says Jesus, "it would be better for him to be thrown into the sea with a large millstone tied around his neck."

I once read a short story by O. Henry (William Sydney Porter), which told of a little girl whose mother had died. When the father would come home from work, he would fix their meal, then sit down with his paper and pipe, put his feet up on the hearth, and read. The little girl would come and say, "Father, would you play with me?" And he would say, "No, I'm too tired, I'm too busy. Go out in the street and play."

This went on for so long that finally the little girl grew up on the streets and became what is called a streetwalker (a prostitute). Eventually she died, and her soul approached the gates of heaven. Seeing her, Peter said to Jesus, "Here's a prostitute. Shall we send her to hell?" Jesus said, "No, let her in. But go find the man who failed to love this child, the man who told her to go out into the streets—send *him* to hell."

Here in Mark's gospel, Jesus is saying that neglect is sometimes the greatest injury done to a child and to young believers.

The least of these, the children, are to be loved and nurtured in the name of the Lord.

Lesson 3

The third lesson of a child follows immediately in Mark's account, and Jesus' words are shocking to our ears.

> *"If your hand causes you to sin, cut it off. It is better for you to enter life maimed than with two hands to go into hell, where the fire never goes out. And if your foot causes you to sin, cut it off. It is better for you to enter life crippled than to have two feet and be thrown into hell. And if your eye causes you to sin, pluck it out. It is better for you to enter the kingdom of God with one eye than to have two eyes and be thrown into hell, where*
>
> > *" 'their worm does not die,*
> > *and the fire is not quenched.'*
>
> *Everyone will be salted with fire."* (MARK 9:43–49)

Remember, these words are also spoken as Jesus has His arms around the child. The third mark of greatness, then, is that all judgment starts with ourselves. If we are to take seriously the issue of spiritual growth, then we must deal drastically with ourselves. These words about cutting off the hand and foot and eye are but an intensified, dramatic way of saying what Jesus said on another occasion: "Why do you look at the speck of sawdust in your brother's eye and pay no attention to the plank in your own eye? How can you say to your brother, 'Let me take the speck out of your eye,' when all the time there is a plank in your own eye?" (Matthew 7:3–4).

The analogy Jesus draws is clear and is taken from life. If you have an infected arm that develops gangrene, and it is threatening your life, and the doctors cannot do any more for you, then there is only one thing left to do: amputate. If you keep the arm, you will lose your life. We must deal drastically with bitterness, hate, pride, envy, backbiting, gossip, lust, and other sins. If we do not, these things will drag us down into hell.

The word Jesus uses for "hell" is *gehenna*. Gehenna, or Gehinnom, was the name of a valley outside Jerusalem. It was the place where some of the wicked kings of Israel had offered their children to the god Moloch to be burned with fire. It was a defiled place, and it became the garbage dump of Jerusalem. Fires smoldered there continuously; repulsive worms ate at the garbage. The garbage dump of Gehenna became a symbol to the Jews of the eternal waste of life.

It may surprise you to know that Jesus spoke of hell more than any other person in the New Testament. So when we read these words of Jesus about hell, we must understand that when they are applied to an unbeliever who has resisted and rejected the good news of Jesus Christ, it means that the person's whole life is like something tossed on a burning garbage dump—a waste, a total loss. There is nothing salvageable about it. An unbeliever may have won the approval of other people, may have lived comfortably, but at the end of life ends up on the trash heap for eternity.

Here, however, Jesus is not addressing unbelievers but His disciples. When these words apply to believers, as they do here, Jesus is speaking of partial loss. Some of our life is wasted, squandered, lost. It has been misused. The way to avoid such a loss is to, as Jesus vividly puts it, salt ourselves with fire, that is, to judge ourselves. We should deal drastically with ourselves so that we can avoid a worse loss in eternity.

We should start, Jesus says, with the hand. To "cut off the hand" refers to eliminating the act that is wrong, the evil deed. If you have a dirty mind or a filthy mouth, then stop thinking evil thoughts and stop using obscene or profane speech. If you are engaged in sexual sin, then end it and forsake it. If you are dishonest in business or prone to gossip or guilty of some other sin, then you must repent, fully and completely. If your attitude toward another person is bitter and resentful, then forgive and seek forgiveness. If you don't cut off the hand of sin, you will waste your life.

If that is not enough, the foot must be amputated. The foot symbolizes the steps along the path to evil. You may have to change where you go and what you spend your time doing, because you are confronted with temptation that is too strong for you to handle. You may have to cancel your cable television, turn off your Internet connection, stop going to certain places, stop hanging out with certain friends. If these things expose you to temptation and pressure that is too much for you to handle, cut them off without mercy! Otherwise you will waste your life and your soul.

Or it may be that the eye, which symbolizes our inner vision, our imagination and fantasies, our memories and dreams, must be plucked out. Jesus is saying that we must deal drastically with these issues, we must judge ourselves severely, or these diseased parts of our life will take over and infect our souls, causing us to waste away.

Jesus concludes with these words:

> *"Salt is good, but if it loses its saltiness, how can you make it salty again? Have salt in yourselves, and be at peace with each other."* (Mark 9:50)

Salt—the salt of self-judgment, the salt of the chemical fire that purifies and cleanses—is good. So judge yourself, look at yourself and evaluate what you are doing, and learn to control yourself. But remember, your life before God must be real; it cannot be phony. Salt that has lost its saltiness is worth nothing. It must be real, genuine salt. So have salt in yourselves, judge yourselves, be honest with yourselves about your sin. And if you do that in all humility, then you will surely live at peace with one another.

Remember how this account opens? The disciples were arguing as to who was going to be greatest. They were engaged in a clash of competing egos. Jesus says that the remedy for such contention, dissension, and discord between Christian brothers and sisters is for us to have salt in ourselves, to judge ourselves, to deal first with our weaknesses and sins, not those of others.

For the marks of greatness in the kingdom of God are these: to treat everyone the same; to take life and humanity seriously; to be concerned for the best interests of others; to build others up, not harm them or tear them down; to judge our hearts rather than focusing on the supposed flaws and faults of others. A person who does these things may not be great in the eyes of the world, but he or she will rise in stature and greatness in the eyes of God.

And it is His opinion of us—His and His alone—that matters.

eighteen

What About Divorce?

➤ **Mark 10:1–12**

The English Shakespearean actress Dame Sybil Thorndike enjoyed a long marriage to fellow actor Sir Lewis Casson. They often toured and performed together. Although they were known to have their occasional disagreements and even quarrels, they generally considered their marriage a happy and successful one. After Sir Lewis passed away, a friend asked Dame Sybil if she and her husband ever considered divorce.

"Divorce!" she replied, laughing. "Oh, no, never! But murder? Often!"

If you have been married any length of time, you may identify with Dame Sybil. What do you think of divorce? Your attitude toward divorce speaks volumes about your attitude toward marriage. In Mark 10, we come to Jesus' teaching about divorce, and as we discover His attitude toward divorce, we will learn much about God's plan for marriage.

Two Schools of Thought

In this passage we have the account of a new journey our Lord took with His disciples, leaving Galilee for the last time. The first verse sets the scene:

> *Jesus then left that place and went into the region of Judea and across the Jordan. Again crowds of people came to him, and as was his custom, he taught them.* (MARK 10:1)

This verse summarizes an extensive ministry our Lord had after He left Galilee. It took Him into Samaria and northern Judea. During that journey, He sent out seventy disciples, as earlier He had sent out the Twelve, to go into all the villages and preach the gospel. Also, as we discover in John 10, Jesus made a quick trip to Jerusalem in the dead of winter and appeared at the Feast of Dedication. Having spoken at that feast, He left Jerusalem and came with His disciples into the area on the eastern side of the Jordan River. There, in the region called Perea, He was ministering, and great crowds gathered to hear His teaching. During this time, He was approached by a group of Pharisees.

> *Some Pharisees came and tested him by asking, "Is it lawful for a man to divorce his wife?"* (MARK 10:2)

Mark is careful to point out the motive that brought them. They have come to test Him, that is, to probe Him, trip Him up, discredit Him, and catch Him in an error. Their hostility is more intense than ever, and they are determined to put Him to death. So they select a controversial question: the issue of divorce.

These Pharisees are masters of manipulation. They have devised the perfect trap. Their plan is to maneuver Jesus into a position where He must choose between two widely held schools of thought regarding divorce. That way, no matter which view He chooses, those who hold the opposite view are sure to be offended.

One school of thought was that of the great rabbi Hillel. Moses, in Deuteronomy 24, had said that a man could divorce his wife if he found any indecency in her. Hillel interpreted that to mean anything that displeased the husband. If the wife made bad coffee, he could divorce her. If she did not keep the house clean, he could divorce her. If she had one hair out of place when she woke up in the morning, he could divorce her. This was the easy-divorce school of thought. It made men the absolute masters in their homes and made life miserable for a lot of Jewish wives.

Opposed to Hillel's view was the school of Shammai, another great Hebrew rabbi, who taught that divorce was to be strictly limited. According to this school of thought, divorce could be granted under only the most extreme and narrowly defined conditions.

Of course, we have the same split in modern North American culture. Throughout the Christian church, modified versions of these two viewpoints continue to battle each other. Particularly in this age of rampant divorce and the disintegrating respect for marriage, how should we view divorce? Should divorces be granted readily and easily, on the basis of simple incompatibility? Or is marriage so sacred that it should be dissolved only under severely limited conditions? That is the question with which the Pharisees confront Jesus and attempt to trap Him.

Jesus Avoids the Trap

In His answer to the Pharisees, Jesus develops two important arguments. First, He takes them back to Moses and discusses divorce as Moses handled it. Next He goes back even further, to Genesis and creation. Let us look first at what He says about Moses.

"What did Moses command you?" he replied.

They said, "Moses permitted a man to write a certificate of divorce and send her away."

"It was because your hearts were hard that Moses wrote you this law," Jesus replied. (MARK 10:3–5)

Notice that Jesus did not answer the Pharisees on the basis of His authority or opinion. He referred them to Moses. In other words, He upheld the authority of Scripture. Jesus always referred to the Old Testament as a book of answers, as the authority on all questions pertaining to life. He never superseded that word. Again and again, He said, "It is written." Even in the Sermon on the Mount, He said that He came not to destroy the law but to fulfill it, and He warned against anyone who attempted to destroy or change what the Bible says. This is why He sent these Pharisees back to Moses for the answer.

But Jesus did not stop there. He went on to clarify the law. He interpreted the word of Moses for them and revealed to us something that the law does not tell us. He gave us the ultimate reason Moses permitted divorce. It was because men's hearts were hardened that Moses allowed divorce. What does that mean?

Jesus is saying that divorce reveals in public what has been going on in the privacy of a marriage: hardness of heart. That is what the law always does. As Paul writes, "Through the law we become conscious of sin" (Romans 3:20). So it is in line with his role as lawgiver that Moses should also give laws concerning divorce, in order to make visible what is going on in a family. And what was going on in Israel whenever a divorce took place? Hardness of heart.

What is a hardened heart? God created the human heart to be full of love, generosity, patience, tolerance, compassion, forgiveness, gentleness, and openness. Sin replaces these beautiful, soft qualities with hardness, that is, with hatred, selfishness, impatience, narrowmindedness, indifference, vengefulness, hostility, and deceitfulness.

The term "hardness of heart" is used many times in Scripture. We are often warned against hardening our hearts. There is the Old Testament story of Moses going before Pharaoh, again and again, to deliver the message of God: "Let my people go." Each time Pharaoh heard that word from God, he hardened his heart (see Exodus 8:15, 32; 9:34; 10:1). Pharaoh determined that he would handle it his way, according to his stubborn will. Having heard what God was telling him, Pharaoh willfully decided to ignore it and go his own way. Whenever you know what God desires for you to do and you willfully choose to disobey, you are hardening your heart. And that, says Jesus, is what was going on in the marriages in Israel.

Moses looked at the issue of divorce from the standpoint of the husband and said that if the husband saw something displeasing in his wife (and Moses did not specify what it must be), then divorce was to be permitted. Why? To make the husband's attitude publicly, openly clear.

What would the divorce law of Moses reveal about the husband's attitude? It would reveal that this husband is following his natural, sinful inclination. Rather than showing love, patience, and forgiveness, he chooses to be critical and demanding, even shutting his wife out of the home if she does not meet all of his exacting standards. The divorce law in Israel showed that some husbands were exhibiting contemptuous and contemptible behavior and attitudes toward their wives.

In that culture, the value of women was heavily discounted. Wives were viewed almost as property and were sometimes mistreated. To make these conditions clear and visible, Moses granted permission for divorce. It released women from what was often a hell on earth.

But the New Testament gives us a more complete revelation about how a husband is to treat his wife. For example, Peter writes,

Husbands, in the same way be considerate as you live with your wives, and treat them with respect as the weaker partner and as heirs with you of the gracious gift of life, so that nothing will hinder your prayers. (1 PETER 3:7)

In other words, a husband should not merely react in annoyance when his wife does something that displeases him. He should treat her with love, compassion, and thoughtfulness. He should seek to understand why she said what she said or did what she did. Christian husbands should love and honor their wives, sharing all things with them and remaining faithfully committed to them. This is what a marriage is for—to provide a safe place where difficulties and problems can be worked out and resolved in an atmosphere of accepting love and complete forgiveness.

But Moses granted divorce, Jesus said, to expose the hardness of heart in many of the marriages in Israel. The law of divorce was not God's ideal choice for Israel. It was God's reluctant accommodation to the reality of so many hardened and sinful hearts.

The Jangling Alarm of Divorce

How do you soften a hardened heart? A heart is always soft when it recognizes its inability to handle a situation and relies on the wisdom and power of God. An attitude of obedience to God keeps the heart tender, loving, malleable, and reasonable. That is what the atmosphere in a marriage is supposed to be, but in Israel in those days (as in America in our day), there was hardness and harshness instead of wisdom and love.

Even in our time, divorce has a way of opening eyes and clarifying issues. Many times people come to me for counseling after a divorce and say, "I never understood what I was doing to my mate until after the divorce. Somehow this opened my eyes, and I began to see that the problem wasn't my spouse; it was me." Through the tragic pain of divorce, people often learn something about themselves. When they go on to a later marriage or restore their broken marriage, they often do so on a different basis, with a changed attitude.

We are living in an age, as you well know, when half of all marriages end in divorce. This breakdown of the family should frighten us and trouble us, because it marks the deterioration of our society. It is a jangling alarm, warning us that something is terribly wrong in our communities. It should drive us to acknowledge that we have failed to live out God's plan for marriage. Men do not know how to act as men, and women do not know how to act as women. Something is precipitating this enormous breakdown. Our skyrocketing divorce rates did not happen in a vacuum.

It is not enough to say, "Well, divorce is a massive social problem. What can one person do?" We should not throw up our hands in despair and apathy. Before divorce can become a social issue, it first becomes a personal issue between two people. When a marriage breaks down, it is *always* the result of the hardness of one or both human hearts. To solve this problem, each of us must look within, to the hardened condition of our hearts. And we must repent.

The purpose of the law of divorce is to unveil our sin and drive us to grace. Law can never heal the problem; it simply points it out. And the law of Moses, by permitting divorce, unfolded a private problem and made it a public predicament, so that everyone became aware of the issue. This is why God permitted divorce.

But we as individuals do not need to tolerate divorce. We can choose a soft heart, full of love, patience, and forgiveness, pliable and obedient to God. A whole family or a broken family? Each of us has the power to make that choice, in reliance on God's grace.

No Longer Two but One

After showing why Moses allowed divorce, Jesus gave God's plan for a healthy marriage, drawn from the creation story in Genesis. Mark records these words of Jesus:

> *"But at the beginning of creation God 'made them male and female.' 'For this reason a man will leave his father and mother and be united to his wife, and the two will become one flesh.' So they are no longer two, but one. Therefore what God has joined together, let man not separate."*
>
> (MARK 10:6–9)

You recognize those words. They are quoted at many weddings, and all too often, they are tragically ignored thereafter. Here Jesus goes back before Moses and the law, taking us to the dawn of creation, the beginning of the human race. He points out that the problem began there, long before Moses gave the law regarding divorce. The law came only to reveal the problem that already existed. The real problem is not divorce but marriage. Why should we bother to maintain it? What is our motivation for keeping a marriage together? That is the question answered by the Lord's quotation from Genesis.

In quoting this passage, Jesus forces us to focus on three important factors: the actions of God, the plan of God, and the warning of God. This three-point outline will help us to understand God's plan for marriage, as explained in our Lord's discourse on marriage and divorce.

First, Jesus points us to the actions of God. "At the beginning of creation God 'made them male and female.' " God made human beings to consist of two distinct and different sexes. This was no afterthought. The whole creative process, beginning with the first day of creation, was aimed at that one great fact. Everything God did, from the first verse of Genesis through that whole creative sequence until human beings appeared on the scene, was aimed at that one great event. This is how important the sexual nature of humanity is to God. He made human beings to be biologically and psychologically different from each other so that they could complement and complete one another. This was His plan.

People are creatures of three dimensions: body, soul, and spirit. In body, men and women are different, visibly and notably so. In the soul, the psyche, they are different as well, although the modern feminist movement seeks to deny it.

In decades past, the feminist movement has helped to correct a number of social ills, including unequal pay between men and women and the problem of sexual harassment in the workplace. But in attempting to correct some longstanding social ills, the feminist movement has perpetrated some terrible new ones. The so-called right to abortion is an example of a flagrant injustice that feminism has foisted on society. Feminists want to be sexually promiscuous without consequences, just like men. It is unfair, they claim, that women are subject to pregnancy while men are not, so they try to equalize men and women by giving women an unrestricted right to "terminate a pregnancy." This obsession with biological inequality is the result of twisted thinking about humanity. It is the result of denying the fact that God made us male and female and that men and women are psychologically and biologically different. Not unequal, but different. It is a difference we should celebrate, not obliterate.

While men and women are physically and psychologically different, we should never forget that on another level men and women are absolutely identical. I am speaking of the spiritual level. In a spiritual sense, men and women are the same; there is no difference. And because of this fact, men and women are equal before God. That is why Paul writes:

> *There is neither Jew nor Greek, slave nor free, male nor female, for you are all one in Christ Jesus.* (GALATIANS 3:28)

Here is the source of true, godly feminism—not a feminism that demands the right to take life but a feminism that is free to experience an equality of life alongside men in the family of faith. Whatever our distinctions and differences, as Christians we are one in the Spirit, we are one in Jesus Christ the Lord.

God made us male and female. That was His design for humanity, and the result is the wonderful richness and balance of maleness and femaleness in human society. When we live out our sexuality as God intended, the result is beautiful, harmonious completeness in Christ.

What God Had in Mind for Marriage

We move from the actions of God to the plan of God, the second point in the Lord's discourse on marriage and divorce. " 'For this reason a man will leave his father and mother and be united to his wife, and the two will become one flesh.' So they are no longer two, but one." Notice that phrase "for this reason." For what reason? For the reason that human beings are made male and female. They were made male and female so that they might leave father and mother, join to each other, and become one. That was God's plan in making us male and female.

There are many implications in that simple statement. For one thing, it disallows such current notions as homosexual marriage. Two people of the same sex cannot be married. That is a distortion and a violation of God's plan. It takes a man and a woman to make a marriage.

This statement also disallows practices such as polygamy. Notice that Jesus does not say that God made them males and females. He uses the singular, not the plural, because marriage is intended by God to be one man joined for life with one woman.

Our Lord also makes it clear that this relationship is the highest relationship possible in life. It takes priority over all others. The marriage relationship is even closer than a blood relationship in the mind and heart of God. Jesus does not say that the two will become a partnership or a union or a team or a corporation. He says "the two will become one flesh." There is no more intense relationship than that. That is the plan God had in mind from the beginning, when He made the first man and the first woman.

What, then, was God's purpose for marriage? That the two become one. Two distinct and different individuals, with different personalities and different gifts, blend their lives so completely that they become one flesh. That does not happen instantaneously when you get married. The wedding service does not make you one. The first act of sex after marriage does not make you one. It begins the process, but it does not complete it. It takes the whole marriage to accomplish this. Marriage is the process of two people becoming one over a lifetime together.

So God did not intend the man and the woman to live together as roommates. Marriage is not a matter of living separate lives, having separate careers, and sharing a house and a bed. Nor is a couple to split up over every problem or difficulty that arises between them, for that is a matter of hardness of heart. God intended that two soft-hearted, loving, forgiving, patient people would come together within the safe enclosure of a committed, covenant relationship, and there they would work out their differences and problems together as one flesh.

The goal of a husband and wife is to merge their lives in Christ. They must not act as rivals but become full partners. A successful marriage therefore is not without problems; it is a place where a husband and wife cooperate to solve their problems. In a successful marriage, neither partner says, "This is too hard. I'm quitting." Both partners have made a covenant to stick together, face their problems squarely, and rely on God to soften any hardness of heart between them.

A successful marriage is not a product but a process. It is a journey, not a destination. Just as a divorce—a failed marriage—reveals to the world a hardness of heart, a successful Christian marriage is a witness to the world of the love, acceptance, and forgiveness that two people can express to each other under the lordship of Jesus Christ.

Sex and Marriage

The third and final point of our Lord's discourse on marriage and divorce is a word of warning. Mark records:

> *"Therefore what God has joined together, let man not separate."*
>
> *When they were in the house again, the disciples asked Jesus about this. He answered, "Anyone who divorces his wife and marries another woman commits adultery against her. And if she divorces her husband and marries another man, she commits adultery."* (MARK 10:9–12)

Notice that Jesus lifts the whole matter far beyond the prevailing Jewish view of marriage. The Jewish view, as reflected in the law, was that only the husband could divorce his wife. But our Lord places the husband and wife on an equal basis. Not only can a wife be held accountable for committing adultery, but also a husband can be held equally accountable. Jesus makes both parties equally responsible for maintaining purity and faithfulness in the marriage.

He says that adultery, that is, sexual infidelity, destroys God's work of building oneness in a marriage. The phrase "what God has joined together" does not refer to a wedding ceremony. It refers to the mystical union that takes place within marriage. God blends two people into one flesh, sometimes with great pain and mutual exasperation. The marriage union is His work. He uses every aspect of this relationship, including the trials and conflicts the couple have gone through, to shape their souls, to reveal the hard places in their hearts, and to break down and soften those hard places. It is all part of His process of producing Christlike character in marriage partners.

Every newlywed couple, when they move into their first apartment or home, ought to put up a sign: Caution! God at work! That is what is taking place in that newly formed relationship. He is building a oneness, creating an ecstasy, artistically shaping a thing of exquisite beauty.

That is why sex is such a crucial component of a marriage. Sex is the visible picture of what a marriage ought to be, and that is why God reserves sex for marriage. What He is saying, in a beautifully metaphoric way, is that every marriage ought to follow the natural course of the act of sexual union. It begins with the separation and polarity of two individuals, one male and one female; it proceeds through a time of increasing closeness, enjoyment, and response; it rises to an ecstatic sense of climax and oneness; and it concludes with a lingering sense of contentment and peace.

Every act of marital sex is a picture of this miracle of God, in which He makes one where there were two. And that is why the act of adultery, of sexual infidelity, damages and destroys the work of God.

I know that among the readers of this book there will be many who have gone through the pain of divorce. It will include many who have experienced adultery, either as an innocent victim of a spouse's betrayal or as a partner in sin. I do not intend to inflict a sense of condemnation on any reader. But I do want to make clear what Jesus said. And He is unequivocal in stating that divorce is sin. Divorce is a violation of God's intention for marriage. Every time a divorce takes place, sin is involved.

This is not to say that divorce is never necessary. When one spouse threatens to harm the other spouse or the children—undoubtedly the ultimate form of a hardened heart—then there is no marriage worth saving. No one should remain in a violent relationship, and children must always be protected from the threat of harm. Such an extreme situation only underscores the point that divorce always involves some form of sin.

But thank God, even though the law condemns the sin that produces divorce, God offers us His grace and leads us to the place of forgiveness. There is the possibility of restoration, of healing, and a new beginning. God's way of restoration is the way of repentance. Repentance means that if you receive a second chance at marriage, either by remarrying your first spouse or by marrying anew, then you approach this marriage with a new and godly attitude of absolute commitment. This time when you say "till death do us part," you mean it.

I am troubled by people in the church who trivialize this issue that God treats so seriously. I have heard Christians say, "If you can't get along with your mate, if you don't like him, if you're not compatible with her, if you find someone you like better, get a divorce and get married again. Even if it's wrong, God will forgive you." Scripture never teaches that grace is that cheap, that forgiveness is dispensed like tap water to people who are insincere and unrepentant.

The Scriptures teach that forgiveness is given only to those who repent. Repentance means that you understand and acknowledge the awfulness and hurt your sin has caused, you feel shame and horror over what you have done, and you turn your back on that sin and walk with God in a new direction. Anything less is not true repentance and is unworthy of God's forgiveness. So don't think that an insincere "Oops, sorry, God! Excuse me while I sin!" will cover your willful, unrepentant, premeditated offenses. All you will ever accomplish in that way is to demonstrate to God that you truly have a hardened heart.

Jesus calls us to soften the hard places of our hearts. He calls us to the joy of discovering the ecstatic, exciting miracle of oneness in a genuine Christian marriage. He calls us to experience what it means for God to join two separate lives together into a beautiful artwork of oneness—a testimony to the whole world of the grace and love of God and of His power to change human lives.

God is in the business of softening hearts and building up families as safe havens of love, acceptance, and forgiveness. That's His plan for every marriage, including yours.

nineteen

The Plight of the Overprivileged

➤ **Mark 10:13–31**

William Henry Vanderbilt was a rich young ruler in nineteenth-century America. The son of shipping and railroad magnate Cornelius Vanderbilt, William multiplied his inherited wealth many times over in the railroad business. By the time of his death, his fortune was estimated at more than $200 million, which made him the Bill Gates of his day. Shortly before his death, he lamented, "I have received no more gratification or enjoyment from my wealth than my neighbor on the next block who is worth only half a million."

It seems that "wealthy" is truly a relative term, is it not?

In this study, we will be introduced to a wealthy young man of Jesus' day, a man who no doubt inherited his wealth as William Vanderbilt did, a man who was powerful, young, rich, and too attached to his wealth for his soul's good.

Jesus Loves the Little Children

Before we meet the rich young ruler, Mark first brings us the story of Jesus' blessing of the children. As you will see, Mark links these stories and ties them with a single thread. When preachers preach on this portion of Mark, they tend to treat these stories as two separate, unrelated incidences. That, I believe, is a mistake. There is a clear linkage between these two stories that is crucial to observe. Let's see how Mark begins this account.

> *People were bringing little children to Jesus to have him touch them, but the disciples rebuked them. When Jesus saw this, he was indignant. He said to them, "Let the little children come to me, and do not hinder them, for the kingdom of God belongs to such as these. I tell you the truth, anyone who will not receive the kingdom of God like a little child will never enter it." And he took the children in his arms, put his hands on them and blessed them.* (MARK 10:13–16)

Artists love to paint this scene: Jesus gathering the children around Him, one wriggly little boy on His lap, a little girl standing demurely at His side looking up into His eyes, others clustering around, eager for His attention. This scene has proven to be a source of tremendous blessing to millions of children around the world. It is the inspiration for such beloved children's songs as "Jesus Loves Me, This I Know" and "Jesus Loves the Little Children."

I want to touch on only two major points in this account, because I want to link it to the story that follows, the story of the rich young ruler. The first point is Jesus' rebuke of the disciples. Mark indicates that the disciples were trying to protect Jesus by preventing parents from bringing their children to Him. When Jesus saw this, He was indignant. The Greek shows that He took a severe tone in reprimanding the disciples.

The disciples meant well, but they had missed the point that Jesus had been making about the true worth of a child. These disciples thought that Jesus needed protection from bothersome children. But Jesus points out that the children need protection from bumbling adults. This is significant, because it shows that children were made for God, and it shows how God views children.

The children in this story were drawn to Jesus. They loved Him immediately and wanted to be in His presence. Notice that Jesus uses this occasion as yet another object lesson for the training of His disciples. He shows them that it is easy to come to Jesus when you are a child. He is the one children need and want, above all else. So adults need to get out of the way and let the children come to Jesus. Children are always being told, "These are grownup matters. You don't need to know these things. You are just in the way. Go someplace and play. Don't bother the grownups." Jesus says, "Don't push the children to the side. Bring them here to me. 'Grownup business' can wait. The children are my business."

The second significant point Jesus makes is that children exemplify the qualities we all need to enter the kingdom of God: "I tell you the truth, anyone who will not receive the kingdom of God like a little child will never enter it." He does not elaborate what these qualities are. He leaves it up to us to discover them in the eyes of a child, for these are qualities that every child represents, regardless of background, culture, or language. Bible commentators have offered many guesses as to what those childlike qualities might be, but Jesus leaves it to us to discover them.

As a card-carrying grandfather, I have conducted extensive research into the subject, observing my little grandchildren in an attempt to discover what qualities Jesus has in mind. Here are the findings of my exhaustive (and sometimes exhausting) research.

The first and most obvious quality about children is that they have a simple, uncomplicated approach to life. They go right to the heart of things. This is why children ask such frank questions. If you lift a child in your arms, he is likely to look at you and say,

"How come you have such a big nose?" All your adult friends have avoided the subject of your nose for years, but a child will ask. Children are forthright and unpretentious.

The uncomplicated nature of children holds true in every area of their lives. When their bodily needs are demanding, they want that need satisfied now. They want to eat when hungry, drink when thirsty, sleep when sleepy, and when nature calls— look out! They are direct and immediate when they need affection. They will come to you, throw their arms around you, and hug you for all they're worth. When they're curious, they will ask direct, uncomplicated questions and expect direct, uncomplicated answers. In the realm of the spirit, they continually express that sense of wonder, excitement, and awe that we so commonly associate with childhood.

I once saw a mother dragging a little girl down the street. The child saw some mica flashing in a stone and stopped to pick it up. "Oh, Mother, look!" said the girl. "There's stars in the stone!" I was saddened when the mother pulled the child's arm in annoyance and said, "Come on! We haven't time for that now!" That mother missed a beautiful opportunity to share the world of her child.

Children have a marvelous sense of the wonder and mystery of our world, of the glories of nature and the glories of the realm of God and the spirit. How tragic that we, as adults, so easily lose that, and worse, that we often wring all of the wonder and enthusiasm out of our children.

A second aspect of childlikeness that Jesus wants us to grasp is this: a child is wonderfully teachable. Every child wants to learn and is ready to be led. Children recognize their basic need for help and instruction, and they are open and malleable. As someone once observed, children are wet cement. This is one of the beautiful characteristics of children, and one that Jesus wants us to emulate.

Are you and I teachable? Are we open to new ideas, new concepts, and new ways of looking at the world? Are we receptive to the new things God wants to teach us and the fresh and exciting work He wants to do in our lives? Or are we rigidly, permanently set in our ways, our ideas, and our opinions? Jesus said, "Anyone who will not receive the kingdom of God like a little child will never enter it."

Third, every child is by nature obedient. If you are a parent, I know you are already taking exception to that. But think about it. Children are by nature responsive. They respond to what they are taught. They are trusting. They hear what they are told, and they will later parrot it as truth. They respond immediately to what they are told. They do not say, "Let me think about this for a while," as adults will. If you tell them something, they will act on it without delay.

These, I believe, are the characteristics Jesus had in mind. They are essential, He says, in order to enter the kingdom of God. When you listen to the teaching of Jesus and you understand what He says, when you respond directly and simply and wholeheartedly, when you are teachable and obedient to His loving commands, then the door to the kingdom of God is wide open to you. As you enter that door with childlike wonder, trust, and faith, you enter a realm—God's realm—where you can grow, develop, and become strong and spiritually healthy.

That is what Jesus underscores for us as the children gather lovingly around Him, hugging Him, laughing with Him, crawling into His lap. "Let the little children come to me," He says, "and do not hinder them, for the kingdom of God belongs to such as these."

The Young Aristocrat

Next Mark introduces a new incident, but as we shall soon see, this incident is closely related to the scene we have just explored.

> *As Jesus started on his way, a man ran up to him and fell on his knees before him. "Good teacher," he asked, "what must I do to inherit eternal life?"*
>
> *"Why do you call me good?" Jesus answered. "No one is good—except God alone."* (MARK 10:17–18)

This is the well-known story of the rich young ruler. The accounts in Luke and Matthew tell us that this young man was very wealthy and that he was a ruler, a member of the aristocracy.

This is an amazing scene. A wealthy, powerful, young aristocrat comes and kneels at the feet of an itinerant peasant teacher from Galilee. To whom might we compare this young ruler? We might liken him to the young John F. Kennedy, before he was elected president. When JFK was running for his party's nomination in 1960, he visited a West Virginia coal mine. He shook hands with one of the miners, a grimy, sweaty man whose skin was black with coal soot. As the miner's rough hand gripped Kennedy's soft hand, the miner asked, "Is it true that you were born to money, and everything you ever wanted was handed to you by your rich daddy?"

"I suppose so," said Kennedy.

"And is it true you've never done a hard day's work in your entire life?"

Uncomfortably Kennedy admitted, "Yes, it's true."

"Well," said the coal miner, "you haven't missed a thing."

The man who knelt at the feet of Jesus was in the same class. No doubt born to wealth and power, the rich young ruler had lived a privileged life and hadn't missed a thing. Yet he was empty inside. His life was meaningless. Despite his wealth and privilege, he knew that he didn't have this thing called eternal life that Jesus, the traveling, homeless preacher from Nazareth, had been talking about. So this was the young man's question: "Good teacher, what must I do to inherit eternal life?"

This young man had heard Jesus preach. He was almost certainly present when Jesus answered the Pharisees' question on divorce. He had seen Jesus blessing the children and rebuking the disciples, telling them they must become like little children in order to enter the kingdom of God. Something stirred in this young man's heart as he listened, a sense of his need, a yearning for truth and the reality of life. So, his soul bursting with questions, the young man runs to Jesus, kneels before Him as a sign of respect and humility, and asks Jesus for the secret of eternal life.

This young man possessed at least the first of the childlike qualities Jesus said you must have: simple directness. His inner yearning for spiritual reality and meaning had been stirred. He wanted the truth, and he wanted it now. So he asked, "What must I do?"

The initial reply of Jesus has puzzled many Bible scholars over the centuries. Jesus says, "Why do you call me good? No one is good—except God alone." Liberal commentators have seized on this reply as a statement in which Jesus denies that He is God. Their argument is that when the young man calls Jesus good, Jesus answers as if to say, "Don't call me good. I'm not good. Only God is good, and I'm not God."

The problem with this view is that in many other passages Jesus does identify Himself with God the Father. In John 10:30, for example, Jesus says plainly and definitively, "I and the Father are one." In fact, the reason He was crucified is that He clearly and definitely claimed to be God, as this exchange between Jesus and the Jewish leaders, shortly before the crucifixion, shows:

> *The high priest said to him, "I charge you under oath by the living God: Tell us if you are the Christ, the Son of God."*
>
> *"Yes, it is as you say," Jesus replied. "But I say to all of you: In the future you will see the Son of Man sitting at the right hand of the Mighty One and coming on the clouds of heaven."*
>
> *Then the high priest tore his clothes and said, "He has spoken blasphemy! Why do we need any more witnesses? Look, now you have heard the blasphemy. What do you think?"*
>
> *"He is worthy of death," they answered.*
>
> (MATTHEW 26:63–66)

Jesus claimed to be God, and that claim was used against Him by the priests and scribes who wanted Him dead. So Jesus cannot be denying either His goodness or His godhood in this dialogue with the rich young ruler. Here is what Jesus is truly saying to the young man: "Why do you call me good? What do you mean by 'good'? If you understand what 'good' means, then you know that only God is good. Therefore, if you call me good, you are saying that I am God." Particularly in view of what Jesus says about Himself elsewhere in Scripture, the only valid interpretation is that Jesus is forcing this young man to recognize and confess who He is: the Son of God, the Messiah, God in human form.

It is apparent that Jesus is probing this young man, searching to see if he is willing to investigate and learn about Him. In short, Jesus wants to know if this direct and uncomplicated young man is also as teachable as a child. Jesus is asking, "Are you teachable? Are you willing to investigate and think through your questions in order to discover spiritual reality? Are you willing to open your mind to the awesome reality of who I am?"

Next Jesus tests the young aristocrat on the third quality of childlikeness, probing him with this question in mind: "Are you obedient?" Mark records that Jesus says to him:

> *"You know the commandments: 'Do not murder, do not commit adultery, do not steal, do not give false testimony, do not defraud, honor your father and mother.' "* (MARK 10:19)

In other words, "What has God said to you? Have you obeyed the commands of God? Are you obedient?" Again the young man responds eagerly, instantly, without hesitation:

> *"Teacher,"* he declared, *"all these I have kept since I was a boy."*
> *Jesus looked at him and loved him.* (MARK 10:20–21)

Jesus believes the young man. He never suggests that this young aristocrat is lying or even self-deceived. He is satisfied with the young man's reply. No wonder Mark goes on to say, "Jesus looked at him and loved him." Here is an openhearted, moral, excellent young man. Jesus sees in him the childlike qualities that would enable him to enter the kingdom. But Jesus has one thing more to ask of this young man.

> *"One thing you lack,"* he said. *"Go, sell everything you have and give to the poor, and you will have treasure in heaven. Then come, follow me."*
> *At this the man's face fell. He went away sad, because he had great wealth.* (MARK 10:21–22)

Jesus is saying, "You have the qualities it takes to enter the kingdom. You are simple and direct, you are teachable, and you have been obedient—up to this moment. Just one more thing: How obedient are you now? How willing are you to act on what you know to be true? You lack only one thing. Go and sell all that you have, give to the poor, and follow me. If you do that, all the treasure you could possibly want or need is yours, stored up for you in heaven."

There is a supreme irony in what happens next. "At this the man's face fell. He went away sad, because he had great wealth." If you had great wealth, would you be sad? This man was rich and sad, and he was sad because of his riches. Why? Because it was suddenly clear to him that he could not serve two masters. Jesus had pierced to the core of this young man's life. He had shown the rich young ruler that his life was owned by another god. Yes, the young man wanted to live a moral and obedient life before God; yes, he wanted to experience eternal life. But he also wanted to be rich. He did not want to let go of the power, influence, status, and material pleasures that his wealth gave him. Jesus made it clear to him that he could not serve Almighty God and the almighty dollar. He had to choose one or the other. He chose to cling to his meaningless wealth and let go of eternal life.

As I pointed out earlier, I do not believe that this is the end of the story for this wealthy young aristocrat. I believe, based on various clues in Scripture, that this rich young man was none other than Mark. We know that Mark's mother was a wealthy woman of influence named Mary, who owned a large house in Jerusalem. And I think it is noteworthy that only Mark's account of this encounter includes the intimate detail found in verse 21: "Jesus looked at him and loved him." How could Mark have known this fact unless he learned it from Jesus?

I offer this, however, as nothing more than an interesting speculation.

The Trap of Wealth

The disciples have been gathered around, watching this drama between Jesus and the young aristocrat. So the Lord seizes on this opportunity to give them a lesson on wealth.

> *Jesus looked around and said to his disciples, "How hard it is for the rich to enter the kingdom of God!"*
>
> *The disciples were amazed at his words. But Jesus said again, "Children, how hard it is to enter the kingdom of God! It is easier for a camel to go through the eye of a needle than for a rich man to enter the kingdom of God."*
>
> *The disciples were even more amazed, and said to each other, "Who then can be saved?"*
>
> *Jesus looked at them and said, "With man this is impossible, but not with God; all things are possible with God."*
>
> (MARK 10:23–27)

This is a remarkable statement. Jesus highlights two facts. First, He underscores the terrible danger of affluence. People are easily ensnared by the things money can buy. Most of us are envious of rich people, secretly if not openly. We all wish we had money. Yet, if we understood what Jesus is saying, we would not feel that way. We would feel sorry for the rich. We tend to think of wealthy people as overprivileged; Jesus says they are underprivileged. They are deprived people. The things they have rob them of so much. Jesus points out the terrible danger of affluence. "How hard it is," He says, "for the rich to enter the kingdom of God." And so important is the point that He repeats it for emphasis: "Children, how hard it is to enter the kingdom of God!"

Then Jesus employs a vivid metaphor: "It is easier for a camel to go through the eye of a needle than for a rich man to enter the kingdom of God." I am aware that some Bible commentators have attempted to soften this metaphor by explaining that "the eye of a needle" referred to a tiny gate, about four feet high, located in the wall of Jerusalem. The reasoning goes that if a camel's burdens are removed (in the same way that Jesus told the rich man to unburden himself by giving his wealth to the poor), then that camel could, by squirming and wriggling, barely squeeze through that tiny gate.

I do not see much evidence to support that view. I am convinced that when Jesus says "the eye of a needle," He is referring to a literal sewing needle. Could a camel—no matter how much you lighten its load—manage to squeeze through the eye of a sewing needle? Absolutely not, and that is the image the disciples pictured when they heard Jesus speak those words. They interpreted Him correctly. Jesus was saying to them, "It's impossible."

At that point, the disciples were baffled. The rich were held in the highest esteem. "A rich man," they thought, "with his ability to make great donations to God's treasury, should be able to buy his way into the kingdom of God. But if it's impossible for a rich man to enter the kingdom, then what hope is there for the rest of us?"

And Jesus affirmed their impression of His words. "With man," He said, "this is impossible."

Why is it impossible? What do riches have to do with our spiritual vitality and salvation? It is clear from the context that riches tend to destroy the qualities you must have in order to enter the kingdom of God. They destroy the childlikeness of life, and you can see why. Affluence creates a concern for secondary values. Rich people are not worried about where their next meal is coming from; they worry about what it will taste like and what the setting will be. Rich people are not concerned about whether they will have shelter and clothing to wear; they are taken up with fashion and style and decor and whether they are in the right mode or not. They are not concerned about whether they worship God rightly or not, but whether they are in a beautiful building that pleases them aesthetically. The possession of riches shifts a person's concern from the elementary, necessary things to the complex, secondary things.

Furthermore, riches hinder teachability. Wealth has a tendency to produce pride and arrogance in those who possess it. You may have noticed how some wealthy people seem to enjoy exercising power and even bullying others because they are rich and powerful. They can get other others to fear them, agree with them, and bow and scrape before them because of their wealth. If you took away their riches, would anyone be intimidated by them? Would anyone kowtow to them? Hardly. Stripped of their riches, these arrogant people would appear as simpletons, almost fools. But because people jump at their slightest whim, the rich often think themselves wise and powerful when they are not.

I am not attacking all rich people. I know a number of godly, wise, wealthy people—people who, by the grace of God, have escaped the snare that riches often set for people. I am stating a general principle: riches can easily destroy a teachable spirit by creating a false sense of power and authority. People who have power because of their money begin to feel that they ought to be the teachers. They do not need to learn; they already know everything! The result, as I have seen many times, is arrogance, insensitivity to the feelings of others, and a tendency to talk instead of listening, boss others around instead of serving others, and demand their way instead of seeking God's way.

As Scottish historian Thomas Carlyle (1795–1881) once observed, for every hundred men who can withstand adversity, only one can withstand prosperity. Wealth a trap for the unwary and unwise. It is a dry rot that eats away at the simplicity of life and the sensitivity of the heart. It removes people from the realities of life. It fills the human heart with pride and arrogance.

Finally, affluence gradually enslaves those who become attached to it. It builds an increasing dependence on comfort and the good life, until it is impossible to let go. Like the rich young ruler, the wealthy gradually become owned by their possessions, even though clinging to those possessions leaves them sad and empty. That is why Jesus said it is impossible for rich people to enter the kingdom of God.

But note this! Jesus says, "With man this is impossible." With man—but not with God. Here Jesus gives us a note of grace, a ray of hope. Humanly speaking, the enslavement of riches is inevitable, and all who possess riches are doomed to be possessed by their riches. But by the grace of God, the enslavement of riches can sometimes be broken.

A pastor once told me, "I have a number of wealthy people in my congregation, and they trouble me, because they dabble with Christianity." That is often true. Of the many wealthy Christians I know, I find it rare to find one who is truly, radically committed to obeying the Word of God. Most go along only to a point. Thank God for those few whose hearts have been kept safe from the snare of material possessions, whose hearts truly belong to God and God alone.

I don't know how God preserves a wealthy person from becoming possessed by wealth, but I do know that only God can do it. He can break through, and He sometimes does. He sometimes creates in a wealthy man or woman a tremendous distaste for material things; He makes that person so aware of an emptiness and spiritual hunger that he or she loses all interest in the ups and downs of the stock market, finding tax loopholes, acquiring property and possessions, and the like. They see the hollow mockery of material things and, like the rich young ruler, they begin to search for the realities of life. Sometimes a person has to suffer catastrophe—almost lose family or business or health—before gaining that godly perspective.

But however God chooses to work His miracle and draw the overprivileged to Himself, one thing is sure. The rich person comes to Christ in precisely the same way as does the homeless person on skid row. In the words of the hymn, "Nothing in my hand I bring / Simply to thy cross I cling." We all come to the throne of grace as guilty sinners, powerless to save ourselves. Rich man, poor man—every man and every woman must come to Christ acknowledging moral bankruptcy and spiritual poverty.

The First and the Last

Next our Lord draws a contrast and sets forth what happens to those who serve Him.

> *Peter said to him, "We have left everything to follow you!"*
> *"I tell you the truth," Jesus replied, "no one who has left home or brothers or sisters or mother or father or children or fields for me and the gospel will fail to receive a hundred times as much in this present age (homes, brothers, sisters, mothers, children and fields—and with them, persecutions) and in the age to come, eternal life. But many who are first will be last, and the last first."* (MARK 10:28–31)

The key to this passage is the last sentence: "But many who are first will be last, and the last first." People often ask, "What is Jesus teaching here? Is He telling us that if we have money and wealth, we must give it all away, as He required this rich young ruler to do? Must I take a vow of poverty in order to be a true Christian?" Some people have interpreted this passage to mean exactly that.

For hundreds of years in the Christian church, almost from the end of the first century, men and women have understood it this way. They took a vow of poverty, gave away everything, and became monks and nuns, ascetics and hermits. Some gave up everything and went around as beggars. But did this mean they were truly obedient and fulfilling this passage?

"No," Jesus says, "many who are first, apparently, in giving up things, turn out to be last." You see, He is not talking about external things. There is plenty of testimony from the history of the church to prove that He is not commanding all Christians to impoverish themselves. These self-impoverishing practices provide no guarantee of true spirituality. He is talking, rather, about the attitude you have toward material things. That is the key: an attitude that recognizes that everything is a gift of God, and the gifts of God are to be shared, not hoarded or selfishly squandered.

Money exists to be spent on the needs of one's family and invested in God's work. God is the Lord of the harvest, the source of our income. We do not own our possessions and money. We are stewards of things that God has entrusted to us. A day is coming in which every one of us must give an account of how we used all that God has entrusted to us. It is not wrong to use a certain amount of what God has given you for enjoyment and pleasure. As the apostle Paul writes, God "richly provides us with everything for our enjoyment" (1 Timothy 6:17). So enjoy! But be responsible, be a good steward or caretaker of everything you have received from God.

If you have the attitude that the things God has given you belong to Him and not to you, then adversity is no great hardship for you. If God takes away some of your material things, so what? You remember that they were not yours to begin with. You know that what matters is that you have your salvation. That is the attitude Jesus wants us to have, regardless of whether we are rich or poor or somewhere in between.

Once this is your outlook on your life and your possessions, you begin to realize that you can never give up anything to God except what you have already received from Him. It was all His to begin with. What's more, as Jesus tells Peter, you realize that you can never give up anything that God does not restore to you a hundredfold. Jesus said, "No one who has left home or brothers or sisters or mother or father or children or fields for me and the gospel will fail to receive a hundred times as much in this present age." Notice, Jesus does not say a hundred percent, but a hundred times as much.

How will this come to you? That's always a surprise! But the promises of the Lord never fail. I have found that if you are willing to hold things lightly rather than tightly, you will find that people will open doors to you, Christian brothers and sisters will have things that you can use, and you won't have to pay taxes or rent on them. You will have homes and families and boats and pleasure outings offered to you for God's sake, through the friendship and love of other Christians.

Of course, Jesus promises persecution too. He makes that promise in the midst of this passage, almost as if He is offering persecution as one of the advantages of the Christian life. In a way, it is. If you are a Christian, you will have enemies. But you should feel complimented to be hated by such people. Your enemies are a credit to your character, a testimony to your faithfulness to God. You will be glad that you have such enemies and that they are persecuting you, because you will be in good company: the company of the Lord Jesus Christ and all His saints.

What a difference it makes once we learn to hold things lightly for His sake. What a difference it makes to live to please Him and not just ourselves. If we sacrifice for His sake, we help to advance His cause, and we will be surprised to discover how God rewards those who have given up much for His sake. We will be surprised to discover that "many who are first will be last, and the last first."

In his first letter to Timothy, the apostle Paul made a statement that stands as a powerful commentary on our Lord's words in Mark 10:

> *Command those who are rich in this present world not to be arrogant nor to put their hope in wealth, which is so uncertain, but to put their hope in God, who richly provides us with everything for our enjoyment. Command them to do good, to be rich in good deeds, and to be generous and willing to share. In this way they will lay up treasure for themselves as a firm foundation for the coming age, so that they may take hold of the life that is truly life.* (1 TIMOTHY 6:17–19)

Whether rich or poor in the things of the world, the Christian who learns to have this attitude toward earthly possessions can be assured of great riches in eternity with Jesus.

twenty

The Ambitious Heart

➤ **Mark 10:32–52**

Julius Hickerson was a brilliant young doctor. His friends and family had no doubt that he was poised for a successful career and a comfortable life as a physician in the United States. But Dr. Hickerson felt God calling him to serve as a missionary doctor in the South American nation of Colombia. When he announced his plans, his friends thought he was crazy. "Just look at the career you'll be throwing away!" they said. "Think of all the money you could make in the States! If you go to Colombia, you'll just be wasting your life!"

For a long time after Dr. Hickerson arrived in Colombia, it looked as if his friends were right. He worked long hours in remote South American villages, treating patients and sharing the gospel. The people, however, were resistant to the gospel. At the end of two years' work, he didn't have a single convert to show for all his labor.

One day he was in a small mission plane, flying supplies to a remote village, but he never arrived. The plane crashed in the forest outside the village, and Julius Hickerson was killed. Just as his friends had predicted—a wasted life. Dr. Hickerson had died for nothing.

A couple of years passed, and the missionary organization that had sent Dr. Hickerson to Colombia, the Southern Baptists, decided to send another missionary to Colombia. The plan was for this missionary to resume the work that was interrupted with the death of Julius Hickerson. The missionary traveled into the region where the doctor had met his death and was astonished to find that all of the local tribesmen were Christians.

The more the missionary explored, the more Christians he found. There were thriving churches throughout the region. Somehow, during the time following Dr. Hickerson's death, that whole area had been Christianized.

The missionary asked the tribesmen, "How did this happen? Where did you learn about Jesus Christ?"

"From this book," they answered, and they showed him a well-worn Bible that had been translated into their language. After the plane crash, the tribesmen had gone through the wreckage, looking for food and other items they could use. They found the Bible and began to read it. They passed it around to other members of the tribe, who also read it. As they read, the tribesmen began, one by one, to turn their lives over to Jesus Christ. They formed churches, and they sent out people to nearby villages, spreading the good news throughout the region.

After hearing this incredible story, the missionary opened the Bible and saw a name written on the flyleaf: Julius Hickerson.

A wasted life? No life is ever wasted when that life is committed to following Jesus Christ.

At this juncture in our study of Mark's gospel, we find Jesus on His way to Jerusalem. His footsteps take Him inexorably closer and closer to the cross, to the end of His mortal life. His disciples hear Him predicting His end. Some wonder, "Is He crazy? Is He throwing away His mission and His ministry as the Messiah? Is He really going to Jerusalem just to die? What a waste!"

But, as we shall see, a life that is ended is not necessarily a life that is wasted. As the drama of the cross begins to unfold, astonishing events lie ahead for Jesus and His disciples and for you and me.

Jesus Is Resolved to Go

This account shows that Jesus foresaw the cross and all that it would involve, yet He resolutely kept His footsteps pointed toward Calvary. It also shows how blind the disciples were and how they continued to ignore and deny the revelation Jesus gave them. Mark writes:

> *They were on their way up to Jerusalem, with Jesus leading the way, and the disciples were astonished, while those who followed were afraid. Again he took the Twelve aside and told them what was going to happen to him. "We are going up to Jerusalem," he said, "and the Son of Man will be betrayed to the chief priests and teachers of the law. They will condemn him to death and will hand him over to the Gentiles, who will mock him and spit on him, flog him and kill him. Three days later he will rise."* (MARK 10:32–34)

This is the third time we have seen Jesus make this special announcement to His disciples. Each time He informs them, in increasing detail, what the cross will involve. And each time He includes the promise of the resurrection, which they never seem to hear. The atmosphere is tense among the disciples as they walk along the road. Notice carefully how Mark sets the scene.

He says that Jesus went first, all alone, at the head of the procession. Behind Jesus came the Twelve, who, says Mark, were amazed. Behind them came the crowd, waiting on His words, but as

Mark ominously observes, "those who followed were afraid." There was a strange sense of impending doom, of approaching crisis. The disciples were aware of this, and even the crowd felt the tension.

What astonished the disciples and made the crowd fearful was Jesus' attitude. The Greek suggests that Jesus had a tough, resolute determination to go to Jerusalem. He was adamant, and no one could dissuade Him. The people had seen the hostility of the Jewish religious leaders, and everyone around Jesus knew He was going into danger.

Jesus' third announcement of His impending death is the most detailed yet. He knows what He is heading into. He may not know the exact timing, but that will unfold as He goes on. What He does know, He states with remarkable precision and accuracy. He will be betrayed into the hands of the priests and the scribes. They will hand Him over to the Romans (the Gentiles), and He will be condemned to death. Then Jesus adds three details that were not included in any previous announcement: the Romans will mock Him, spit on Him, and scourge Him.

How did Jesus know these things? He learned them from the Scriptures. Every one of these events is predicted by the Old Testament prophets. Luke tells us that at this time, Jesus said to His disciples, "We are going up to Jerusalem, and everything that is written by the prophets about the Son of Man will be fulfilled" (Luke 18:31). Our Lord did not require any supernatural insight to know what was about to happen. What He predicted to His followers was what He had learned by studying Isaiah 53, Psalm 22, and other Old Testament passages that predicted these events.

Contrasting Goals

Contrast the goal of Jesus with the goal of the disciples. Jesus has His face set toward Jerusalem and the cross. But, as Mark shows, the disciples are looking toward a different goal. They believe they are on a pathway to personal glory.

> *Then James and John, the sons of Zebedee, came to him. "Teacher," they said, "we want you to do for us whatever we ask."*
>
> *"What do you want me to do for you?" he asked.*
> *They replied, "Let one of us sit at your right and the other at your left in your glory."* (MARK 10:35–37)

Matthew tells us that the mother of James and John asked this of Jesus, suggesting that the brothers had talked her into asking. Mark shows us that whatever role their mother may have played, these two disciples were ambitious on their own behalf. Jesus knew the request had come from them, so He answered them. Many interpreters have misconstrued this story, thinking the disciples were wrong in making this request. But that is not true. They were asking for something Jesus had given them every reason to ask for, a few days earlier.

Matthew records that Jesus had promised them that when He came into His glory, they would sit on twelve thrones and judge the twelve tribes of Israel. This is what they had on their minds as they walked to Jerusalem. In their thinking, they have twelve thrones waiting for them there. So these two disciples, James and John, asked for three specific things.

First, they asked for preeminence. They wanted to sit on the thrones and have the honor and exaltation that a throne represents. This is nothing more than what Jesus had promised them.

Second, they wanted proximity. Once the disciples knew that twelve thrones were waiting for them, it is easy to understand why they would discuss where those thrones would be placed in relationship to Jesus. James and John, talking this over with their mother, decided there was no good reason why they could not belong to the inner circle, with one on the right hand and one on the left. So they came with a request. They wanted to be close to Jesus. It is not wrong to want to be close to Jesus. They knew they are going to sit with Him, and they thought it reasonable to ask for positions nearest Him.

Third, they wanted power. That, of course, is what a throne represents. In some sense, they had already experienced the gift of power from Jesus. They had been sent out and given power to raise the dead and heal the sick and cast out demons. So they are asking for what had already been promised. There is nothing wrong with that.

When our Lord replied, He did not rebuke them. He did not say, "What a bunch of swelled heads you have! How arrogant can you be?" He did not rebuff their ambition to be near Him, to have preeminence, or to have power. Instead, He told them they were going about it the wrong way and with a lack of understanding of what they were asking for.

The Cup and the Baptism

Jesus did not want His disciples to ask in ignorance for something they did not understand. So He alerted them to the fact that there would be a heavy price to pay in fulfilling their ambition. Mark writes:

> "You don't know what you are asking," Jesus said. "Can you drink the cup I drink or be baptized with the baptism I am baptized with?"
>
> "We can," they answered.
>
> Jesus said to them, "You will drink the cup I drink and be baptized with the baptism I am baptized with, but to sit

at my right or left is not for me to grant. These places belong
to those for whom they have been prepared."

(MARK 10:38–40)

Jesus is saying, "You are not asking for the wrong thing. You are asking for the right thing but without any understanding of what is involved or what it will cost you." He implies that He is on the same path as the one they desire to follow. He is on the path to glory, but that path leads through the horrors of the cross. He is ready to pay the price. They haven't looked at the price tag.

"Can you drink the cup I drink," He asks, "or be baptized with the baptism I am baptized with?" Here Jesus employs two metaphors to help us understand what He faced: a cup and a baptism. What does the cup mean? We all know the words of the psalmist: "My cup runneth over" (Psalm 23:5 KJV). What does that imagery mean? The cup symbolizes the realm of your experience, the circumstances into which you are placed, circumstances that, we all hope, will result in a life of joy, peace, and serenity.

In the Old Testament, however, the cup is also used of things that are not so joyful. Jeremiah speaks of Israel having to drink the cup of the fury of the Lord at His hand. In that instance, the cup represented something that had to be drunk, even against your will. So a cup is also a metaphor of what life hands to you, a circumstance in which you have no choice. It may produce either joy or despair, but a cup speaks of something you must drink.

What, then, is the cup that Jesus says He must drink? He speaks of the cross. He sees it as a cup given to Him by His Father. Later, in the Garden of Gethsemene, He will pray, "Father, if you are willing, take this cup from me; yet not my will, but yours be done" (Luke 22:42). He is speaking of the whole spectrum of events surrounding the cross: the rejection, the torture, the mocking, the flogging, the spitting, the nails, the tearing of the flesh, the dislocation of the bones, the slow draining of the blood, the laboring for breath. But most of all, His cup was the burden of the sin of the world, the lonely separation from the Father, and the darkness of death. All of this is the Father's choice for Him, the cup that the Father has handed Him to drink.

When Jesus uses the metaphor of baptism, He again employs imagery that is common in the Scriptures, in the Old and New Testaments. To baptize means to dip or submerge a person or thing in a liquid. Paul writes that the Israelites who fled Egypt by passing through the middle of the Red Sea "were all baptized into Moses in the cloud and in the sea" (1 Corinthians 10:2). A way was opened for them, so that they were surrounded by water, even though they walked on dry land. Thus they were "baptized into Moses."

Baptism, then, is an image of an event that Jesus must pass through and that will engulf Him. He will be immersed in it so that no part of Him will remain untouched. The cross would seek Him out at every level of His being, and the horror and loneliness of the cross would overwhelm Him. It is as the psalmist wrote in Psalm 42:7: "Deep calls to deep in the roar of your waterfalls; all your waves and breakers have swept over me." Jesus would be saturated by the baptism of the cross.

So, with this insight into the meaning of the cup and the baptism, we now have a sense of what He is saying to James and John: "This is the price of glory, and it is a very high price. Are you willing to pay it?" And look at the self-confidence these disciples exude. They respond, "Sure, Lord! Just bring it on! We can take it!"

And notice the reply of Jesus. He doesn't try to explain it all to them. They will find out soon enough as events unfold. He takes them at their word. "All right," He says, "if you want to drink of my cup and be baptized with my baptism, you shall."

Did these disciples know what they were asking for? They didn't have a clue! And sometimes we don't either, when we ask of God. But God often grants it anyway. I'm sure that if these disciples had known what it meant, they would never have asked. Dr. A. B. Bruce once put it this way: "If crosses would leave us alone, we would leave them alone too." But crosses, cups, and baptisms do not leave us alone. They are handed to us. We cannot escape them. We are called to suffer along with Jesus. We too are called to bear reproach, shame, anguish, suffering, and death.

As it turned out, this is what happened in the lives of these disciples. James was the first of the apostles to die, as recorded in Acts 22. He was arrested and beheaded by Herod. James was the first martyr, and John was the last to be martyred. These two brothers formed a kind of parenthesis of martyrdom, within which all the apostles were put to death, each in turn, for the sake of Jesus. We are not told how John died, although some writings of the early church fathers suggest that he was boiled in oil. Others say that he died a natural death. Although the mode of his death is uncertain, we do know he was exiled to the island of Patmos for the testimony of Jesus, and he underwent much suffering for the Lord's sake. So Jesus granted them their request.

But one thing He could not grant them. "To sit at my right or left is not for me to grant. These places belong to those for whom they have been prepared." This is an illuminating statement. Jesus implies that the Father chooses people for this honor. He chooses the person, then prepares that person by a series of circumstances, by the cups and the baptisms, that He leads that person through.

God always starts with people, not events. His goal is the shaping and molding of lives, and He fits the events to fulfill that purpose.

The Indignant Ten

One disciple will sit at Jesus' right hand and another at His left hand. God is going to mold those two and prepare them for those honored places. And what of the other ten? Mark turns our attention to them.

> *When the ten heard about this, they became indignant with James and John. Jesus called them together and said, "You know that those who are regarded as rulers of the Gentiles lord it over them, and their high officials exercise authority over them. Not so with you. Instead, whoever wants to become great among you must be your servant, and whoever wants to be first must be slave of all. For even the Son of Man did not come to be served, but to serve, and to give his life as a ransom for many."* (MARK 10:41–45)

Picture again the scene. Jesus and His disciples are walking on the road to Jerusalem. Jesus looks ahead and sees a cross waiting for Him. James and John look ahead and see two thrones waiting for them. And what do the other ten see? They see James and John. They are angry and upset because these two got to Jesus first. They wanted the same things that James and John wanted, and they are angry because James and John beat them to it. This is often a cause for anger. We are upset because someone else beat us to a good idea.

Jesus sets aside their envy and politicking and maneuvering for special favors. He acknowledges that this is the way the world works (and it works the same way even now), but this is not how the kingdom of God operates. In the kingdom—in the church, if you will—there is not to be struggling and striving for position and honor. Paul writes a powerful exposition of this truth in 1

Corinthians 12, where he compares the members of the church with members of a human body, eye, hand, foot, and so forth. All parts of the human body are necessary and worthy of honor. The same is true of the body of Christ, the church. All competition is eliminated from the church by these terms.

Notice the patience of our Lord as He explains these principles to them. He says, "Now, fellows, sit down. I want to clarify something for you. You've seen the Gentile nonbelievers, and you see how they exercise authority, always bossing others around. They measure their power and influence by how many people they give orders to. That is the mark of their authority."

I do not think our Lord is saying that organizational structures are wrong. He recognizes that this is how it is done, and this is also how people judge their worth and success. If you sit in the corner office and boss others around, you are successful. So says the world. But what is the result? Rivalries, cutthroat competition, back stabbing, boot licking, maneuvering, manipulation, anything to get ahead. You can't blame people for operating that way because that is all they know.

But Jesus introduces a radical new concept. We find the key to this new concept in the words "not so with you." Or as the Revised Standard Version puts it, "But it shall not be so among you." The church is not to be that way. It is not to operate as a hierarchy of power. There is no chain of command in the church of Jesus Christ. Jesus had already said to these disciples, "You have only one Master and you are all brothers" (Matthew 23:8). As Paul tells the Corinthians, "Not that we lord it over your faith, but we work with you for your joy" (2 Corinthians 1:24). No one is ever to boss, bully, or command others in the church. Only the Lord commands.

The institutional church, Catholic and Protestant, has failed to live out this precept of the Lord and of the Scriptures. The

Protestant and evangelical churches have rightly rejected the Catholic notion of the prelacy or papacy, the office of a human head over the church. But what have the Protestant and evangelical churches put in place of a pope over all churches? A lot of little popes in every church! This is just as bad, or worse. I submit to you, as a pastor, no less, that there is no authority in being a pastor. A pastor is a brother who is given certain gifts in order to help people understand what they are doing and where they are going. Pastors have no authority over the brothers and sisters in the congregation, for we are all jointly brothers and sisters in the Lord. There are bosses in the unbelieving world, but Jesus says, "It shall not be so among you."

Matthew records that Jesus tells us where true authority lies: "Not so with you. Instead, whoever wants to become great among you must be your servant, and whoever wants to be first must be your slave" (Matthew 20:26–27). Jesus has said this before, but He underscores it again for us. True authority arises out of servitude, out of meeting someone else's need. Jesus says that when you are willing to give yourself to meet another person's need, something remarkable happens. You establish a mystical kind of authority in that person's life. They want to respond to you. Their attitude toward you changes. They want to do something in return. They do not have to; they want to.

This, Jesus said, is a principle in the kingdom of God. This is the way authority arises. Those who have authority are those whom people have learned to respect and honor because they have been served by them. And Jesus offers Himself as the ultimate example of this principle:

"For even the Son of Man did not come to be served, but to serve, and to give his life as a ransom for many." (MARK 10:45)

Here is absolute servanthood in human form. Here is the one who had every right to authority, yet He lovingly relinquishes everything in order to meet our needs. This is how we are to function in the kingdom of God.

A strange, fallacious teaching has infected the church. It claims that Jesus died in order that we who believe in Him might never have to suffer, become sick, experience trials, or face death. That is not what the Scriptures remotely imply, much less say. The Bible teaches that Jesus died in order that He might go with us through death and bring us out onto the other side. He does not eliminate death; that final enemy awaits all of us. But we do not face it alone. We face it in the company of one who has passed through death and emerged into a beautiful resurrection.

The Blind Beggar of Jericho

Next Mark records a remarkable incident that occurs as Jesus and the disciples are leaving the city of Jericho.

> *Then they came to Jericho. As Jesus and his disciples, together with a large crowd, were leaving the city, a blind man, Bartimaeus (that is, the Son of Timaeus), was sitting by the roadside begging. When he heard that it was Jesus of Nazareth, he began to shout, "Jesus, Son of David, have mercy on me!"*
>
> *Many rebuked him and told him to be quiet, but he shouted all the more, "Son of David, have mercy on me!" Jesus stopped and said, "Call him."*
>
> *So they called to the blind man, "Cheer up! On your feet! He's calling you." Throwing his cloak aside, he jumped to his feet and came to Jesus.*
>
> *"What do you want me to do for you?" Jesus asked him.*

The blind man said, "Rabbi, I want to see."

"Go," said Jesus, "your faith has healed you." Immediately he received his sight and followed Jesus along the road.

(MARK 10:46–52)

This incident has no noticeable connection to what has gone before, so it seems that Mark abruptly changes the subject at this point. Or does he? Was it just by chance that as Jesus was leaving Jericho, a blind man named Bartimaeus was sitting by the road? Or was this incident prearranged by God?

A closer inspection of this account reveals some surprising ties with what has gone before. First, there is an unusual repetition involved when Mark gives us the name of this man. He is Bartimaeus, a blind beggar, the son of Timaeus. The name Bartimaeus means "son of Timaeus." It is redundant to say "Bartimaeus, the son of Timaeus," because they mean the same thing. So it seems that Mark underscores this name for some reason. There must be something about this name that Mark wants us to notice. When you look up the Greek meaning of Timaeus, Mark's purpose becomes clear. Timaeus means "honor." This beggar was named "the son of honor." And what had James and John asked Jesus for? Honor. "Let one of us sit at your right," they said, "and the other at your left in your glory." Coincidence?

Notice too that Mark skips over a number of events that are recorded in other gospel accounts. For example, he does not refer to the story of Zacchaeus, which is recorded in great detail in Luke 19, although that incident occurred at this time in Jericho. Mark goes directly to the time that they left the city in order to emphasize a connection between the discussion about honor and Jesus' encounter with the blind son of honor.

Notice also the question Jesus poses to Bartimaeus: "What do you want me to do for you?" That is word for word the question Jesus put to James and John when they came to Him with a request for honor. Look at that passage again:

> *Then James and John, the sons of Zebedee, came to him.*
> *"Teacher," they said, "we want you to do for us whatever we ask."*
> *"What do you want me to do for you?" he asked.*
> *They replied, "Let one of us sit at your right and the other at your left in your glory."* (MARK 10:35–37)

Again I ask: coincidence?

What was the trouble with these disciples? They were blind. They could not see what was involved, what they were so eagerly committing themselves to. They could not see the cup, the baptism, the suffering, the shame, the cross. They were spiritually blind. And what was the trouble with Bartimaeus? He was physically blind. Jesus asked, in both cases, "What do you want me to do for you?"

The significance of this story, I believe, lies in what Bartimaeus did. That is the reason Mark placed it here. Here was a blind man who was conscious of his blindness, whereas the disciples were not conscious of theirs. When he heard that Jesus of Nazareth was passing by, he became excited and began to demand his attention. "Jesus, Son of David," he shouted, "have mercy on me!" When people tried to silence him, he shouted louder: "Son of David, have mercy on me!"

When our Lord stopped to serve this man and meet his needs, He asked, "What do you want me to do for you?" Doesn't that seem like a silly question to ask a blind man? Jesus has the power to restore the man's sight. Jesus knows it. Bartimaeus knows it. What else could the man want? Yet Jesus asks the question anyway. Bartimaeus provides the obvious answer: "Rabbi, I want to see." Immediately Jesus said, "Go, your faith has healed you." And Bartimaeus saw the world for the first time in his life.

Why did Mark put this account in this place? Because this healing is intended to instruct the disciples and to instruct us. Jesus is saying, "When you come asking for good things from God, ask also to be able to see what they involve. Ask to have your sight given to you, so that you see yourself accurately. Ask for the sight to see the true implications of all that you ask in prayer." Jesus is teaching His disciples and us that we need to pray this prayer of David:

> *Search me, O God, and know my heart;*
> *test me and know my anxious thoughts.*
> *See if there is any offensive way in me,*
> *and lead me in the way everlasting.*
> (PSALM 139:23–24)

This is what Jesus wanted His disciples to pray. How blind they were! How foolish and ignorant and self-confident they were, not knowing what was in them and what God would have to do to remove it.

And what of you and me? What foolish blindness lurks in our souls, clouding our prayer life, causing us to ask God to give us things we do not understand? May our ambitious hearts learn the lesson that eluded the disciples as they accompanied Jesus on the way to Jerusalem, on the road to the cross.

twenty-one

The King Is Coming

➤ **Mark 11:1–25**

I have seen audiences moved to tears of joy by Bill and Gloria Gaither's gospel anthem "The King Is Coming." Although it was written as a song of anticipation of the Lord's triumphant return, the sheer power of the music would make a fitting soundtrack for the subject of this study in Mark. For now we come to the story of Jesus' triumphal entry into Jerusalem. In this account, we shall see a city that has been shaken to its foundation by the news that the King is coming.

As we pick up the narrative from the end of Mark 10, we see that the Lord and His disciples have left Jericho and are approaching Jerusalem. They are moving inexorably toward the climactic events of the Lord's final week, the week that is destined to result in His death and resurrection.

The Fulfillment of Prophecy

We are about to examine the event that has come to be known as Palm Sunday. Mark sets the scene for us:

> *As they approached Jerusalem and came to Bethphage*
> *and Bethany at the Mount of Olives, Jesus sent two of his*

disciples, saying to them, "Go to the village ahead of you, and just as you enter it, you will find a colt tied there, which no one has ever ridden. Untie it and bring it here. If anyone asks you, 'Why are you doing this?' tell him, 'The Lord needs it and will send it back here shortly.' "

They went and found a colt outside in the street, tied at a doorway. As they untied it, some people standing there asked, "What are you doing, untying that colt?" They answered as Jesus had told them to, and the people let them go. (MARK 11:1–6)

It seems obvious that Jesus had made advance arrangements for this day. He knew He was coming into the city to fulfill the ancient biblical prophecies, so He made arrangements to fulfill the prophecy concerning this colt. Thus we do not need to see the availability of this colt as a miraculous occurrence. The colt was tied where it was because Jesus had arranged for it to be there. When the word was given that the Lord had need of it, that was all the owner required.

John 10 tells us that Jesus had made a quick trip to Jerusalem in what would have been our month of January, and there He appeared at the Feast of Dedication. This was about three months before the events we are studying. So it is likely He made arrangements for the colt then. Jesus knew the day and the hour He was coming into Jerusalem, and He knew what would be required of that moment, because it was foretold by the prophet Zechariah:

> *Rejoice greatly, O Daughter of Zion!*
> *Shout, Daughter of Jerusalem!*
> *See, your King comes to you,*
> *   righteous and having salvation,*

> *gentle and riding on a donkey,*
> *on a colt, the foal of a donkey.* (ZECHARIAH 9:9)

Jesus knew that He would be coming into the city on a colt. He also knew exactly what day this event would occur, because the Old Testament book of Daniel tells us that almost five hundred years earlier, an angel had appeared to the prophet Daniel and had told him that a certain amount of time had been marked out by God. That time would bring about the fulfillment of dramatic events concerning the people of Israel.

This period of time began when the Persian king Artaxerxes issued an edict for the rebuilding of the walls of Jerusalem. You will find that edict recorded in Nehemiah 2. When this heathen king issued the edict, he unknowingly set in motion God's timetable for the Jewish nation and for the appearance of the Messiah. Daniel was told that 490 years must run their course before all of God's events would be fulfilled. The passage of 483 of those years would be marked off by the triumphant arrival in Jerusalem of the Messiah.

This timetable was discovered by a nineteenth-century lawyer and detective, Sir Robert Anderson. For many years, he served as director of England's famed Scotland Yard. Not only was he a brilliant logician, but also he was an avid Bible student. By analyzing the book of Daniel and determining precisely when the decree of Artaxerxes was issued (March 28, 445 B.C.), Anderson was able to calculate forward, correcting for calendar errors, and determined the precise date that Jesus rode into Jerusalem: April 6, A.D. 32, exactly 483 years after the decree of Artaxerxes.

If a nineteenth-century Englishman could examine these Scriptures and calculate the precise date on which Messiah would come to Jerusalem, then the Son of God would know. Jesus had not only studied the book of Daniel, but also, as the preexistent Son of God, He had inspired the writing of the book. So it is a reasonable inference that He made the appropriate arrangements to enter the city, to ride down the slopes of the Mount of Olives on a colt on which no one had ever sat, in precise fulfillment of the predictions of Zechariah and Daniel.

All three Synoptic Gospels (Matthew, Mark, and Luke) tell us that this was a young donkey, an animal on which no one had ever sat. When I was growing up in Montana, my friends and I would break horses for amusement. Some of the full-grown ones were a little too much for us to handle, so we concentrated on the yearling colts on which no one had ever sat. I can testify that these animals do not welcome the experience. Even when they're a year old, they are capable of sending you base over apex.

Yet Jesus selects an animal that no one has ever sat on, and this animal is docile, responsive, and obedient. In contradiction to its nature and instincts, the lowly animal carries Jesus through the streets of the city. Although the procurement of the animal may not have been supernatural, the behavior of that colt was not natural. But it should be remembered that the rider of the colt was also the one who had commanded the wind and waves.

"Well," you might say, "if Jesus arranged all of these details, how can you call it a fulfillment of prophecy? Jesus engineered everything so that it would appear that prophecy was being fulfilled."

The answer is that Jesus arranged a few things, but He could not have arranged everything. He could not have arranged the response of the crowd as He entered the city or the attitude of the rulers. These factors were beyond His control, yet they too had been predicted in the Old Testament.

A Tragic Pronouncement

The Messiah is about to enter Jerusalem. This event has been prophesied for almost five hundred years, yet the city is strangely unaware of the momentous thing that is about to happen. Mark's narrative continues:

> *When they brought the colt to Jesus and threw their cloaks over it, he sat on it. Many people spread their cloaks on the road, while others spread branches they had cut in the fields. Those who went ahead and those who followed shouted,*
> *"Hosanna!"*
> *"Blessed is he who comes in the name of the Lord!"*
> *"Blessed is the coming kingdom of our father David!"*
> *"Hosanna in the highest!"* (MARK 11:7–10)

From other accounts, we know these people were not so much citizens of Jerusalem as people from around Galilee who had come to Jerusalem for the Passover feast. Many of them were children. Historians tell us that the population of Jerusalem at the time of Jesus was about 80,000 people, but during the great religious feasts, the number of people in the city would swell to as much as 250,000. There was no room to house so many pilgrims and strangers within the city, so they would spend the night sleeping in the hills around the city, then stream through the city gates throughout the morning. So it was probably a crowd of religious pilgrims and their children, not citizens of Jerusalem, who greeted Jesus as He approached Jerusalem.

Where, then, were the citizens of Jerusalem? They were in the city, conducting their business, going about their lives, oblivious to

the fact that the long-awaited Messiah was just outside the city walls!
So it was up to these strangers and visitors, these Galilean tourists,
to cry out the words that fulfilled the prophecy of Psalm 118. You
cannot read this account without seeing that these words must have
been much in the Lord's mind as He rode into the city that day:

> *The stone the builders rejected*
> *   has become the capstone; . . .*
> *This is the day the Lord has made;*
> *   let us rejoice and be glad in it. . . .*
> *Blessed is he who comes in the name of the Lord.*
>   (PSALM 118:22, 24, 26)

These were the words that the people cried out as Jesus rode
through the streets. Luke adds an interesting dimension in his
account of this same event:

> *As he approached Jerusalem and saw the city, he wept*
> *over it and said, "If you, even you, had only known on this*
> *day what would bring you peace—but now it is hidden from*
> *your eyes. The days will come upon you when your enemies*
> *will build an embankment against you and encircle you and*
> *hem you in on every side. They will dash you to the ground,*
> *you and the children within your walls. They will not leave*
> *one stone on another, because you did not recognize the time*
> *of God's coming to you." (LUKE 19:41–44)*

The Lord's sad prophecy was fulfilled to the letter forty years
later, when the Roman general Titus brought his armies and laid
a prolonged siege against Jerusalem. Eventually the Romans bat-
tered their way into the city. In violation of the general's orders,

the temple was burned. The gold of the temple treasury melted and ran into the cracks of the stones. In their efforts to get at the gold, the soldiers pried apart the stones. When they had finished, there was literally no stone left standing on another.

As He rode down the mountain, Jesus knew all that was coming, and He wept because Jerusalem did not recognize the time of God's coming. That is one of the most tragic pronouncements in the Bible. God had sent out invitations to this great event five hundred years before. He had told when it would happen, had given an exact time schedule, and had told the people how to recognize the King. But when Messiah came, nobody in the city knew who He was. The only ones who recognized Him as Messiah were some itinerant Galilean peasants and their children who were there to celebrate Passover. What an ironic twist! Yet that is often the case. We ignore the signs the God gives us, and we don't even recognize Him when He is suddenly in our midst.

An Official Visit from the King

After the death of Jordan's beloved King Hussein, many of the Jordanian people wondered if the king's successor, his son Abdullah, would be as compassionate and dedicated to the welfare of his people as Hussein had been. After ascending to the throne, King Abdullah adopted a bold and daring strategy that would have surprised even his father. Abdullah sometimes disguised himself as a laborer, such as a taxi driver or a hospital orderly. Then he went out among the people to see how they lived and what they needed from their government. For example, he would appear at a government hospital and observe how some of the doctors mistreated their patients. Or he would walk the streets and talk to the common people about their concerns and problems. Then the young king would go back to his palace in Amman and issue laws and decrees that would punish wrongdoers and improve the lives of the common people. There are some things a king in disguise can discover that a king on a throne cannot.

In the next passage in Mark 11, we see that Jesus does something similar. He enters the city, a King in disguise, to find out what is going on within His kingdom. Mark records:

> *Jesus entered Jerusalem and went to the temple. He looked around at everything, but since it was already late, he went out to Bethany with the Twelve.* (MARK 11:11)

At first glance, it doesn't seem that Jesus does anything significant here. But looking carefully at this narrative, we can discover His purpose in these actions. This was an official visit of the King of Israel. He was making an inspection tour of the heart of the nation. He went to the temple, the throbbing heart of the nation of Israel, the focus of all Jewish worship. There He looked at everything. And we know what He saw. The crass commercialism of the moneychangers. The exploitation of the people by corrupt religious leaders. The filth and squalor, the injustice and hypocrisy, the arrogance and extortion. He saw that religious ceremonies were being carried on without any meaning or spiritual significance.

"He looked around at everything," says Mark, but He did not say a word. Nobody paid any attention to Him, because He had been there many times before. The priests and moneychangers did not know that this was an official tour of inspection by the King.

God often comes into our lives that way, doesn't He? Wouldn't it be wonderful if God looked at us only when we came to church on Sunday morning, when we are scrubbed and presentable, when our hearts are turned to thoughts of God, when

His Word is open on our laps and we are thinking sweet, spiritual thoughts? But God doesn't inspect us only on Sunday mornings. He also knows when we are arguing in the kitchen, when we are cutting ethical corners at the office, when we are behaving rudely in the car. He knows us when we are saying what we shouldn't say, thinking what is unclean to think, doing what we should be ashamed to do, and viewing what is foul to view.

He comes into our lives. He looks around. And He does not say a word.

But that is just the inspection. Mark next shows us the result of that inspection. In Mark 11, that result takes place on the following day. It begins with a symbolic action.

> *The next day as they were leaving Bethany, Jesus was hungry. Seeing in the distance a fig tree in leaf, he went to find out if it had any fruit. When he reached it, he found nothing but leaves, because it was not the season for figs. Then he said to the tree, "May no one ever eat fruit from you again." And his disciples heard him say it.*
>
> (MARK 11:12–14)

A surprise awaits the disciples. On the following day, as we will soon see, the disciples will pass the fig tree again, and they will find that it has withered to the roots. Many people have been troubled by this miracle. It seems so vindictive and destructive, so unlike Jesus. It is the only miracle in Jesus' ministry in which He pronounces judgment and destruction on anything. Another troubling aspect is that Jesus seems to be irrationally angry with the tree. He curses this tree for not having figs, yet the passage clearly states, "it was not the season for figs." Why would He curse the tree for not bearing fruit when it is unreasonable to expect fruit on the tree? Is Jesus that arbitrary and capricious?

I had read this story many times and puzzled over it for years before I finally decided to conduct some research into the nature of fig trees. When I moved to California, I planted a fig tree to see what it would do. I wanted to learn from it, and as I watched it grow, I learned a great deal. From the fig tree in my yard, I discovered the answer to the riddle of this passage.

The first spring I watched with interest as the barren limbs of that tree began to swell, the buds began to fill out, and the leaves appeared. To my astonishment, tiny figs appeared right along with the leaves. With most fruit trees, the fruit sets on long after the leaves appear, so the appearance of these tiny figs along with the leaves was surprising. Day by day, I watched these tiny figs grow and turn from green to yellow. Soon they began to appear ripe, so I picked one and sampled it. I was disappointed to find that instead of being full of juice and pulp as a normal fig would be, it was dry and withered inside, with no juice. I waited a few more days and checked the other figs, and they were the same. I thought, *My fig tree is a lemon!*

Time passed, and more figs appeared on the tree; they swelled and ripened. I opened one of these later figs, assuming it would be dry and withered like the first ones, but it was a sweet, rich, juicy, pulpy fig. And that tree has borne a great crop of figs ever since. So I learned something from my fig tree. It produces two kinds of figs: the early figs (I call them pre-figs) that look like figs but are not true figs, and the later, true figs, which are sweet and tasty. I have since learned that if a fig tree does not produce the early figs, it will not produce the later, true figs.

I am convinced that this explains what Jesus did. He came at a time when figs were out of season, but He knew what to look for in a fruitful tree. He looked at the tree and found none of the early figs that would promise a later harvest of true, juicy figs. He knew that this tree would never have figs but would produce nothing but leaves. The life of the tree had been spent producing luxuriant foliage, so that it looked like a healthy tree, but it was not productive. He cursed it, and the next day it was withered to the roots.

That tree was a symbol of the nation Israel, as we will see. And what Jesus does next is a vivid, even violent, representation of what He did symbolically with the cursing of the fig tree. The symbolic message of the cursing of the fig tree is identical to the message of the cleansing of the temple.

The Cleansing of the Temple

Before showing us the fate of the fig tree, Mark takes us back to Jerusalem for this powerful scene.

> *On reaching Jerusalem, Jesus entered the temple area and began driving out those who were buying and selling there. He overturned the tables of the moneychangers and the benches of those selling doves, and would not allow anyone to carry [a vessel] through the temple courts. And as he taught them, he said, "Is it not written:*
>
> *" 'My house will be called*
> *a house of prayer for all nations' ?*
>
> *But you have made it 'a den of robbers.' "* (MARK 11:15–17)

Jesus took two significant actions that are tantamount to the cursing of the nation of Israel, just as He had cursed the fig tree when He found it with nothing but leaves. First, He cleansed it from all the false manifestations that had crept in. He cleaned out the commercialism of the temple. This was the second time He had done this. According to John's gospel, He had entered the temple three years before, at the beginning of His ministry, and had swept out the moneychangers in a similar fashion.

In the course of this second cleansing, Jesus refused to allow anyone to commercialize the sacrificial offerings. Merchants were selling animals as a so-called service to the people. And because they would accept only the official temple currency, money-changers had set up shop (another service) so people could exchange normal Roman currency (defiled with the graven image of Caesar) into temple currency. The moneychangers and traders were making an excessive profit at this business, and Jesus stormed in and swept out the whole mess.

But then comes the second significant action of Jesus. Mark says that Jesus "would not allow anyone to carry [a vessel] through the temple courts." I have inserted the phrase "a vessel" in that statement because that is what the text literally says. The New International Version uses the term "merchandise," which is not what the Greek text says. The New International Version is a very good translation in general, but it erred when it inserted the word "merchandise" here, because Mark is not talking about the merchandise of the traders and moneychangers at this point. The King James Version accurately states that Jesus would not allow anyone to "carry any vessel through the temple." The word "vessel" refers to a utensil of worship. Mark expresses something highly significant. Jesus shut down not only the commerce of the temple; He shut down the religious rituals as well.

Why is this significant? If you will refer to the Old Testament books of Leviticus and Numbers, you will see that God had instituted rituals for the temple at Jerusalem that required the priests to carry many things through it. They had to bring the animals into the temple, bind them on the altar, and slay them. They had to catch the blood of these animals and carry it in basins into the holy place to sprinkle it on the altar of incense. They had to take the bodies of the sacrifices, after they were burned, and carry them back out again. So there was a continual procession of priests through the temple all day, carrying out the system of rituals that God had given to the nation of Israel.

But on this day, when Jesus came into the temple, He halted the temple's religious activity. Why? Because Jesus refused to acknowledge the temple worship as having any meaning or value any longer. Although the Jewish priests, moneychangers, and traders went back to their former activity as soon as Jesus left, and although these practices would continue for forty more years until the Romans destroyed the temple, God no longer accepted those sacrifices. The rituals of the temple were meaningless and worthless.

The temple was the heart of the nation of Israel, and Jesus cursed the heart of Israel by rejecting its worship. This was what the cursing of the fig tree represented. Israel, like that tree, no longer bore fruit. It produced nothing but leaves. It appeared to have life and value, but in reality it did not. It appeared to offer hope to the men and women of the nations of earth, because people came from all over the world to worship at the temple in Jerusalem. They came hoping to find an answer to the emptiness of their hearts, but they found no help, because the rituals of the temple had become empty and meaningless, corrupted by greed and exploitation.

So Jesus cursed the nation, just as He had cursed the fig tree.

The Withering of the Nation

The cleansing of the temple draws an immediate and fateful response from the religious leaders in Jerusalem. Mark records:

> *The chief priests and the teachers of the law heard this and began looking for a way to kill him, for they feared him, because the whole crowd was amazed at his teaching. When evening came, they went out of the city.*
>
> (MARK 11:18–19)

The chief priests and the teachers of the law heard that Jesus had shut down all activity in the temple, overturning the tables of the traders and moneychangers and stopping all the religious rituals of the temple. This was too much for them. They were filled with fury. In the past, Jesus' words had angered and confounded them, and they had met together to discuss what ought to be done about Him. But their hostility suddenly turned a corner at this point. There was no longer any question what to do with Jesus. He had to be destroyed. The only question remaining was how to accomplish the deed.

That was the point of no return for the nation of Israel. This act of Jesus—shutting down the ritualistic worship in the temple—resulted in His death the following Friday. The teachers of the law and the priests would no longer put up with anything Jesus did or said from that moment on. His actions in clearing the temple almost certainly sealed His death.

But the religious leaders' hostile and murderous response also sealed their destiny. They thought they were getting rid of Him. But it was He, as the King in all His majesty, who had pronounced sentence on them and had sealed their doom. Just as the fig tree had been cursed and would soon be found withered beside the road, so the withering of the life of the nation of Israel had already begun.

"Have Faith in God"

The meaning of these events is wrapped up in the next three verses, although that meaning is easy to miss if we don't read carefully.

> *In the morning, as they went along, they saw the fig tree*
> *withered from the roots. Peter remembered and said to Jesus,*
> *"Rabbi, look! The fig tree you cursed has withered!"*
> *"Have faith in God," Jesus answered.* (MARK 11:20–22)

Does Jesus' answer seem strange to you? Many people have read this passage and, neglecting to read it in its context, have taken this to be a formula for working miracles. It is as if Jesus is saying, "You too can curse fig trees and make them wither if you have faith in God." But that is not even remotely what Jesus is saying. If you read His words in connection with all the events of this passage, the meaning becomes clear. It is significant that the story of the cursed tree wraps around and encloses the story of the cleansing of the temple. That is deliberate, for they are one story, not two.

Jesus is not telling us the secret of how to curse fig trees; He is telling us the secret of how to live so that we will not be cursed. This nation was cursed because it had lost faith in God. It had substituted empty rituals and meaningless performance for a true, loving, obedient relationship with God. Israel's religion was one that went through the motions. It was an outward religious show, but inwardly it was unreal and hypocritical. The corrupt priests were in collusion with the moneychangers and merchants, bilking the people out of their money in the name of God. True faith in God was dead, so the life of God that had once made the nation green and fruitful was now dried up and withered.

This is what Jesus is telling us: "Have faith in God! If you truly want to live, have faith in God! If you don't want to be cursed and withered and dead, have faith in God! If you want a life that is full and rich and meaningful, have faith in God! Trust that the living God knows what He is doing in your life. Believe what He says and obey what He commands! Open your life to Him and let Him flow through you and make you fruitful! Have faith in God!"

This is the answer. When a nation begins to dry up and wither, when it ceases to become fruitful, the only answer is to have faith in God. Whether that nation is Israel in the first century or the United States of America in the twenty-first century, the only answer is to have faith in God. And what is true of a nation is true of an individual. If you feel dried up, wasted, withered, and dead inside, have faith in God. Trust Him. Obey Him. Seek Him. Let Him make your life fruitful once more.

How to Move Mountains

Jesus next says something that many people have found perplexing and troubling.

> *"I tell you the truth, if anyone says to this mountain, 'Go, throw yourself into the sea,' and does not doubt in his heart but believes that what he says will happen, it will be done for him."* (MARK 11:23)

If we wrench these words out of context and treat them as a magic formula for doing amazing things, we will miss the truth that Jesus wants to teach us. Imagine going around and commanding mountains to lift themselves up and cast themselves into the sea! Many preachers claim that the secret to mountain moving is to believe that it's going to happen and it will happen. But in all the years that preachers have been preaching that twist on Jesus' words, I have never heard of a single mountain that ever got up and flew into the sea.

So there is some deeper and more profound truth that Jesus is trying to communicate. Jesus is saying that to have faith in God at times is difficult to do. He knows that. There are mountains that stand in the way of faith and make believing difficult. There are obstacles to faith.

Israel had experienced powerful, formidable obstacles. One such obstacle was the Roman enslavement of Israel. Another was the apparent silence of God for several hundred years. All the circumstances that aroused doubt and fear in their lives were like a mountain that stood in the way of their faith. Jesus says, "I tell you, if you ask in faith, that mountain will be removed." And then He explains how.

> *"I tell you, whatever you ask for in prayer, believe that you have received it, and it will be yours. And when you stand praying, if you hold anything against anyone, forgive him, so that your Father in heaven may forgive you your sins."* (MARK 11:24–25)

Whatever you do, don't remove those words from their context. Jesus is saying, "The great hindrance to having faith in God is pride, a pride that refuses to forgive. Pride is like a mountain that fills up your life. All you can see is that big mountain looming before you, blocking the life of God in your life. You have the power to remove that mountain of pride if, when you stand and pray, you will forgive those who have offended you. Because the only thing that stops you from forgiving is pride."

Most of us wrestle with forgiveness in one way or another. We feel justified in wanting others to forgive us, but when others hurt us, we feel entitled to exact a price for the hurt they have caused us. So, in subtle ways or direct, we insist on being avenged. "Okay," we say, "I'll forgive—as soon as I've seen him crawl or heard her beg for forgiveness." That kind of forgiveness is not forgiveness. It's another form of vindictiveness and vengefulness.

"And that," says Jesus, "is a great mountain that needs to be removed, for it is blocking the flow of the life of God to your faith." God has forgiven you; now you need to let His forgiveness flow through you to others, to the ones who have hurt you.

The basis of all forgiveness is the fact that God, through Christ, has forgiven us. Another has paid the price. Another has assumed our debt. Another has borne the hurt, so that we might be free. We have received from Him freely, without doing anything to earn or deserve it. How much more, then, should we extend that same mercy and love to all who have offended us? If we do not forgive, then we do not have faith, and we will wither as surely as that unfruitful fig tree. But if we have faith to obey God and forgive, then our prayers will be answered and our mountains will move.

Have faith in God!

twenty-two

By What Authority?

➤ **Mark 11:27–12:27**

Before sunup on the morning of May 10, 1775, a small band of American revolutionaries crept out of the woods and approached Fort Ticonderoga, New York, a supposedly impregnable British garrison. The Americans, led by Colonel Ethan Allen, were heavily outnumbered. But Allen's famed Green Mountain Boys were supremely confident in their cause and in their commander.

In the predawn darkness, Allen's men surprised and quickly overpowered the sentries who guarded the perimeter of the fort. One of the frightened guards was brought to Colonel Allen, who presented the sentry with a choice: "Take me to the quarters of Captain Delaplace—or would you prefer to die?" The sentry chose life, and he led Colonel Allen through the front gate, across the parade grounds to the officers' quarters, up the steps, along the second-story balcony, and to the door of the commander of the British fort, Captain William Delaplace.

Allen drew his sword and banged the hilt loudly against the door. "Captain!" shouted Ethan Allen. "Come out here and surrender, or I'll kill every Englishman in Fort Ticonderoga!" A few moments later, the door opened, and there stood the astonished

Captain Delaplace, freshly rousted out of bed and undressed, holding his breeches in front of him to protect his modesty. Allen suppressed a chuckle, then repeated his demand: "Sir, I order you to surrender!"

"By what authority?" asked the British commander.

Ethan Allen's reply: "In the name of the great Lord Jehovah and the Continental Congress!"

Captain Delaplace surrendered.

In much the same way, the Lord Jesus has come to Jerusalem and presented His demands to the religious rulers of that city. He has gone into the fortress of Israel's religious life, the temple, and He has overturned the corrupt religious practices of that place. Now those religious leaders confront Jesus with a question, the same question Captain Delaplace put to Colonel Ethan Allen: "By what authority?" They ask Him, "Who gave you the authority to overturn these tables and stop the religious rituals in the temple? By what authority are you doing these things?"

The priests and teachers of the law consider themselves the absolute authority over the religious life of Israel. But they are about to discover that there is an even higher authority in Israel.

As we examine our Lord's final visit to Jerusalem during that last, climactic week of His life, we see Him in unremitting conflict with these Jewish authorities. In these confrontations, He addresses the central issue of life: what is the final authority over humanity? This question breaks down into an array of subquestions on the issue of authority. Should I obey the state, or should I obey my conscience? Which is preeminent, the church or the government? Should I walk by reason or by faith? Should I subscribe to the authority of science or of the Bible? These are questions we all face, and in this account, Jesus gives us guidance for everyday living.

Of God or Men?

In our previous study, we saw our Lord in the midst of His second cleansing of the temple. He overturned the tables of the moneychangers, swept out all the commercialized traffic, and did something shocking, something that only Mark's gospel records: Jesus halted the offerings and sacrifices of the Mosaic system. He prevented the priests from carrying out the normal duties associated with the temple sacrifices. Now Mark records the hostile reaction of the religious authorities in Jerusalem.

> *They arrived again in Jerusalem, and while Jesus was walking in the temple courts, the chief priests, the teachers of the law and the elders came to him. "By what authority are you doing these things?" they asked. "And who gave you authority to do this?"* (MARK 11:27–28)

You can hear it in their words: the voices of the temple authorities drip with loathing and rage. Furious that Jesus has challenged their authority, they confront Him and demand, "By what authority are you doing these things?"

When you refine any issue down to its essentials, what you have left is the issue of authority in life. Why do you act the way you do? How do you justify what you say and do? No one ever is his or her own ultimate authority. Presidents can be impeached; kings can be deposed. We all defer to an authority beyond ourselves, something that sets boundaries for our actions, something that governs our decisions. When we confront the question of authority, we are dealing with that which is fundamental to all human behavior.

Who were these Jewish religious authorities? By comparing this account with the other gospels, we know that this was an imposing delegation. It included Caiaphas, the high priest, and his venerated father-in-law, Annas; the scribes, who interpreted the law of Moses; and the elders, those officially appointed to serve in the Sanhedrin, the ruling body of the nation. These were the Jewish heads of state, and they answered only to the overarching rule of Rome.

The answer that Jesus gave these powerful men is one of the most amazing statements in Scripture. This is riveting drama, and it is fascinating to watch our Lord handle Himself so coolly and confidently under pressure. First He turns the tables on His interrogators by demanding their credentials.

> *Jesus replied, "I will ask you one question. Answer me, and I will tell you by what authority I am doing these things. John's baptism—was it from heaven, or from men? Tell me!"*
> (MARK 11:29–30)

Notice His directness. The Jewish rulers think they have Jesus on the spot, but with one response, He puts them on the defensive. Mark shows us the confusion this creates among them.

> *They discussed it among themselves and said, "If we say, 'From heaven,' he will ask, 'Then why didn't you believe him?' But if we say, 'From men' . . . ." (They feared the people, for everyone held that John really was a prophet.)*
> *So they answered Jesus, "We don't know."*
> *Jesus said, "Neither will I tell you by what authority I am doing these things." (MARK 11:31–33)*

Don't you love that answer! The Lord has conceived a remarkable test. He asks them their view of the baptism of John: is it merely a human baptism, or is it of God? The baptism of John was something new and startling in Israel. The priests had many ritual washings under the Levitical system, but those were performed in the temple according to strict rules. But John's baptism was different. John was not a priest, yet he baptized. He baptized not in the temple but in rivers and streams, wherever he could find enough water. Because it was unprecedented, John's baptism was controversial, and feelings ran high on both sides of the question.

So when the Jewish leaders asked Jesus, "By what authority do you shut down the ritual worship in the temple?" the Lord responded by asking, "What do you think of John's baptism? By what authority did John bring this new baptism to Israel? Was it mere human authority, or God's?" All authority is either of God or humankind; there are no other authorities. We are trying either to obey God or to please people.

Jesus had brilliantly impaled these leaders on the horns of a dilemma. In the game of chess, this is called placing your opponent in a fork. No matter what move he makes next, he will lose one of his pieces. These Jewish leaders knew that whatever they said next, they were going to lose something. If they said, "John's baptism was from God," Jesus would respond, "Then why didn't you accept John?" And if they said, "John's baptism was from men," they knew the multitude standing around them would be displeased, because the martyred John was popular among the people.

Unable to give Jesus the answer He demanded, they offered an answer so lame and cowardly it could not have improved their standing with the people. They said, "We don't know." That answer, of course, took Jesus off the hook. "All right, then," said Jesus, "I won't answer your question either. I will not tell you by what authority I do these things."

A Bold and Dangerous Parable

But Jesus did not let the matter rest there. He went on to expose their dishonesty. By their weaseling answer, the Jewish leaders showed they didn't care about the truth. They didn't care about God's authority; they cared only about their power and self-interest. So our Lord proceeded to expose their evil and corruption by telling a parable. With this story, Jesus went on the offensive, attacking these crooked men and predicting their ultimate downfall.

> *He then began to speak to them in parables: "A man planted a vineyard. He put a wall around it, dug a pit for the winepress and built a watchtower. Then he rented the vineyard to some farmers and went away on a journey."*
>
> (MARK 12:1)

As Jesus began talking, the scribes and Pharisees and chief priests immediately recognized the story. Jesus was borrowing almost the exact words of Isaiah 5, where the nation of Israel is described as a vineyard brought out of Egypt and planted in a choice land. There was no doubt in these Jewish leaders' minds where they fit into this parable. Jesus continued:

> *"At harvest time he sent a servant to the tenants to collect from them some of the fruit of the vineyard. But they seized him, beat him and sent him away empty-handed. Then he sent another servant to them; they struck this man on the head and treated him shamefully. He sent still another, and that one they killed. He sent many others; some of them they beat, others they killed.*
> *"He had one left to send, a son, whom he loved. He sent him last of all, saying, 'They will respect my son.'*

> *"But the tenants said to one another, 'This is the heir.*
> *Come, let's kill him, and the inheritance will be ours.' So they*
> *took him and killed him, and threw him out of the vineyard."*
> (MARK 12:2–8)

This is a bold and dangerous parable. Jesus has told a tale of men who will stop at nothing, not even murder, to get what they want, and He tosses the tale into the faces of the murderous men He has exposed. He describes to them who they are and what they are doing—and indirectly He answers their question, "By what authority are you doing these things?" He says, "Here is my authority. I am the owner of the vineyard. I am the rightful heir to it. I am the beloved Son whom the Father has sent. You've beaten, stoned, and killed God's prophets. Now I am here. I am the Son."

And He tells these men what they planned to do. They will beat Jesus, kill Him, and cast Him out of the vineyard. Jesus is under no delusions as to what is going to happen to Him. But God, the owner of the vineyard, will have the final word. Jesus predicts the ultimate end of these corrupt leaders:

> *"What then will the owner of the vineyard do? He will*
> *come and kill those tenants and give the vineyard to others."*
> (MARK 12:9)

In Mark's account it looks as though Jesus answers His own question, but Matthew makes it clear that Jesus asks the question and the scribes and the chief priests give the answer. Jesus tells the story and says, "Now, in that story, what would the owner of the vineyard do?" Matthew records that the scribes and chief priests said, "He will bring those wretches to a wretched end, and he will rent the vineyard to other tenants, who will give him his share of the crop at harvest time" (Matthew 21:41). As Mark records, Jesus continues:

> *"Haven't you read this scripture:*
>
>> *" 'The stone the builders rejected*
>> *has become the capstone;*
>> *the Lord has done this,*
>> *and it is marvelous in our eyes'?"*
>
> *Then they looked for a way to arrest him because they knew he had spoken the parable against them. But they were afraid of the crowd; so they left him and went away.*
>
> *(Mark 12:10–12)*

Jesus has exposed the falseness and corruption of their religious authority. God had not given these evil men authority over the religious life of Israel; they had usurped what was never rightfully theirs. Jesus makes this clear. But He adds, "That is not the end of the story. When human authorities act in evil and corrupt ways, you can be sure that God is not through with them."

And what Jesus predicted later took place. On the day of resurrection, the one whom the builders rejected became the capstone of God's eternal edifice. Later, when the resurrected Lord stood with His disciples, He declared, "All authority in heaven and on earth has been given to me" (Matthew 28:18). The risen Christ is Lord of all, the Ruler of history, the sovereign Monarch of human affairs.

Forty years after the crucifixion and resurrection of Christ, Roman armies surrounded the city of Jerusalem, invaded it, sacked it, and led the chief priests, scribes, and elders away in chains to be dispersed among the nations. God did what He said He would do in this parable.

This is a lesson to us and to all who read this account. Human authority is always limited and subject to the judgment of God's authority. Evil people may sit on the throne of the unrighteous, wielding their unjust power for a limited period of time, but invariably they are swept out of office and into the dustbin of history. As J. B. Phillips once observed, "Remember that the powers-that-be will soon be the powers-that-were." The prophet Ezekiel tells us that God's process throughout history is declared in these words: "I will overturn, overturn, overturn, it: and it shall be no more, until he come whose right it is; and I will give it him" (Ezekiel 21:27 KJV). God is at work in history to overthrow corrupt authorities and to replace one power with another. Human power may flourish for a time, but it always comes to an end.

Our Responsibility to the Government
As Mark continues his account, we see that the Jewish leaders shift to a new strategy. They send a different group of religious leaders, the Pharisees and the Herodians, to attack Jesus in an even more underhanded and fraudulent way.

> *Later they sent some of the Pharisees and Herodians to Jesus to catch him in his words. They came to him and said, "Teacher, we know you are a man of integrity. You aren't swayed by men, because you pay no attention to who they are; but you teach the way of God in accordance with the truth."* (MARK 12:13–14)

What oily scoundrels these were, coming with such saccharine words. Yet this delegation was made up of two groups that bitterly hated each other, the Pharisees and the Herodians. They considered Jesus such a threat to their vested interests that these bitter enemies were willing to join forces. They came to Jesus with a sly question:

> *"Is it right to pay taxes to Caesar or not? Should we pay or shouldn't we?"* (MARK 12:14–15)

This is a question people in the United States wrestle with every April 15. Should we pay taxes to the government when we know that the government will use that money in immoral and unethical ways? Is it right to pay your hard-earned money to a government that wastes it or spends it to further a cause you oppose, such as abortion on demand or an unjust war? Although the question was posed as a trap for Jesus, it is a valid moral question. Mark records the Lord's response:

> *But Jesus knew their hypocrisy. "Why are you trying to trap me?" he asked. "Bring me a denarius and let me look at it." They brought the coin, and he asked them, "Whose portrait is this? And whose inscription?"*
> *"Caesar's," they replied.*
> *Then Jesus said to them, "Give to Caesar what is Caesar's and to God what is God's."*
> *And they were amazed at him.* (MARK 12:15–17)

I once read about a brilliant young lawyer, reared by atheist parents, who had grown up with disregard for Christianity. Someone had given him a New Testament, and he had decided to read it through to find all the logical flaws in the Christian Scriptures. But when he came to Mark, he read this section with intense interest, for he had recently been involved in a court case involving the ethics of taxation. He was so eager to see what Jesus would say, he could hardly read fast enough. When the full impact of the actions of Jesus hit this man, he was astonished. "That is the most amazing wisdom I've ever encountered!" he said.

What was it about the Lord's response that so amazed this young lawyer? It was the way Jesus easily avoided their trap while He wisely answered their question. They asked Him a yes/no, either/or question, but Jesus rejected the premise of the question and showed that He knew their motives. "Why are you trying to trap me?" He asked. Then Jesus called for a coin (He had to borrow one, for He had no money), and He held it up. "Whose picture is on this coin?" asked Jesus. They said, "Caesar's." And He told them, "All right, then it must be Caesar's money. Give to Caesar whatever belongs to Caesar, but give to God whatever belongs to God. And, because God has His stamp on your life, that means you should give everything you are to God."

Secular government is ordained by God. The apostle Paul tells us that plainly, and so does the apostle Peter:

> *Submit yourselves for the Lord's sake to every authority instituted among men: whether to the king, as the supreme authority, or to governors, who are sent by him to punish those who do wrong and to commend those who do right. . . . Show proper respect to everyone: Love the brotherhood of believers, fear God, honor the king.* (1 PETER 2:13–14, 17)

We may be tempted to say, "When Peter wrote those words, he didn't know how corrupt our government would become." Oh? We must remember that the king Peter referred to was Nero, one of the most wretched moral degenerates who ever held a position of power. Nero was the epitome of corruption, yet Peter says, "Honor the king."

Human government has only limited authority over us. It has certain powers over our freedoms, our actions, our speech. It can regulate our conduct to some degree and has the right to influence and regulate our society. But secular power cannot legislate how we worship or whom, nor can it dictate our conscience. Jesus acknowledges, as does all of Scripture, that God is ultimately sovereign over all government, even bad government, and no government exists except by His permission. Certain things belong to Caesar; the rest belongs to God. So give to Caesar only what is his, and give everything else that you are and have to the one who truly owns you.

The Attack of the Rationalists

In the concluding incident in this passage, Jesus is confronted by still another form of human authority, rationalism, the scientific mind, the authority or power of human logic and thought. This authority is very much a part of our world. Mark writes:

> *Then the Sadducees, who say there is no resurrection, came to him with a question. "Teacher," they said, "Moses wrote for us that if a man's brother dies and leaves a wife but no children, the man must marry the widow and have children for his brother. Now there were seven brothers. The first one married and died without leaving any children. The second one married the widow, but he also died, leaving no child. It was the same with the third. In fact, none of the seven left any children. Last of all, the woman died too. At the resurrection whose wife will she be, since the seven were married to her?"*

> *Jesus replied, "Are you not in error because you do not know the Scriptures or the power of God?"* (MARK 12:18–24)

This question is not intended to elicit a serious answer about the resurrection; it is intended only to mock Jesus. Mark makes this clear at the outset, when he tells us that the Sadducees did not believe in the resurrection. They were rationalists, materialists, secular humanists. They did not believe in the supernatural, in angels or spirits or life after death. Yet they come to Jesus inquiring into a subject that they consider nonsense: "What's going to happen in the resurrection?"

The question drips with malicious contempt. Their hypothetical scenario is an absurd, contrived story, concocted to trap Jesus. I suspect Jesus was tempted to dismiss it, as it deserved. For example, He could have answered, "When a woman has seven husbands in a row and they keep dying, you might want to find out what she's been putting in their coffee." But Jesus proceeds to answer their question on its own absurd terms.

> *Jesus replied, "Are you not in error because you do not know the Scriptures or the power of God? When the dead rise, they will neither marry nor be given in marriage; they will be like the angels in heaven. Now about the dead rising—have you not read in the book of Moses, in the account of the bush, how God said to him, 'I am the God of Abraham, the God of Isaac, and the God of Jacob'? He is not the God of the dead, but of the living. You are badly mistaken!"*
> (MARK 12:24–27)

Jesus is blunt. "You are wrong," He tells them. "Your view of life has skewed your thinking. You're so sure you're right. You have narrowed life down to a limited horizon, and you say that's all there is. Looking at life from your narrow perspective, you cannot see the reality that lies beyond. You're wrong because you fail to recognize two great facts. First, God has knowledge that human beings lack, and that is why we have the Scriptures. You don't know the Scriptures, obviously, for that is where God's knowledge is revealed. Second, God has power that infinitely exceeds the power of human beings. You have limited your lives to what human beings can know and what human beings can do—to human knowledge and human power. You've exalted yourselves to the place where you think you know all that can be known, and that nothing is beyond your power. And that is why you are so wrong."

I remember reading this passage as a young Christian, and I was intrigued by Jesus' words, "Are you not in error because you do not know the Scriptures or the power of God?" Over the years, I have tested this statement, and I have always found it to be true. Whether in business, science, religion, politics, psychology, or family life, every error of human thinking can be attributed to one of those two things. Either you don't know the Scriptures, or you don't know the power of God.

Here too we find the fatal weakness of a great deal of scientific thinking. I am not attacking science or scientists. I have known a number of Christian scientists, and they have all shown great wisdom and insight into the nature of reality. Within its purview, science is helpful. I support and appreciate the value of science, but we must also recognize the truth that Blaise Pascal so wisely stated: "The ultimate purpose of reason is to bring us to the place where we see that there is a limit to reason."

I am not opposed to science per se, but I must confront those who have proclaimed themselves scientific rationalists. These are the scientists who have excluded the supernatural from their thinking. They say, "In the scientific realm there is no room for speculation about life after death. Nobody can prove it, or verify it; nobody who has been there has ever come back. Therefore it is an irrelevant fact that has no meaning to life." They dismiss the subject of God, soul, spirit, and life after death by ruling it to be undiscoverable by means of the scientific method.

But Jesus says, "You're wrong, because you do not see the total scope of reality." True, such matters as life after death and the reality of the soul cannot be tested in a particle accelerator or examined under a microscope, but that does not mean they don't exist. A scientist is more than just a scientist; he or she is also a human being. As a human being, a scientist cannot escape the great spiritual questions because they don't conform to the scientific method. If God is real, if the soul is real, if the resurrection is real, but the scientific method cannot detect them, it means only that the scientific method is limited in what it can measure.

If, as a scientist and a rationalist, you push spiritual reality away and refuse to examine it, you will one day find yourself haunted by fears you cannot resolve and guilt you cannot dispel. Your thinking and attitudes will become distorted, and you will make wrong decisions, because you will be operating without an understanding of the fundamental nature of reality. Even your scientific judgment will be colored and distorted because, as a human being, you refuse to recognize the facts about your life and your soul. You are mistaken if you believe that science is the ultimate authority on all reality. It is partial and incomplete. It deals only with time. It cannot measure eternity.

In contrast to the authority of science and reason, God's authority is eternal and absolute. It encompasses all of time, all of reality. It never changes. It is the same in the age of space probes and the Internet as it was in the age of Noah, Abraham, and Moses. God's authority is sovereign over every aspect of our humanity. It touches our body, soul, and spirit. God's authority reaches beyond time through all the limitless ages of eternity, beyond the visible and into the realm of the invisible. It touches the great realities that determine our eternal fate but that cannot be sensed by human eye or hand or detected by manufactured instruments. There is not a subatomic particle anywhere in the universe over which God is not absolutely sovereign.

And He is absolutely sovereign over you and me.

This is why Jesus once said, "Do not be afraid of those who kill the body but cannot kill the soul. Rather, be afraid of the One who can destroy both soul and body in hell" (Matthew 10:28). It is not that Jesus wants us to see God as a terrible and frightening judge. After all, it was our loving, sovereign Father who sent His Son to redeem us. But Jesus wants us to recognize that nothing we can ever do can overrule God's power. Human beings cannot overthrow God.

When that is our perspective on life, when we recognize that God is the absolute authority over all knowledge and all reality, then all the puzzle pieces of reality begin to fit together. Those who seek to be truly rational in their approach to life must begin with obedience to the final authority on life, our loving and sovereign God.

twenty-three

Top Priority

➤ **Mark 12:28–44**

A medical miracle took place on December 1, 1982. On that day, a sixty-one-year-old dentist from Washington State, Dr. Barney Clark, was wheeled into an operating room at the University of Utah Medical Center. There, a device called the Jarvik-7, a mechanical heart, was implanted in his chest. The artificial heart would ultimately extend his life by 112 days, or roughly a third of a year.

When Dr. Clark awoke from surgery, he found his wife at his side. She bent over him and asked, "Do you still love me?"

Drowsily he replied, "Yes, of course I do."

A look of relief spread across her face.

"Why would you ask a thing like that?" Clark wondered aloud.

"After they put that mechanical heart in your chest," she replied, "I just wanted to be sure that you could still love me with all your heart."

In the next section of Mark, Jesus teaches us about the top priority of believers and followers of Christ. Whether your chest throbs with a heart of flesh or a heart of metal and plastic, your top priority in life is to love the Lord your God with all your heart, soul, mind, and strength.

The Greatest Commandment

Let's begin by recalling the context of this passage. We are examining the final week of the Lord's life. Jesus is in Jerusalem; He has cleansed the temple, cast out the moneychangers, and halted the rituals of temple worship. He has been confronted by the scribes, chief priests, Pharisees, Herodians, and Sadducees as they have attempted and failed to trap Him in His words. In the midst of that great discourse, He addresses matters that are of direct and eternal importance in your life and mine. Mark writes:

> *One of the teachers of the law came and heard them debating. Noticing that Jesus had given them a good answer, he asked him, "Of all the commandments, which is the most important?"*
>
> *"The most important one," answered Jesus, "is this: 'Hear, O Israel, the Lord our God, the Lord is one. Love the Lord your God with all your heart and with all your soul and with all your mind and with all your strength.' The second is this: 'Love your neighbor as yourself.' There is no commandment greater than these."* (MARK 12:28–31)

Here was an insightful scribe who asked an honest and thoughtful question; apparently at least one man who served in the temple was not corrupt. This scribe asked Jesus, "What are the priorities of life? Of all of God's commandments, which one ranks as the top priority?" The Lord answered, "Love the Lord your God with all your heart, soul, mind, and strength."

In other words, your top priority is to begin with God. When you are troubled, when you do not know what to do first, when you lack the resources to handle life, when you are baffled, wounded, and reeling from hurt and disappointment, then start with God. Love Him with all your heart, all your being.

Let's be honest. We have to admit that when we are dealing with the struggles and hurts of life, we seldom start by loving God. We usually obsess over the problem. We focus on it, we are haunted by it, we torture ourselves over it. We are so wrapped up with the struggle that confronts us that we can't get our minds off the problem and onto God.

But Jesus says the place to start is by loving God. When you start with God, you start with the one who sees the problem in its totality. He sees it in all its dimensions at once. Whatever the solution to our problem might be, God knows it because He sees it with perfect clarity. So if we want the right perspective on our problems, we must seek God's perspective. We must start by loving God.

When Jesus tells the scribe that our top priority is loving God, He is quoting the command of Moses found in Deuteronomy 6:4–5, a command that Jews everywhere know to this day as Shema Yisrael, from the Hebrew words for "Hear, O Israel." It has been called the Jewish pledge of allegiance, the Jew's testimony of faith and faithfulness to the one true God. Religious Jews desire to have the Shema as the last words on their lips before they die, a parting affirmation of their love for God.

Yet I know some people find this command troubling. "How can I love God on the basis of a command?" they say. "If love doesn't flow freely and spontaneously from the heart, is it really love?" This objection, however, is based on a misunderstanding of our relationship to God. The mental image this question suggests is that God plunks us down and yells, "I command you to love me!" Nothing could be further from the truth.

The image we should have in our minds when we think of our love for God is that of a little child's trusting love for a parent. God is, after all, our heavenly Father, the One who brought us into the world, who gave us life, who nurtured us and provided for us, who believed in us and affirmed us, who taught us and gave us His loving blessing. It is only natural for a child to respond to such a parent with a warm, affectionate, trusting love.

It is easy to love someone who has loved us first. The reason the Bible commands us to love God with all our heart, soul, mind, and strength is that we so easily forget what God has done for us and the love with which He has loved us. If we would live in a continual awareness of His love for us, then our love for Him would be a natural, spontaneous response. As 1 John 4:19 tells us, we love God because He first loved us.

God's love reaches out to us from every conceivable direction. It pours down out of the sky in the form of rain and sunshine. It springs from the ground as fruit and wheat and beautiful flowers. It surrounds us in the love of friends, family, Christian brothers and sisters. It even comes from within, in the form of insights, emotions, pleasures, and joys that God gives to us. All the things that come to us, all the things we need in order to live and enjoy life, come from the hand of God. And the infinite grace of our salvation, paid for at an infinite cost on the cross, came directly from the heart of God. Only a truly ungrateful and thoughtless person could look at all that God lovingly provides for us and then respond with anything less than a love that consumes the heart, soul, mind, and strength.

Not a Feeling but an Action

Next, notice that Jesus tells how to love God. To most of us, the word "love" suggests an emotion or a feeling: "I love my wife," or

"I love my children," or "I love my dog." Sometimes the word is used to express something as trivial as a preference: "I love pepperoni pizza."

But in the Bible, the word "love" is a powerful and meaningful word. When the Bible speaks of love, it refers to a logical choice, a specific action. The key to understanding this active, logical form of love can be found in these words of Jesus. When He quotes Deuteronomy 6:4–5, He shows us that authentic biblical love consists of four dimensions. The parallel passage in Luke 10:27 lists these four dimensions of love in a slightly different order, so it appears that the particular order of the four dimensions of love is not important. What is important is that we understand what this four-dimensional love is all about and that we put it into practice. The four dimensions of biblical love are:

Love God with all your heart.
Love God with all your soul.
Love God with all your mind.
Love God with all your strength.

Let's look at each of these dimensions in turn. First, what does it mean to love God with all your heart? When the Bible speaks of the heart, it usually refers to the human will. In some passages, "heart" refers to the emotions, but in Deuteronomy 6:4–5, it clearly speaks of the will. There are a number of passages where we find the will referred to as "the heart." For example, Genesis 8:21 speaks of "every inclination of his heart," meaning every deliberate and willful intention. And the Bible also speaks of a "hardened heart," a human will that has stubbornly chosen to disobey God. The heart is the seat of decision making; it is where we make moral and spiritual choices. The heart can reject God or receive Him. As Paul writes in Romans 10:10, "For it is with your heart that you believe and are justified." So when you love God with all your heart, it means that you make a choice, a decision of the will, to cling to God in love.

Next, what does it mean to love God with all your soul? The Greek word for soul is *psuche*, from which we get the term "psychology," describing the study of human mental and emotional health. The soul then is our innermost being, the seat of our emotions and feelings. To love God with all your soul means that you go to God with all your emotions—your hurts, your fears, and your joys. During happy moments, when we experience joy, elation, or a blessed serenity, then with the psalmist we can say, "To you, O LORD, I lift up my soul; . . . As the deer pants for streams of water, so my soul pants for you, O God" (Psalm 25:1; 42:1). And when we feel fearful, sad, or troubled, we can bring those feelings to Him just as the psalmist did: "When anxiety was great within me, your consolation brought joy to my soul" (Psalm 94:19). God created us as emotional beings, and He wants us to respond to Him with our emotions. So when you love God with all your soul, you go to Him with your joys and sorrows, you crawl into His lap with a childlike affection, and you receive from Him a warm and healing hug.

Then what does it mean to love God with your mind? The mind is the place from which we observe the world, record information and experiences, and sift truth from error. With the mind, we read God's Word and perceive the truth about God. And it is with the mind that we think about all that God has done for us. That mental understanding of God's loving presence in our lives enables us to respond to God in love through the heart, or our will, and the soul, or our emotions. Again and again the Bible affirms the importance of the mind and thoughts in our relationship with God.

Isaiah 26:3 tells us that the one whose mind is focused on God experiences trust in God and a perfect peace from God. Romans 8:6 reminds us that when our minds are controlled by the Spirit of God, we experience life and peace. Philippians 4:8–9 tells us to focus our minds on things that are true, noble, right, pure, and so forth. Isaiah 1:18 underscores the importance of a meeting of the minds between God and ourselves: " 'Come now, let us reason together,' says the LORD. 'Though your sins are like scarlet, they shall be as white as snow.' " God, who created our minds, wants us to meet Him in the quiet sanctuary of our thoughts, to have fellowship and loving communion with Him.

Once the heart, or our will, has been moved to reach out to God, once the soul, or our emotional being, has been lifted up toward God, once the mind, or our thinking, perceptive, rational being, has been focused on God, then we must love Him with all our strength. What does it mean to love God with all your strength? It means that you obey God in all that He says. You apply your daily efforts and energies to fulfilling His will for your life. You demonstrate your love for God by daily living out His loving commands.

Love Is for the Unloving and Unlovely

After stating the top priority, the command to love God with all our heart, soul, mind, and strength, Jesus stated the second most important priority: "The second is this: 'Love your neighbor as yourself.' " So this is the order Jesus gives. First we love God by responding to the love with which He first loved us. Then and only then can we truly love our neighbor as ourselves. That is how we put the two great commands in their proper order.

One of the ways we show love for others, for our neighbors, is by resolving problems in our relationships with them. And

Jesus gives us the key to solving relational problems. We begin with our top priority; we begin by responding to God's love. When you start with God's love, then you are ready to turn to your particular problem—the argument with your spouse, the disobedience of your children, the squabble with your neighbor, the insensitive actions of your friend, the obnoxious behavior of your boss—and you become free to love that person as you love yourself. You are able to love and forgive that person because you remember how graciously God has forgiven you. Because God's love reached down from heaven and invaded your heart, you can now reach from your heart to those around you.

You can love as you have been loved. You can forgive as you have been forgiven. You can initiate reconciliation just as God took the initiative and sent Christ to die for you while you were in rebellion against Him. You must start with God's love. If you start with your neighbor, you get the process out of order, and it doesn't work. If you try to love your neighbor without first loving God, then you will begin with a focus on all the hurts, difficulties, and friction in that relationship rather than a focus on the healing, forgiveness, and love you have received from God. So the order must never be reversed. It is love God, then love your neighbor. If you don't begin with God, you cannot love your neighbor.

A young man once came to me because of a problem with his adult sister. She had become angry with the family over some perceived offense. So she came to the house and staged a loud, hostile confrontation. She verbally attacked this young man and their parents. The scene became even uglier when this young man responded by shouting back at her. Before it was over, they had threatened each other, insulted each other, and had practically blown the roof off the house. Finally the sister stamped out of the house, slammed the front door, and roared off in her car.

After the young man finished telling me what had happened, I put my arm around him and said, "You know, a few years ago a young man came to our church. He had the most miserable and hateful scowl on his face. He was hostile and upset. He snarled and snapped at anyone who tried to talk with him. But you know, I have been watching that young man the past few years, and he has been changing. He smiles at everyone now, and he is always cheerful and eager to help others. What do you suppose made the change in that young man?"

He grinned sheepishly, because he knew I was talking about him. He knew the answer I was seeking, but he didn't want to admit it. So he shrugged.

I said, "You didn't change because people treated you the same way you treated them, did you? It was love that changed you. Somebody loved you in spite of the way you acted. Somebody reached out to you, showed interest in you, encouraged you, and hugged you. That is what made the change, wasn't it?"

He hung his head for a moment. "Yes," he admitted, "that's right. And now I know what my sister needs." From there, he went to his sister's apartment. He responded to her with love, and the family rift was soon healed.

Love is not just a word to write on a plaque and put on your wall. Love is how you are to respond to those who irritate you, who are hostile to you, who mistreat you, who are unfair to you. Love is the goodness and kindness you show to someone when your emotions and feelings are urging you to lash out and strike back. Love is the lovely act you do for someone who is unlovely or unloving.

And love starts with God. Remember His love to you; then show the same love to the one who has hurt you. Remember His forgiving spirit, how He wiped every trace of your sin from His memory; then do the same to the one who needs your forgiveness.

Loving God is your top priority. Do that, and love for your neighbor will naturally flow out of you like cool, clear water flowing from a bubbling spring.

The purpose of life is to lead us to the ultimate truth that God is the One who loves us and who can satisfy our need for love. His love meets the deepest needs of our life. That is why we must start with God.

No More Questions

The wise teacher of the law who questioned Jesus about the greatest command has heard the Lord's answer, and he approves of what he hears. Mark's account continues:

> *"Well said, teacher," the man replied. "You are right in saying that God is one and there is no other but him. To love him with all your heart, with all your understanding and with all your strength, and to love your neighbor as yourself is more important than all burnt offerings and sacrifices."*
>
> (MARK 12:32–33)

This wise scribe, unknown and unnamed, understood a great truth. He saw that God is not interested in the rituals and outward performances of our life. Contrary to what most people think, God is not primarily concerned with religion. He is concerned with our relationships. He is concerned with our lives. He is concerned with our love for Him and for each other. This teacher of the law understood it well, and Jesus affirmed the man for his understanding.

> *When Jesus saw that he had answered wisely, he said to him, "You are not far from the kingdom of God." And from*

then on no one dared ask him any more questions.

(MARK 12:34)

Our Lord commends this scribe, but He points out that the man is still not laying hold of the kingdom of God. He is close. He is seeing truth that is vitally important—that God is concerned about the inner attitude and not the outward performance of life—but the scribe doesn't grasp the whole truth. He is still not able, in other words, to love the Lord his God with all his heart, soul, mind, and strength. Why? Because he is still missing something. Jesus goes on to explain what this missing thing is.

Unfortunately the linkage between the preceding paragraph and the next paragraph is lost in our English translation. In the Greek text, it is obvious that these two paragraphs are linked together. Here is how the New International Version renders the next paragraph:

> *While Jesus was teaching in the temple courts, he asked, "How is it that the teachers of the law say that the Christ is the son of David?"* (MARK 12:35)

But here is how a more literal translation of that verse ought to read, so that the connection with the previous paragraph becomes clear:

> *Jesus answered as he taught in the temple courts, and he asked, "How is it that the teachers of the law say that the Christ is the son of David?"* (MARK 12:35, STEDMAN TRANSLATION)

Notice the words I supplied, which come from the Greek text: "Jesus answered." Answered whom? The wise teacher of the law,

who, Jesus said, was "not far from the kingdom of God."
Answered what questions? The obvious questions that were in the
scribe's heart: "You say that I am very close to the kingdom of God.
What do I lack? What more must I do to lay hold of the kingdom?" So Jesus answered by putting a question to the scribes:

> *"How is it that the teachers of the law say that the*
> *Christ is the son of David? David himself, speaking*
> *by the Holy Spirit, declared:*
> *" 'The Lord said to my Lord:*
> > *"Sit at my right hand*
> > *until I put your enemies*
> > *under your feet.' "*
> *"David himself calls him 'Lord.' How then can he be his*
> son?"
>
> *The large crowd listened to him with delight.*
>
> (MARK 12:35–37)

According to Mark's record, no one answered that question.
But Jesus is driving home a key point to these teachers of the law.
He quotes David's words from Psalm 110:1 and says that David's
words were inspired by the Holy Spirit. And what David said was
this: "The Lord [Jehovah] said to my Lord [the Messiah], sit at my
right hand." The teachers of the law would have agreed with what
Jesus said. They understood that David, in Psalm 110:1, was
speaking of the Lord God Jehovah and the Messiah. So building
on that verse, Jesus poses a question to them: How can David call
the Messiah "Lord" if the Messiah is David's son? The answer is
the mystery of Jesus' identity. Jesus was descended from David
according to the flesh, the Messiah according to prophecy and
promise, and the Lord of glory according to the Spirit.

Jesus' identity is the central issue of this passage, and it is the central issue of life. Who is Jesus to you? Is He Lord? The whole issue of how to enter the kingdom and how to live in the kingdom of God hangs on that point. Is Jesus the Lord? Is He God?

That wise teacher of the law was not far from the kingdom of God. If that teacher of the law knew and acknowledged that Jesus is Lord, then he would not be close. He would have arrived.

Paul tells us that the whole of creation is moving toward that final day when the question will be answered, when the long, tragic record of human conflict and human evil is ended. Then God will have completed His plan for human life and history. It will culminate in a great scene described by Paul in his letter to the Philippians: "Therefore God exalted him to the highest place and gave him the name that is above every name, that at the name of Jesus every knee should bow, in heaven and on earth and under the earth, and every tongue confess that Jesus Christ is Lord, to the glory of God the Father" (Philippians 2:9–11).

Jesus is the issue. Is He Lord of your life? His lordship releases the kingdom of God in our lives. All the greatness and glory of God comes pouring into us when He is truly Lord of our lives. As Paul writes, "And whatever you do, whether in word or deed, do it all in the name of the Lord Jesus" (Colossians 3:17).

True Godliness Versus Self-righteousness

Mark concludes this account with the vivid contrast that Jesus draws between proud, self-righteous teachers of the law and a poor but godly widow.

> *As he taught, Jesus said, "Watch out for the teachers of the law. They like to walk around in flowing robes and be greeted in the marketplaces, and have the most important*

seats in the synagogues and the places of honor at banquets. They devour widows' houses and for a show make lengthy prayers. Such men will be punished most severely."

(MARK 12:38–40)

We all know that it is easy to pretend to be godly. It is easy to go to church and put on a false show of being a Christian. At one time or another, almost all of us have surely succumbed to that temptation. We love to be honored and well thought of. We want others to know how saintly we are, how long and fervently we can pray. We like to impress each other with our God-talk, our church attendance and involvement. We want other people to know that we are good people. And when we make such an outward show of being godly, as these self-righteous teachers of the law did, we are nothing but hypocrites. Jesus contrasts such phony religiosity with true, godly, humble faith, as exemplified by a poor widow.

Jesus sat down opposite the place where the offerings were put and watched the crowd putting their money into the temple treasury. Many rich people threw in large amounts. But a poor widow came and put in two very small copper coins, worth only a fraction of a penny.

Calling his disciples to him, Jesus said, "I tell you the truth, this poor widow has put more into the treasury than all the others. They all gave out of their wealth; but she, out of her poverty, put in everything—all she had to live on."

(MARK 12:41–44)

The Jewish historian Josephus tells us that the religious exhibitionism among the scribes and Pharisees had reached such an absurd level that some of the Pharisees hired a trumpeter to go before them as they made their way to the great temple collection box. They would make sure they had an audience before depositing a bag of gold in the temple treasury.

But Jesus draws our attention to someone who is likely to be overlooked, an anonymous widow, a woman of neither affluence nor influence. She comes to the collection box; she quietly drops in two tiny coins that added together are worth less than a penny. It was not the change she found behind the sofa cushions. It was her last cent. Yet she gave it to the temple of the Lord, because she was a woman who loved the Lord her God with all her heart, soul, mind, and strength. "This poor widow," said Jesus, "has put more into the treasury than all the others." Why? Because she gave it with love for God, not for show.

Many Christian people are involved in very public forms of Christian service. There are evangelists. There are pastors of large churches. There are Christian authors, radio teachers, television preachers, conference speakers, university presidents, seminary presidents, theologians, and recording artists. All such people serve God in public ways, and some become nationally and internationally known. But the truth is that there are people that you've never heard of and never will hear of who may be doing more to advance the kingdom in their anonymous way than many of the most famous Christian leaders or performers you could name.

It is easy for Christian pastors and authors and evangelists to think, *I'll bet God is impressed with the impact I've been making for Him through my public ministry!* What a foolish thing to think. God looks at the heart, not the performance. He is much more interested to see if we live as genuine Christians when no one is watching than when we stand behind a microphone. He is much more interested in our love for others than our love for the spotlight.

That fact is discouraging and encouraging. It is discouraging for those, like myself, who are in a public ministry. But it is encouraging for all other believers. Isn't it great to know that God is watching the widow with her few coins? He isn't looking for a grand performance. He is looking for people who will love Him with all their heart, soul, mind, and strength, and who will love their neighbors as themselves.

twenty-four

Watch!

► Mark 13

The great English mathematician and astronomer, Sir Isaac Newton (1642–1727), held the Lucasian chair of mathematics at Cambridge University. It was Newton, you'll recall, who formulated the law of gravity after being hit on the head by a falling apple, or so legend has it. During the Dutch-English war, Newton strode into the hall at Cambridge's Trinity College and made a startling announcement to his fellow professors. "Less than an hour ago," said Newton, "there was a great naval battle between the Dutch and English navies—and I regret to say that our own English navy got the worst of it."

"Sir Isaac," said one professor, "you can't possibly know such a thing! Cambridge is many miles from the sea. Even a rider on the fastest horse imaginable couldn't possibly have brought you such news in so short a time."

"I never said that anyone brought me news," replied Newton. "But everything I told you is absolutely true. There *was* a naval battle within the past hour, and our fleet *was* forced to flee."

"If that is true," said another professor, "then tell us how you know."

161

"It is really quite simple," said Newton. "Less than an hour ago, I was up in my observatory. The observatory is so high that ordinary street sounds cannot be heard there, yet loud sounds such as cannon fire can be heard from quite a distance away. There, I heard the incessant, repeated sound of cannon fire, such as could only have taken place between two great fleets. The sound not only continued but grew louder, which meant that the ships were moving closer to our own shores. That could only happen if the English ships were retreating toward the coast."

The professors laughed. They were relieved to learn that Newton's battle scenario had been based on the slenderest of evidence: some distant sounds he had heard while he was up in his observatory.

The following day, the news reached Cambridge University. During a battle with the Dutch navy, the English fleet had been routed and forced to flee to the coast in disarray, just as Sir Isaac Newton had said. There is moral to this story from history: If you want to know what is happening in the world, pay attention to the signs.

The Big Question: When?

At this point in our study of Mark, we come to the great prophecy of Jesus dealing with the last days of earth, just before the return of the King in all His power and glory. Jesus tells His disciples that if they want to know what will happen at the end of the age, they must pay attention to the signs.

This passage, Mark 13, is known as the Olivet Discourse because Jesus gave this talk as He was seated on the Mount of Olives, looking out over the city of Jerusalem. It was only a day or two before His crucifixion, and Jesus was answering questions from the disciples—and contemplating the fate of the city.

In the opening verses of Mark 13, we hear the questions that the disciples put to Him.

> *As he was leaving the temple, one of his disciples said to him, "Look, Teacher! What massive stones! What magnificent buildings!"*
>
> *"Do you see all these great buildings?" replied Jesus. "Not one stone here will be left on another; every one will be thrown down."*
>
> *As Jesus was sitting on the Mount of Olives opposite the temple, Peter, James, John and Andrew asked him privately, "Tell us, when will these things happen? And what will be the sign that they are all about to be fulfilled?"*
>
> (MARK 13:1–4)

This strongly suggests that the disciples might have felt embarrassed and upset by Jesus' recent actions. He had cleansed the temple and had rebuked and condemned the Jewish religious leaders. It seems that the disciples felt He had been too harsh, so they are trying to put Him in a more positive frame of mind toward the Jewish religious structure by pointing out some positive aspects of the temple.

After all, the disciples still didn't understand His mission on earth. They saw the Messiah as the one who would sweep away the oppressive Roman occupation of Israel. Why then was He attacking the Jewish religious leaders? Why was He insulting His countrymen? Shouldn't He focus His wrath on the Roman oppressors?

So, to try to influence Him to soften His attacks on the temple leaders, they pointed out the greatness of the temple buildings and the gigantic stones of which they were made. (Josephus records that some of these stones were forty feet long and eighteen feet high.) But Jesus' answer is even more disturbing and perplexing than anything He has said before. He tells His disciples that these stones, as great as they are, will be cast down, and the temple will be destroyed.

Editor's Note: A cover story in *Time* for Easter 2001 included this significant statement: "When the unnamed disciple remarked on the size of the temple stones, Jesus replied that 'not one stone will be left upon another; all will be thrown down.' He was right. After one last rebellion, in A.D. 135, the Romans leveled Jerusalem, leaving only the bald platform behind."

See David Van Biema, "Jerusalem at the Time of Jesus," *Time*, April 16, 2001, 46ff.

The disciples were understandably troubled by the Lord's prediction of the destruction of the temple. One gets the impression that the Twelve selected a delegation of four men to go and talk with Jesus. They chose the two pairs of brothers, Peter and Andrew, and James and John, who were in the inner circle. Finding Jesus seated on the Mount of Olives, they asked Him privately, "Tell us, when will these things happen? And what will be the sign that they are all about to be fulfilled?"

For twenty centuries, these questions have baffled human minds. For twenty centuries, men and women have anticipated the events Jesus talks about in this prophecy and expected its fulfillment in their lifetime. We must honestly face this fact. Every generation has thought Jesus was coming back in their time, because of signs they saw or thought they saw in the events of their day.

But I think it is clear, as you read this account, that the disciples have asked the wrong question, and so have we. To ask *when* is to ask the wrong question. Jesus makes it clear that if you focus on when, you will be misled. History records that this has happened again and again, as various leaders and teachers have thought they had the answer. So they led their followers to a mountaintop somewhere to await the second coming, which would occur on a schedule that they had carefully calculated. Time passed. Nothing happened. And these leaders and teachers end up looking like fools.

Jesus does not ignore the question of when these things will happen. He answers it, in His own fashion, but He leaves it to the end. So let's work our way through Mark 13 and examine what Jesus says. In the course of this study, we will discover His surprising answer.

A Warning: "Watch Out!"

Four sections of Jesus' message relate to the question of the disciples in Mark 13:4: "Tell us, when will these things happen? And what will be the sign that they are all about to be fulfilled?" Let's examine these four sections in the order Jesus gives them. As we go along, remember that if we want the full account of what He said to the disciples, we must also read the parallel passages in Matthew 24 and 25 and Luke 21. We need all of these passages in order to see the full picture. Each of the gospel writers selects certain things he wants to emphasize. Matthew focuses on what is to happen to Israel. Luke is the only one who tells us of the fall of Jerusalem, the subsequent captivity of the Jews, and the domination of the city by the Gentiles. But Mark emphasizes the danger to faith that is going to arise in the age that follows the crucifixion and resurrection of our Lord.

Jesus begins His discourse with a word of warning.

> *Jesus said to them: "Watch out that no one deceives you."* (Mark 13:5)

This is the keynote of everything Jesus is about to reveal. As we will see, He begins and ends with this same emphasis: "Watch out!" or "Watch!" In Mark 13:5, the Greek word for the phrase "watch out" is *blepo,* which conveys a sense of "Look out! Beware! Open your eyes to a dangerous situation!" His closing words in Mark 13:37 are, "What I say to you, I say to everyone: 'Watch!' " The Greek word for "watch" in this verse is *gregoreuo,* which conveys a sense of "Wake up! Don't fall asleep! A calamity is coming!" This urgent warning brackets everything Jesus says in His prophecy of the coming time. So, during the course of the age, He wants us to be watchful and wakeful and aware, for it is a dangerous time.

Section 1: The Nonsigns

In the first section of Jesus' message (Mark 13:6–13), He talks about certain events that many people have mistaken as signs of the end of the age. By failing to read His words with care, they have been deceived into seeing signs where there were no signs. You have probably heard sermons or read books based on these so-called signs of the times, but if you read with care, you see that Jesus tells us these events are not the signs. In fact, I like to call the events Jesus describes nonsigns because they are events people have mistaken as signs but are not signs.

The first nonsign in this passage is the coming of various religious pretenders or false Christs. Jesus says:

> *"Many will come in my name, claiming, 'I am he,' and will deceive many."* (MARK 13:6)

It is important to understand that literally dozens of false messiahs came before, during, and after Jesus, fulfilling His prophecy that many would come claiming, "I am He; I am the Messiah." Acts 5:36–37 mentions two: Theudas, who said he would miraculously part the Jordan River but ultimately led four hundred followers to their deaths; and Judah the Galilean, an anti-Roman radical who founded the Zealot movement. (One of the Twelve, Simon the Zealot, was a member of this movement.)

A century after Jesus died and rose again, another would-be messiah, Simon Bar-Kochba, began a rebellion that lasted for more than three years and cost hundreds of lives. Proclaimed the long-awaited Messiah by Rabbi Akiva in Jerusalem, Bar-Kochba gained control of the Jewish population in Palestine. He was fanatically convinced of his messianic calling and ruled with an iron fist. He demanded that Christians deny Christ, and he brutally tortured and killed any Christian men, women, or children who remained faithful to their Lord. In the end, the Romans put an end to Simon Bar-Kochba and his followers, killing thousands and sending many more into captivity and slavery. Bar-Kochba's patron, Rabbi Akiva, survived but was discredited and disgraced.

Other supposed messiahs included Moses of Crete, who promised to part the Mediterranean and lead his followers across dry land from the island of Crete to the Holy Land. Many jumped off a cliff at his command and were drowned. There was Moses Al-Dar'I, who commanded his Jewish Moroccan followers to rid themselves of their possessions because Messiah was coming at Passover in 1127; Passover came and went, and his people were left destitute. In the late 1200s, a Sicilian mystic named Abraham ben Samuel proclaimed himself the Son of God and led a failed attempt to resettle Jews in Palestine.

Shabbetai Tsevi of Smyrna burst on the scene in 1666, claiming to have heard God's voice declaring him to be the Messiah. He led a procession of followers into Constantinople, where he was promptly arrested and imprisoned by the Turkish sultan. When the sultan ordered Shabbetai Tsevi either to prove himself the Messiah or be executed, the would-be messiah responded by converting to Islam.

In our era, we have seen many would-be messiahs parade across the stage, often leading their followers to some horrible end such as mass suicide. These messiahs possess charming and charismatic personalities, and they attract hundreds or even thousands of followers. They often mingle teaching from the Old Testament prophets, the words of Jesus, and the book of Revelation with New Age mysticism and even UFO cult lore. It is common for these assorted messiahs to take some of the sayings of Jesus out of context, mingle them with Eastern religion and other false doctrines, and sell it to the unwise and unwary as truth.

Jesus predicted it would happen, and it has. Cults and cult messiahs continually arise, claiming to come in the name of Jesus, but what they teach is not what Jesus taught. This, Jesus said, is a deceptive strategy, designed to lead many astray. His word of warning is, "Watch out that no one deceives you." In other words, "Open your eyes and take heed! Be careful that the messiah you follow is the biblical Jesus, the one of whom the apostles give witness. If not, you will be led into error and destruction." His warning has been proven valid through twenty centuries of bloody human history.

But the proliferation of would-be messiahs is not a sign of the end times. It is a nonsign.

"Wars and Rumors of Wars"

Next Jesus lists a number of disasters and calamities that many people have mistaken for signs of the end. Jesus says:

> *"When you hear of wars and rumors of wars, do not be alarmed. Such things must happen, but the end is still to come. Nation will rise against nation, and kingdom against kingdom. There will be earthquakes in various places, and famines. These are the beginning of birth pains."*
>
> (MARK 13:7–8)

Wars, earthquakes, famines, and other cataclysmic events will occur and increase throughout the whole sweep of the age. But Jesus also makes it clear that these are not signs of the end. There is no mistaking His meaning when He says, "but the end is still to come," and they are merely "the beginning of birth pains." Ask any mother, and she will tell you that when the "beginning of birth pains," or early contractions, take place, there is a long process of labor ahead before the baby is born.

Yet down through history and to the present day, people have misunderstood these plain words of Jesus. They have taken these cataclysmic events to be signs of our Lord's return. As a young Christian, I read books that described World War I, an event in which nation rose against nation and kingdom against kingdom, as the sign of the end. "No other war in history fulfilled this prophecy to this extent," the authors claimed. But then World War II came along, and the authors of those books had to explain that. So they said, "World War I fulfilled the part about 'nation shall rise against nation,' and World War II fulfilled 'kingdom against kingdom.' " These books went through successive editions and revisions as their authors scrambled to stay current with changing world events.

But these authors failed to recognize one simple fact. Jesus clearly states that none of these events are the signs. There have been wars and rumors of wars from the beginning. There have been famines and earthquakes around the world for thousands of years, and there will undoubtedly be more to come. As a boy in the 1930s, I read a book about the great San Francisco quake of 1906, and I thought, *Wow! That earthquake was so destructive, it must have been a sign that the Lord is coming soon!* I expected the Lord to come the day after I finished reading the book. I didn't understand, as I do now, that Jesus was saying that these events were not the signs but merely the beginnings of the sufferings of humanity. The increase of natural disasters does not signify that we are in the end times.

Persecution

Another sign that is often listed as an indicator of the end times is the rising persecution of Christians. Again a close examination of the words of Jesus shows this to be another nonsign.

> *"You must be on your guard. You will be handed over to the local councils and flogged in the synagogues. On account of me you will stand before governors and kings as witnesses to them. And the gospel must first be preached to all nations. Whenever you are arrested and brought to trial, do not worry beforehand about what to say. Just say whatever is given you at the time, for it is not you speaking, but the Holy Spirit."* (MARK 13:9–11)

These words began to be fulfilled from the beginning of the Christian era. The book of Acts describes how the apostles and thousands of early Christians were arrested, dragged before governors and kings, flogged, beaten, stoned, and more. Mark's account of Jesus' words links persecution with the preaching of the gospel, for in the midst of this prophecy of persecution comes this statement: "And the gospel must first be preached to all nations." This linkage indicates that when the gospel penetrates a nation, governing authorities scrutinize Christians, whose witness becomes a testimony to that nation. For example, when Paul stood before the emperor Nero in about A.D. 67, it was evident that the gospel had penetrated much of the Roman Empire because of Paul's witness.

"Whenever you are arrested and brought to trial," Jesus said, "do not worry beforehand about what to say. Just say whatever is given you at the time, for it is not you speaking, but the Holy Spirit." And as we read through the book of Acts and the annals of Christian history, we see that the Lord's counsel has also been fulfilled. As Christians have been brought before governors and kings, God the Holy Spirit has given them His words of testimony to speak. We recall how Paul spoke with supernatural wisdom as he stood before King Agrippa and the Roman governors Felix and Festus.

Centuries later, Martin Luther stood before yet another Roman king. Our family once visited that great cathedral at Worms, Germany, along the Rhine River, where Luther made his stand. I vividly recall my feelings as we walked into that imposing Gothic structure. I imagined the scene, centuries ago, when all the most powerful men of Europe were assembled in that place: Charles V, emperor of the Holy Roman Empire; the papal delegates; the bishops and archbishops of all the Catholic realms. And they gathered to confront a single man. Luther, on trial for his life and acting in total reliance on the Holy Spirit, was given these words to speak, which have come ringing down the centuries: "My conscience is bound by the Word of God. Unless I am convinced from the sacred Scriptures that I am in error, I cannot and I will not recant. Here I stand. I cannot do otherwise. God help me." Although he was condemned as a heretic, those words ignited the Reformation, which spread throughout Europe.

History has seen this amazing phenomenon again and again. Martyrs and witnesses who have no special ability as great speakers or deep thinkers have suddenly received supernatural wisdom to speak. In their hour of trial and persecution, the Spirit has given them power to proclaim God's words as a testimony to the nations.

But even the persecution of believers is not a sign of the end, because it has been going on through the course of the age. The persecution of believers is going on now, all around the world, and persecution will characterize this age until it is ended. That is the point Jesus makes.

Jesus underscores that we can expect persecution of such an intense, hostile, and violent nature that it will threaten to destroy our faith. It will be so intense that family members may even betray one another. He says:

> "Brother will betray brother to death, and a father his child. Children will rebel against their parents and have them put to death. All men will hate you because of me, but he who stands firm to the end will be saved."
>
> (MARK 13:12–13)

The "end" Jesus refers to is not the end times but the end of a Christian's life. All Christians are called to be faithful unto death. In the book of Revelation, Jesus addresses seven churches in Asia Minor and says, "Be faithful, even to the point of death, and I will give you the crown of life" (Revelation 2:10). That is not a word for martyrs only, but for all Christians: "Be faithful until your dying day." Why? "Because he who stands firm to the end will be saved." Jesus is not saying that we earn our salvation by enduring to the end; rather, we prove that our salvation is genuine by the fact that we endure to the end. Only genuine Christians will survive the test of the age.

The apostle John laments the fact that some people seem to be believers for a time, but they do not endure as Christians. He writes, "They went out from us, but they did not really belong to us. For if they had belonged to us, they would have remained with us; but their going showed that none of them belonged to us" (1 John 2:19). Every age of Christian history has seen this phenomenon. People make a profession of faith, and they seem to be growing, they seem happy and committed—and then their commitment seems to crumble under the pressure of the times. They do not endure to the end. John tells us that the fact that they did not endure shows that they never truly belonged to the body of Christ.

Section 2: The Sign

In the second section of the Lord's Olivet Discourse, we come to His answer to the question of the disciples regarding signs. They asked, "Tell us, when will these things happen? And what will be the sign that they are all about to be fulfilled?" The Lord puts His answer into a single brief phrase:

> *"When you see 'the abomination that causes desolation' standing where it does not belong—let the reader understand—then let those who are in Judea flee to the mountains."* (MARK 13:14)

Note the statement that appears to be inserted into Jesus' words: "let the reader understand." These do not seem to be Jesus' words, for He is talking to hearers, not writing to readers. This appears to be Mark's statement, intended to underscore what Jesus is saying. Mark is telling us that this is an important piece of information, and we need to think about it carefully and understand it. Matthew adds a similar emphasis in his parallel account:

> *"So when you see standing in the holy place 'the abomination that causes desolation,' spoken of through the prophet Daniel—let the reader understand—"*
>
> (MATTHEW 24:15)

Matthew also tells us that Jesus is referring to the book of Daniel. You can read Daniel 9:27, 11:31, and 12:11. In those passages, Daniel talks about a sacrilege, a desecration, an "abomination of desolation," which is to be set up in the temple, defiling and profaning the temple. Paul appears to be referring to the same act of sacrilege when he speaks of the "man of lawlessness" who is to appear, proclaiming himself to be God.

> *Don't let anyone deceive you in any way, for that day will not come until the rebellion occurs and the man of lawlessness is revealed, the man doomed to destruction. He will oppose and will exalt himself over everything that is called God or is worshiped, so that he sets himself up in God's temple, proclaiming himself to be God.*
>
> (2 THESSALONIANS 2:3–4)

This is a reference to the worldwide religion of the last days. Of course, we already see religions abounding that claim that humankind is God, that we do not need any God other than ourselves. This deification of the self will reach its personified apex when a human being, "the man of lawlessness," takes his place in the temple of God, desecrating it with his blasphemy.

This is why Bible students have always watched with great interest the possibility of the reconstruction of the temple in Jerusalem. In A.D. 70, the Roman armies of Titus fulfilled one of Jesus' prophecies by destroying the temple. There has never been a temple in Jerusalem since. But Jesus speaks of a desolating sacrilege that will be set up in the temple, which means that the temple must be rebuilt in Jerusalem. Having predicted the temple's destruction, Jesus implies that it will be reconstructed. And as we approach the time when a temple can be constructed, we are seeing the possibility of the fulfillment of this event in our day.

Editor's Note: News reports from Israel confirm the increasing likelihood of the reconstruction of the temple in our time. A report in *The* (London) *Daily Telegraph* states that Orthodox Jews are laying plans to rebuild the temple in Jerusalem and are even training young boys to serve in the restored priesthood; they would assume priestly duties at the age of thirteen. The Orthodox group has "meticulously reconstructed the plan of the temple, made replicas of the holy vessels in gold and woven the cotton garments the high priest wore at rituals to specifications listed in the Book of Deuteronomy."

In 1995, the *Jerusalem Post* reported a major archaeological find that brings the reconstruction of the temple a few steps closer. Archaeologists had uncovered an exact replica of the Jerusalem temple atop Mount Gerazim, overlooking the city of Nablus. This find, said the *Post,* "could provide the first historical indication of what the temple, destroyed by the Romans in 70 C.E. [Christian era], looked like. It itself was a reconstruction of the temple built by King Solomon in 960 B.C." Archaeologists located the replica through clues in the writings of the Jewish historian Josephus.

The biggest obstacle to rebuilding the temple is the fact that the site is now claimed as a Muslim holy place. "Two of Islam's holiest mosques," reports *The Daily Telegraph*, "stand in East Jerusalem at the traditional site of King Solomon's temple, destroyed by the Romans in A.D. 70. In recent years, the hilltop compound has become the focus of contention and sometimes bloody clashes between Muslims and Jews."

See "Orthodox Plan to Raise Boys as Temple Priests," *The Daily Telegraph*, March 2, 1998; and Associated Press, "Archaeologists Uncover Replica of Second Temple," *Jerusalem Post*, April 17, 1995.

The Outbreak of the Tribulation

Jesus says that when the "abomination that causes desolation" appears, there will be three immediate and terrible results. First, there will be an immediate and sudden peril to believers who are in Jerusalem and the surrounding area (tourists to the Holy Land, take note).

> "When you see 'the abomination that causes desolation' standing where it does not belong—let the reader understand—then let those who are in Judea flee to the mountains. Let no one on the roof of his house go down or enter the house to take anything out. Let no one in the field go back to get his cloak. How dreadful it will be in those days for pregnant women and nursing mothers! Pray that this will not take place in winter." (MARK 13:14–18)

It will be a time of such imminent danger that people will have no time to go home and pack. They must flee the city or be trapped. The second result is the outbreak of worldwide tribulation.

> "Because those will be days of distress unequaled from the beginning, when God created the world, until now— and never to be equaled again. If the Lord had not cut short

those days, no one would survive. But for the sake of the elect, whom he has chosen, he has shortened them."

(MARK 13:19–20)

This will be a time of unprecedented global cataclysm. If you want the vivid details, they are found Revelation, in the passages that deal with the pouring out of the vials of God's wrath, the opening of the seven seals, and the sounding of the seven trumpets. It will be a time of economic totalitarianism, when all commerce is controlled by a central authority. Everyone will be issued a number by which to do business, an economic system that is undoubtedly presaged by the current computerized credit and electronic currency system.

The third result will be:

"At that time if anyone says to you, 'Look, here is the Christ!' or, 'Look, there he is!' do not believe it. For false Christs and false prophets will appear and perform signs and miracles to deceive the elect—if that were possible. So be on your guard; I have told you everything ahead of time."

(MARK 13:21–23)

This will be a time of worldwide religious deception. I believe that these false Christs and false prophets mentioned here will be agents of the single, supreme Antichrist who will rule in that day. There will be people all over the world whose task it is to bring men and women into submission to the new global religion whose creed is "humankind is God." What a threat to faith that is! We can see the advance of this secular religion in our time. And we must remember that there have been such trends in the past.

But when all the signs appear as Jesus prophesied, we must be watchful that we are not deceived during this coming time of worldwide deception.

The Climax of History

Finally, says Jesus, there comes the climax of history. The picture Jesus paints is a terrifying one, although it will be a glorious time for those who belong to the Lord Jesus Christ.

"But in those days, following that distress,

> *" 'the sun will be darkened,*
> *and the moon will not give its light;*
> *the stars will fall from the sky,*
> *and the heavenly bodies will be shaken.'*

"At that time men will see the Son of Man coming in clouds with great power and glory. And he will send his angels and gather his elect from the four winds, from the ends of the earth to the ends of the heavens."

(MARK 13:24–27)

The appearing of Jesus Christ as Lord is the climax of history. (I hasten to add that this passage does not deal with what is called the rapture, the departure of the church; that is dealt with in other passages.) Here we have the appearance again of Jesus Christ in great power and glory. It is preceded, as all the prophets have predicted, by terrible signs in the heavens. Evidently some tremendous cataclysm upsets the whole solar system, of which we are a part. Astronomers are continually discovering previously unknown objects and forces at work in the heavens, from asteroids and comets that make frighteningly close approaches to the earth to mysterious black holes with such immense gravitational pull that even light cannot escape from them. These objects and forces, or others yet to be discovered, could have some influence on the terrifying events that are described.

From other prophetic passages of Scripture, we know that this disruption of heavenly bodies will have an effect on the earth, causing volcanoes to erupt and tidal waves to arise. Then the Son of Man appears, and all His mighty angels with Him. He sends those angels out to gather Israel back into the land. This gathering of the elect, I am sure, is the fulfillment of the predictions of the prophets that there will come a time when Israel will be gathered from the four corners of the earth, not by natural migration but by supernatural means. There, in the land God promised to Abraham, Isaac, and Jacob, the kingdom of God will be visibly, wonderfully established on the earth.

Our Lord then draws this analogy from nature:

> *"Now learn this lesson from the fig tree: As soon as its twigs get tender and its leaves come out, you know that summer is near. Even so, when you see these things happening, you know that it is near, right at the door. I tell you the truth, this generation will certainly not pass away until all these things have happened. Heaven and earth will pass away, but my words will never pass away."*
>
> (MARK 13:28–31)

This is an easy analogy to follow and understand. When you see the trees in the spring putting forth leaves, you know two things. First, summer is near. It will not be long until the days are warm and the cold weather is over. Second, it is certain that nothing will stop it. When the leaves appear on the trees, summer is certain to come.

Jesus says we can draw the same conclusions from seeing the events He has outlined for the future. He says, "Even so, when you see these things happening, you know that it is near, right at the door." What does He mean, "these things"? I do not think He means the signs in the heavens, for they are not the beginning of the events. Rather, He is talking about the sign on earth, that is, the appearance of the "abomination that causes desolation" in the temple in Jerusalem. When you see things beginning to move in this direction, things that begin to make this event possible, then you know that the return of the Lord is drawing near. At that point, says Jesus, His return is so near that "this generation will certainly not pass away until all these things have happened." In other words, once this process begins, the generation that sees it begin will not pass away before these events have run their course. In biblical terms, a generation is about twenty-seven years.

Jesus also assures the disciples and us that these events are certain to happen. How certain? "Heaven and earth will pass away," He says, "but my words will never pass away." Those words are given to us to strengthen our faith in a time of testing. Jesus knew that future generations of Christians would have their faith tested. There would be times when it might seem that the Bible is wrong, that world events appear to be taking a route different from the one predicted in Scripture. But in those times when biblical prophecies seem unreal, untrustworthy, and unrelated to the world of events, remember these words of Jesus: "Heaven and earth will pass away, but my words will never pass away." This prophecy is certain. History is going to end just as Jesus said.

Jesus Returns to the Question

In the last section of Mark 13, Jesus returns to the question that began this discourse: "Tell us, when will these things happen?" Jesus says:

> *"No one knows about that day or hour, not even the angels in heaven, nor the Son, but only the Father."*
>
> (MARK 13:32)

If anyone claims to have a revelation as to when this event is going to take place, that person is either lying or deluded. Even the angels do not know. In fact—and this is one of the most startling statements Jesus ever spoke—even the Son does not know. This statement marks the humanity of our Lord. In coming to earth as a man, Jesus has set aside the exercise of His deity. He never exercised it while He was here among us. He was a man like us, limited to the knowledge that God had made known to Him. And because God had not told Him the day or the hour, even He did not know.

Remember that even after His resurrection, Jesus told His disciples, "It is not for you to know the times or dates the Father has set by his own authority" (Acts 1:7). So quit trying to figure it out! When is not important, because it cannot be determined. There is no way that you can know the time or date.

As we read on, we see that even our Lord did not know how long it would be before He came back. All these disciples thought it would take place within their lifetime, and Jesus seems to speak as though that were the case: "When you see . . . When you hear . . . Be on your guard." He is addressing the disciples as if He thinks it is possible that they will be present to witness those events, but it did not happen in their lifetimes. It has been almost two thousand years since Jesus spoke those words, and still no one knows when He will come again.

The important thing Jesus wants us to know, however, is not *when* but *watch*. We must always be watchful, always aware, always awake, because these events might happen at any time. So Jesus concludes:

> *"Be on guard! Be alert! You do not know when that time will come. It's like a man going away: He leaves his house and puts his servants in charge, each with his assigned task, and tells the one at the door to keep watch.*
>
> *"Therefore keep watch because you do not know when the owner of the house will come back—whether in the evening, or at midnight, or when the rooster crows, or at dawn. If he comes suddenly, do not let him find you sleeping. What I say to you, I say to everyone: 'Watch!' "*
>
> (MARK 13:33–37)

Here Jesus gathers up all the intervening time between His first and second comings, and He divides it into four watches— one long night of the world's sin. He says to us, "You don't know," and I think He implies that He does not know, "whether my return will be early, or in the middle of that time, or three-quarters of the way through, or at the end. No one knows."

He compares His absence with a man who assigns tasks to his servants before leaving on a journey. The man expects his servants to carry out their assigned duties. He has set a doorkeeper to watch at the door. What is the doorkeeper to watch for? The master's return? That is how this passage is usually interpreted, but that is not what Jesus is saying.

If you look carefully at Jesus' words, you see that the door-keeper is to begin watching as soon as the master leaves the house. The servants know the master will not return immediately. So what is the doorkeeper watching for? He is to watch lest somebody deceive them and gain entrance to the house. He is to stand guard and prevent robbers from entering and wrecking the master's house. So Jesus says, "Be on guard! Be alert! Watch!" He is warning the disciples, and you and me, that temptations and pressures wait to ambush. Those forces will try to deceive us, try to make us give up and stop living like Christians. We must stand guard against thieves coming in and stealing our faith. And while we are being watchful, we must continue doing the work He has given to us.

We are not to be looking up at the sky, wondering when He will come. That will happen when He is ready. Rather, we are to watch that we are not deceived.

Over the years, I have been troubled and saddened at the number of Christians I have known who have fallen away from the faith. Looking back over decades of ministry, I can picture the faces of people I would have sworn were committed, faithful Christians, yet today they deny the faith they once embraced. On every side, this tragedy increases. Christians fall away into unbelief or immorality. They turn away from the faith, and they no longer walk according to the Word of God. That is what our Lord warns against in the Olivet Discourse.

He says to us, "Wake up! Open your eyes! Don't listen to the secular voices that tell you the world will go on forever as it is now. Don't listen to the voices that tell you there is no God and you can live as you please without fear of judgment. A day of reckoning approaches. If you do not want to be caught up in the wrath that is to come, then cling to the truth of God's Word, and heed My warning."

With one sharp, ringing word of command, Jesus ends His message: "Watch!"

twenty-five

Love's Extravagance

> Mark 14:1–25

Agreat king was riding in his carriage through the forest. As the carriage passed a humble farm cottage, the king happened to look out and see a beautiful girl. She was obviously one of the poorest commoners in his kingdom. Yet none of that mattered. The king was instantly smitten by her. The moment he saw her, he knew he could never love any other maiden. And yet, how could he tell her of his love for her? The fact that he was a king and she was a humble peasant girl created an enormous gulf between them. If he brought her to the royal palace and presented her with gifts of jewels and purple robes, she would surely consent to marry him.

But would she consent out of love?

Or would she consent merely out of awe at his majesty? Or from fear of his power? Or from a desire to live as a queen?

He wanted her to marry him, but only if she genuinely loved him. She would say she loved him, but how could he ever know if she truly loved him or not?

As the carriage took him toward the palace, he pondered these questions. For days, she was all he could think of. Then, one night, an idea occurred to him, a plan by which he could know if she truly loved him.

The next morning, the king clothed himself in the rags of a peasant, and he set out on foot to the cottage of the peasant girl. He knew that he could not raise her to his level without destroying her freedom. So he chose to descend to the level of a peasant.

But the rags he wore were no mere disguise. He went not as a king in peasant's rags but as a peasant. For before he left his palace, he renounced his throne.

That is a story of extravagant love. And it is a parable of the love Jesus has shown to us in descending to our level, becoming not merely God in human disguise but fully human in every way. As the poet Wordsworth wrote, Jesus "left his throne on high, and deigned to wear the robe of flesh we wear." When Jesus exchanged His throne for a lonely wooden cross, it was an act of extravagant love, beyond our ability to comprehend.

Love and Hate: A Poignant Study in Contrasts

In our study of Mark, we have seen again and again how the writer of this gospel brings together certain events, placing them side by side so that we can see contrasts and connections in emphases and themes. Mark shows an artistic flair for weaving themes together in a meaningful pattern. In this chapter, Mark 14, he brings together contrasting stories of love and hate, and he braids them together to maximize the impact on our souls.

We will see Mark's account of the hatred of the priests toward Jesus intertwined with the story of the love of Mary of Bethany for her Lord. We will see the story of Judas Iscariot's mounting treachery intertwined with the story of our Lord's self-sacrificing love for His disciples, including Judas. The mingling of these contrasting themes forms a poignant, moving storyline that reaches our hearts and spirits at a deep level.

Mark opens this portion of his gospel with the murderous hatred of the religious leaders.

> *Now the Passover and the Feast of Unleavened Bread were only two days away, and the chief priests and the teachers of the law were looking for some sly way to arrest Jesus and kill him. "But not during the Feast," they said, "or the people may riot."* (MARK 14:1–2)

The religious leaders were aware that time grew short. The days of the Passover and the Feast of Unleavened Bread were at hand. The population of Jerusalem and surrounding villages swelled enormously during the feast days, as pilgrims from all over the known world made their way to Jerusalem. The chief priests and scribes knew that if they arrested Jesus at the height of the feast, they were apt to incite a riot. They needed to act swiftly. This kind of haste is characteristic of hatred. Hatred can never wait. It must act as soon as an opportunity presents itself. And hatred acts stealthily, secretly, under the cover of darkness, hidden from view. That is what we see now as these religious leaders plot the death of Jesus.

Why did the chief priests and teachers of the law want to kill Jesus? To protect their power. Jesus was a threat to them. They loved to pose as holy, godly men, but Jesus exposed their lies and hypocrisy. When evil is exposed, it always retaliates.

Next Mark takes us to Bethany to witness a contrast, a beautiful counterpoint, to the hatred of the religious leaders. What Mark recounts for us took place six days before the Passover. Mark has inserted this episode out of chronological order to provide thematic contrasts to the plotting and scheming of the priests and scribes. Mark tells us the story of the love of Mary of Bethany.

> *While he was in Bethany, reclining at the table in the home of a man known as Simon the Leper, a woman came with an alabaster jar of very expensive perfume, made of pure nard. She broke the jar and poured the perfume on his head.*
>
> *Some of those present were saying indignantly to one another, "Why this waste of perfume? It could have been sold for more than a year's wages and the money given to the poor." And they rebuked her harshly.*
>
> *"Leave her alone," said Jesus. "Why are you bothering her? She has done a beautiful thing to me. The poor you will always have with you, and you can help them any time you want. But you will not always have me. She did what she could. She poured perfume on my body beforehand to prepare for my burial. I tell you the truth, wherever the gospel is preached throughout the world, what she has done will also be told, in memory of her." *(MARK 14:3–9)

Mark does not give the name of this woman, but John tells us it was Mary, the sister of Martha and Lazarus. There are three movements in this brief account.

First movement: the act of loving sacrifice. You can picture it in your imagination. Mary comes into the room with the jar of expensive perfume as Jesus is reclining on the couch. John tells us that she anointed His head and His feet. She breaks the jar and pours the contents on His head and feet, anointing Him. It is a beautiful act, one that captures the attention of all who are present.

Second movement: the onlookers' indignant response. Mark tells us that some of the people present responded with indignation to Mary's loving act. Why? Because, they said, the gift of the anointing was a waste. John tells us that Judas raised this objection. This is characteristic of Judas, because John says he was a thief. He had been appointed treasurer for the disciples because, apparently, he had a good head for money. Too good, it seems, since his talents included embezzlement. Judas was the kind of person who placed a monetary value on everything, even on the life of Jesus the Master. Judas knew the price of everything but the value of nothing.

Third movement: the Lord's affirming response. He says five things about Mary's loving gift that mark her actions as an offering of love.

First, Jesus says, "Leave her alone. . . . She has done a beautiful thing to me." The beauty of Mary's gift lay in its extravagance. This woman did not spare any of the perfume but broke the flask and poured its contents out on Him. It was a costly perfume, made of pure nard, the spicy, fragrant oil pressed from the leaves of a rare plant that grew in the East. Because nard was rare and imported, it was extremely expensive. Judas, with his calculating mind, estimated its worth at three hundred denarii. A denarius was the day's wage for a laborer, so the value of this flask was about a year's wages for a common laborer. It was a lavish act, and therein lay the beauty of it. Jesus said, "That's beautiful! She hasn't held anything back but has poured it all out. What extravagant love!"

Second, Jesus says it was a timely thing she had done: "The poor you will always have with you, and you can help them any time you want. But you will not always have me." It is right to help the poor. But there are opportunities that come only once in a lifetime, and they must be seized at that moment or the moment will be lost forever. Mary seized the moment. While others criticized her for being wasteful and not giving to the poor, Jesus affirmed her sensitivity to the timing of the moment.

Third, Jesus says, "She did what she could." She offered the only act of worship and love that was open to her. Mary could not fix Him a meal; there was no time for that. She could not make a garment for Him; there was no time for that. But she had this bottle of costly perfumed oil, and she used what she had to do what she could. I am sure our Lord calls attention to this aspect of her gift of love because it is such a practical lesson for all of us: use what you have and do what you can. You cannot feed the starving world, but you can feed one person. You cannot evangelize the world, but you can share the gospel story with the people around you. You can't comfort all the lonely people on earth, but you can comfort one or two. So do as Mary did: use what you have and do what you can.

Fourth, our Lord says, "She poured perfume on my body beforehand to prepare for my burial." It is interesting, as you read the gospels, to note the many times Jesus told His disciples He was going to die. It seems that not one of them believed Him except Mary of Bethany. She believed Him, and she grieved for Him, even before His death. That is what motivated her. She understood that He was moving inexorably toward His death and burial. Jesus knew her motives, and He was comforted by her love for Him. Of all the friends who surrounded Him at this time, only Mary had the sensitivity to understand what was happening. How she ministered to His spirit by this simple, understanding act of extravagant love.

Finally, Jesus says that what she did would always be remembered. He said, "I tell you the truth, wherever the gospel is preached throughout the world, what she has done will also be told, in memory of her." Two thousand years later, this prophecy of Jesus is still being fulfilled. As your eyes pass over this page, as you drink the beauty of this story into your heart, you are living out the promise that our Lord made to Mary after she anointed His head and feet.

A Cold and Calculating Business Transaction

Immediately after this story of love, Mark again shifts the scene. We are wrenched away from a tableau of extravagant love, and we are thrust up against one of the ugliest acts of human history: the betrayal of Jesus by one of His friends, the disciple Judas.

> *Then Judas Iscariot, one of the Twelve, went to the chief priests to betray Jesus to them. They were delighted to hear this and promised to give him money. So he watched for an opportunity to hand him over.* (MARK 14:10–11)

Some people try to excuse Judas. They say that he was merely misled. He expected Christ to usher in an earthly kingdom, and when Jesus did not act in line with that and fulfill Judas's political expectation, Judas tried to force Jesus' hand. They say that Judas didn't want to betray Jesus; he was only trying to put Jesus in a position where He would have to demonstrate His power and launch His political revolution. Judas wasn't evil-intentioned, they say. He was overeager and misguided.

But the Scriptures do not allow such an interpretation. We see that Judas deliberately went to the high priests with the intention of betraying his Lord. Judas took the initiative. No one misled him. Mark even underscores the treachery of Judas with these words: he was "one of the Twelve," he was a trusted member of the Lord's inner circle, he was one the Lord depended on and trusted. And he was a deliberate traitor.

What was the motive of Judas? It was nothing complicated. Mark shows us that his motive was greed. The chief priests and scribes promised Judas money, and he accepted. He was already a thief and an embezzler. It didn't take much inducement to turn him into a traitor as well. Judas was a calculating man. He added the price of the Master's life into his calculations and decided that the price was right. For Judas, the betrayal of the Lord and Savior of the world was a business transaction.

The Drama of the Upper Room

From treachery and greed, Mark takes us back to the beautiful theme of extravagant love. In the closing account of this section, he shows us the love of Jesus for His disciples at the last Passover feast. We begin with the preparations for Passover.

> *On the first day of the Feast of Unleavened Bread, when it was customary to sacrifice the Passover lamb, Jesus' disciples asked him, "Where do you want us to go and make preparations for you to eat the Passover?"*
>
> *So he sent two of his disciples, telling them, "Go into the city, and a man carrying a jar of water will meet you. Follow him. Say to the owner of the house he enters, 'The Teacher asks: Where is my guest room, where I may eat the Passover with my disciples?' He will show you a large upper room, furnished and ready. Make preparations for us there."*
>
> *The disciples left, went into the city and found things just as Jesus had told them. So they prepared the Passover.*
> (MARK 14:12–16)

Again, as in the case of the arrangements for the donkey He rode into Jerusalem, Jesus appears to have arranged everything in advance. I do not think we need to read anything miraculous into the signal Jesus gave His disciples as to how to find the Upper Room. The significance of that signal is that Jesus has planned all of these arrangements, knowing what lay ahead of Him. Nothing that happens to Jesus is an accident, nor is anything forced on Him. His life will not be taken from Him; He will give it willingly.

He tells His disciples, "Go into the city, and a man carrying a jar of water will meet you." That would stand out to the disciples, just as a man carrying a purse on his arm would stand out today. Carrying jars of water was women's work. Gender roles were rigidly separated, and there was a clearly defined division of labor in those days. So Jesus told them, "You won't have any trouble recognizing the man you are to speak to. He will be doing women's work, carrying water. Find him, and follow him." And the disciples found everything just as Jesus said.

Why did Jesus use this symbol? God's symbols always have meaning, if we know how to understand and read them. The Scriptures tell us what this symbol meant; another feast of the Jews centers around the carrying of a water jar by a man. We find it in John's gospel:

> *On the last and greatest day of the Feast, Jesus stood and said in a loud voice, "If anyone is thirsty, let him come to me and drink. Whoever believes in me, as the Scripture has said, streams of living water will flow from within him."*
> (JOHN 7:38–39)

I think this is what Jesus is saying to His disciples: "Where we are going you don't understand. Although some of the symbolism of the Passover lamb is known to you, other elements of it you do not know. But follow me, and out of your hearts shall flow rivers of living water."

Next Mark takes us to visit the Upper Room. There we experience the terrible anguish and sadness of the approaching betrayal.

> *When evening came, Jesus arrived with the Twelve. While they were reclining at the table eating, he said, "I tell you the truth, one of you will betray me—one who is eating with me."*
>
> *They were saddened, and one by one they said to him, "Surely not I?"*
>
> *"It is one of the Twelve," he replied, "one who dips bread into the bowl with me. The Son of Man will go just as it is written about him. But woe to that man who betrays the Son of Man! It would be better for him if he had not been born."*
>
> (MARK 14:17–21)

Your mental image of this may have been colored by the famous painting of Leonardo da Vinci. Someone once observed that da Vinci's *The Last Supper* makes it appear as if Jesus said, "All you fellows who want to get into the picture, come over on this side of the table!" But the disciples were not seated in chairs at a table. They were lying on couches around a low table, in the Roman manner, which the Jews of that time followed. In that arrangement, John and Judas were on either side of Jesus, equally close to Him, so that only two of the disciples could have reached the same dish that Jesus used: John and Judas. He was telling the other disciples that the traitor was one of those two.

Yet, when Jesus announced that there was a traitor in their midst, not one of the disciples said, "I know who it is! He's the one!" Instead, each man looked within. Each feared that treason lurked somewhere within his skin. And each looked to Jesus and asked, "Lord, is it I?" Every one of us recognizes the feeling that there is something evil in us, something we do not trust. We wonder, "Will I be strong enough to withstand pressure and testing when it comes, or will I crumble, panic, and fail the Lord?" Each of these men was riddled with self-doubt. They all seemed to think that the betrayal Jesus talked about was a failure of nerve, a failure of character. It didn't occur to them that Jesus was talking about someone who would betray Jesus deliberately and with cold-blooded premeditation.

So each one said, with a note of doubt in his voice, "Surely not I?" So Jesus reassured them and says, "It is one of the Twelve, one who dips bread into the bowl with me." John's account goes on to say:

> *As soon as Judas took the bread, Satan entered into him.*
> *"What you are about to do, do quickly," Jesus told him.*
>
> (JOHN 13:27)

And Judas left the Upper Room. But before Judas left, Jesus said to the disciples, "The Son of Man will go just as it is written about him." It had been predicted that Jesus would be betrayed by one of His own, and the prophecy was being fulfilled. Jesus also said, "But woe to that man who betrays the Son of Man!" Woe to him—not because Judas was doing something he could not help. Judas was operating according to his free will, even though his actions had long been predicted. God did not drive Judas to betray the Lord; Judas chose to do what he did.

This is why Jesus adds what are probably the most solemn words He ever spoke: "It would be better for him if he had not been born." What frightening words! This scene should fire our passion to remain faithful until death, so that such a thing may never be said of us.

The Bread and the Cup

Now Mark brings us to the final scene in the Upper Room, a scene that Christians everywhere celebrate and commemorate to this day.

> *While they were eating, Jesus took bread, gave thanks and broke it, and gave it to his disciples, saying, "Take it; this is my body."*
>
> *Then he took the cup, gave thanks and offered it to them, and they all drank from it.*
>
> *"This is my blood of the covenant, which is poured out for many," he said to them. "I tell you the truth, I will not drink again of the fruit of the vine until that day when I drink it anew in the kingdom of God."* (MARK 14:22–25)

Here again our Lord teaches by means of symbols, and the symbols are significant. He took the bread and said, "This is my body," and He broke the bread, symbolizing how His body would be broken. And He took the cup, and said, "This is my blood of the covenant."

What covenant was Jesus talking about? A covenant is a formal agreement. Jesus was saying that with the pouring out of His blood, a new agreement would exist between God and humanity. Henceforth, salvation would be based on the perfect sacrifice of Jesus. The old covenant involved the keeping of rituals and sacrifices that symbolically looked to the future; they symbolized a sacrifice that had not yet taken place. But soon and forevermore, saving faith would look back on the perfect sacrifice of Christ as an accomplished fact. Salvation would not involve the works of the law of Moses but faith and grace. As Paul writes:

> *For it is by grace you have been saved, through faith— and this not from yourselves, it is the gift of God—not by works, so that no one can boast.* (EPHESIANS 2:8–9)

Salvation is by faith, and not by works. It is a free gift from

God, purchased at the cost of the Lord's blood. That is the new covenant to which Jesus refers.

Finally, Jesus reminded them that this was the end, that He would never drink of the cup again until He drank it new in the fulfillment of the kingdom of God.

Now we begin to see why Mark placed this account alongside the story of Mary of Bethany. Here our Lord shows the disciples that He is about to do what Mary has already done for Him. She brought to Him a beautiful alabaster flask. She could have removed the stopper to pour out the contents, but that's not what she did. In a beautifully symbolic act, she broke the flask and poured out its costly contents on Him. Jesus is saying to the disciples, "My body is like that alabaster flask. I am going to be broken for you."

When Mary poured out the perfumed oil in that flask, its spicy fragrance filled the room. And when the blood of Jesus was poured out on the ground at the foot of the cross, the sweet fragrance of God's love and forgiveness began to fill the earth. Jesus told His disciples, "The alabaster flask that is my body will be broken, and my blood will be poured out for you, so that the fragrance of love may fill your lives. Through you, may that fragrance go out to fill the world."

In the motion picture *The Hiding Place,* there is a scene set in the Ravensbruck concentration camp during World War II. Corrie ten Boom and her sister Betsy are there, imprisoned for the crime of hiding Jews from the Nazis. The conditions in the camp are degrading beyond belief. The barracks are freezing and lice-ridden. It is a place of death and despair. As Betsy reads the Bible and leads a devotional time for some of the women in the barracks, a bitter woman calls out from her bunk, mocking their worship.

"If your God is so powerful and loving," the woman demands, "why does He allow such suffering?" She tears away the filthy rags she has wrapped around her hands, and we see that her fingers are broken, bloody, and mangled. "Before I came here," she says, "I was the first violinist of the symphony orchestra. Did your God will *this* to happen?"

For a moment no one answers. Then Corrie steps forward, her eyes filled with hurt and compassion. "I can't answer that question," she says to the woman with the mangled fingers. "All I know is that our God came to this earth and became one of us. He suffered with us and was crucified and died. And He did that for love."

That is what Mark is saying to us through the story of the bread and the cup—and the story of the broken alabaster flask. This is the story of love's extravagance. What Mary poured out on her Lord was precious and costly; it was an act of extravagant love. But how much more extravagant is the love of Jesus, who poured out His life for you and me? When we partake of the table of the Lord together, Jesus says to us, "See? I have broken the flask of my body for you. I have poured out my blood for you. I have done this so that you will know that your life is no longer governed by law. It is governed by love."

The extravagant love of Jesus is set before us as an example. Now let us go out and share this love with others.

twenty-six

Strike the Shepherd

➤ **Mark 14:26–52**

Confederate General Richard S. Ewell looked out across a bat-tlefield during the American Civil War. His troops had just exchanged a furious volley of gunfire with Union troops, who were dug in about seventy yards away. As the smoke cleared during the brief lull in the shooting, Ewell saw a Union cavalry officer walking among his soldiers, boldly risking death to rally his troops. Ewell was so impressed by the enemy officer's gallantry that he ordered his soldiers not to shoot at the man.

After the battle, General Ewell was reprimanded by his commanding officer, General T. J. "Stonewall" Jackson. "Why did you order your soldiers not to shoot at the Union officer?" Jackson demanded sternly.

"I admired him, sir," said Ewell. "He was a brave officer."

"If you want to win this war, Ewell," said Jackson, "*shoot* the brave officers—then the cowards will run away and take their men with them!"

Whether he knew it or not, Stonewall Jackson was restating a prophetic principle found in Scripture: "Strike the shepherd, and the sheep will be scattered." As we continue our study in

Mark, we are about to see the drama of this principle in the Lord's last hours before the cross.

Jesus Knew the Divine Program

The Twenty-third Psalm, often called the shepherd's psalm, is undoubtedly the best-loved psalm of all. I can testify that I have often been helped and strengthened by those opening words, "The LORD is my shepherd, I shall not be in want." The thought of the Lord as the Shepherd of His people—watching over His flock, guarding them, guiding them into green pastures—has probably comforted you as well. I believe that as Jesus gathered with His disciples in the Upper Room, He probably thought of the fact that, in laying down His life for the sheep, He was preparing to fulfill that psalm, as well as many other passages of Old Testament Scripture. We rejoin Mark's account immediately after the end of the meal Jesus shared with His disciples in the Upper Room.

> *When they had sung a hymn, they went out to the Mount of Olives.*
>
> *"You will all fall away," Jesus told them, "for it is written:*
>
> *" 'I will strike the shepherd,*
> *and the sheep will be scattered.'*
>
> *But after I have risen, I will go ahead of you into Galilee."*
> *Peter declared, "Even if all fall away, I will not."*
> *"I tell you the truth," Jesus answered, "today—yes, tonight—before the rooster crows twice you yourself will disown me three times."*
>
> *But Peter insisted emphatically, "Even if I have to die with you, I will never disown you." And all the others said the same.* (MARK 14:26–31)

Note two things in this brief paragraph. First, the passage reveals that Jesus knew what was going to happen to Him. He fully understood the divine program, He anticipated it, and He even made arrangements for it. We have seen how, sometimes weeks ahead of time, He has made preparations for a certain person to be in a certain place doing a certain thing, in fulfillment of an Old Testament prophecy. Our Lord knew what was going to happen because He had pored over the Scriptures. He knew the Old Testament thoroughly, including all the messianic prophecies. As He meditated on these events and prayed about them before the Father, the Spirit made known to Him details not recorded in Scripture, so that it was clear to Him what was going to happen.

The hymn that Jesus and the disciples sang as they left the Upper Room was undoubtedly from the Old Testament, a passage we now know as Psalms 113–118. This was the traditional hymn called the Hallel (*Hallel* is Hebrew for "praise to God"). The Hallel was recited as a hymn on the three pilgrim festivals, when the Jewish people offered sacrifices at the temple of Jerusalem. These psalms focus on one theme: *Hallelujah,* praise to the Lord. It is significant and prophetic that the closing verse of the Hallel includes these words, "Bind the sacrifice with cords, even unto the horns of the altar" (Psalm 118:27 KJV)

As they sang those words, Jesus and the disciples left the Upper Room and made their way down the Kidron Valley, into the shadows of Gethsemane. As they went, Jesus quoted from the prophecy of Zechariah. He said to them, "You will all fall away, for it is written: " 'I will strike the shepherd, and the sheep will be scattered.' " It is instructive to look at Zechariah's original words:

> *"Awake, O sword, against my shepherd,*
> *against the man who is close to me!"*

declares the Lord Almighty.
"Strike the shepherd,
*   and the sheep will be scattered,*
*   and I will turn my hand against the little ones."*
(ZECHARIAH 13:7)

When Jesus quoted this passage, He changed it from the imperative mode, "strike the shepherd," to the indicative, "I will strike the shepherd." These words come from the lips of God. It is God who strikes Jesus, and the result is that the sheep will be scattered. So this prophecy of Zechariah refers to the Garden of Gethsemane. The Lord's struggle in the garden is the moment the prophet foretold, when God struck Jesus. The next part of that prophecy—the scattering of the sheep—is fulfilled, as we shall later see, in Mark 14:50: "Then everyone [that is, all the disciples] deserted him and fled."

So Jesus knew what was about to happen that night in the Garden of Gethsemane. But He could also see even further down the dark tunnel ahead, to the bright light of the resurrection: "But after I have risen, I will go ahead of you into Galilee." He is reassuring His disciples that after the cross comes the resurrection. He will go before them as the Shepherd, still guarding His flock, still watching over them, and He will meet them again in Galilee.

Jesus never spoke of the cross to the disciples without setting it against the dawning light of the resurrection. And yet they never seemed to grasp it. Not one of them believed Jesus would be raised from the dead. I suspect that the reason they could not hear what He said about the resurrection was that they did not want to hear about His death, and the one entailed the other. So, although He tried to comfort them, His words were of no avail at the moment.

But later the disciples would remember.

False Bravado

The second thing to note about this passage is the bravado of Peter and the disciples. Peter said to Jesus, "Even if all fall away, I will not." Notice the contrast between "they" and "I." In other words, "They may deny you, Lord. I know these fellows, Lord, and you can't trust them. But, Lord, you're wrong about me. I will never let you down, Lord. You can count on me." Peter is confident that he is not even capable of failure, although he freely expresses doubts about the rest of the disciples.

But Jesus saw far more clearly than Peter. He saw that Peter's confidence rested on his human will, and Jesus knew the weakness of it. So He said to Peter, "I tell you the truth, today—yes, tonight—before the rooster crows twice you yourself will disown me three times." It is interesting to see how Jesus narrows down the time.

Literally, in the Greek, He says three things: today, this very night, and before the rooster crows twice. In other words, Jesus tells Peter, "In just a few hours, my friend, all your firm resolve and confidence will have melted away. You'll crumble, you'll fail, you'll say you never knew me. And it will happen before these few hours have passed."

I am always amazed by the symbols Jesus employs in this statement. They are so appropriate. He uses a classic symbol of arrogance and overconfidence to convey His prophetic words to Peter: a rooster. Whenever someone displays a boastful attitude like Peter's, we say he is cocky; that is, he is like a cock or a rooster. We say he is crowing or sounding off like a rooster. We say he is cocksure.

Yet Peter insisted that Jesus was wrong: "Even if I have to die with you, I will never disown you." Have you ever felt that way? I have. I have been so sure that something the Word says could not happen. I have convinced myself that by sheer determination and force of will, I could work it out on my own. I have said the same thing Peter did, and I'm sure you have too.

I believe that there is a subtle suggestion in the symbol Jesus chooses here. The next time you think this way, remember that the cocky little rooster that strutted around in a barnyard last week could end up in a stewpot tomorrow.

The Sword Falls; The Shepherd Is Struck

Mark records what happens next as Jesus leads His disciples into the Garden of Gethsemane.

> They went to a place called Gethsemane, and Jesus said to his disciples, "Sit here while I pray." He took Peter, James and John along with him, and he began to be deeply distressed and troubled. "My soul is overwhelmed with sorrow to the point of death," he said to them. "Stay here and keep watch."
>
> Going a little farther, he fell to the ground and prayed that if possible the hour might pass from him. "Abba, Father," he said, "everything is possible for you. Take this cup from me. Yet not what I will, but what you will."
>
> (MARK 14:32–36)

Here begins the terrible moment Zechariah had predicted:

> "Awake, O sword, against my shepherd,
>   against the man who is close to me!"
>   declares the Lord Almighty.
> "Strike the shepherd,
>   and the sheep will be scattered,
>   and I will turn my hand against the little ones."
>
> (ZECHARIAH 13:7)

God will strike His shepherd, "the man who is close to me," and the sheep will be scattered. Notice that a sword is an instrument designed to split, to sever, to separate. In this metaphor, I think we see for the first time the sense of division between Jesus and the Father. This separation is manifested when Jesus says, "Yet not what I will, but what you will." Up to this point in our Lord's ministry, He knew that He was going to the cross. But this is the first sign that He was not willing and ready to go to the cross. All along He has spoken of it, He has understood what it would involve, yet there has never been a sign that He was reluctant to go—until now.

Suddenly, and seemingly for the first time, Jesus does not want to do what the Father wants Him to do. There is a sense of distance, of division, of struggle. The disciples sense this, and He does not try to hide it from them. He says to them, "My soul is overwhelmed with sorrow to the point of death." Few of us have ever known such a sense of sorrow, mingled with horror, that we feared it might take our life—but *Jesus knew.*

And in those terrible moments, the thing He had come to do, the thing that had seemed so inevitable and irrevocable, now became unthinkable and unbearable. So Jesus prayed, "*Abba,* Father, everything is possible for you. Take this cup from me."

Some interpreters think that the cup refers to the agony of Gethsemane. But in John's account, when Jesus is arrested by the soldiers who come with Judas, Peter wields a sword in the Lord's defense. Jesus says, "Put your sword away! Shall I not drink the cup the Father has given me?" (John 18:11). The cup still lies ahead of Jesus. It is the cup of agony and terrible separation that awaits Him on the cross.

Some Christians are troubled by the idea that there was ever a time when Jesus did not want to do the Father's will. When you suggest this to them, they argue the point, even though the Lord's reluctance is powerfully, unambiguously portrayed in the gospels. A man once wrote me and said, "Pastor Stedman, you missed the point of what Jesus prayed in Gethsemane. When Jesus said to the Father, 'Not what I will, but what you will,' that was the ultimate example of perfect and voluntary submission." And that is true. We see that Jesus wants to do the Father's will, and He ultimately chooses to obey. But the Scriptures are robbed of all meaning if you fail to acknowledge the intense conflict expressed in those words, "Not what I will, but what you will." The fact that Jesus states that His will and the Father's will are not identical makes absolutely clear a separation is taking place between Father and Son.

Jesus loves the Father and wants to obey Him, but the road ahead is so dark and terrible that He is filled with an unfathomable horror. Surely the physical torture alone would be enough to make any of us draw back in terror. But for Jesus, there is an even deeper, darker terror awaiting Him at the cross: a spiritual black hole beyond human comprehension.

So He asked for a way out. Surely, He said, there must be a way out. Everything is possible for God. There must be some other way.

But when the Father's silence made it clear that there was no other way, Jesus accepted His awesome and awful mission. And He accepted it with gracious submission: "Not what I will, but what you will."

While the story of the Lord's dread and reluctance in the garden is disturbing to some believers, it has been a comfort to my faith. The parallel account in Luke 22:44 tells us that His anguish was so great that "his sweat was like drops of blood falling to the ground." I believe that this is a literal description of what Jesus went through—an anguish so intense that the blood was forced from His veins by the agony and pressure within, so that His sweat fell in great drops of blood on the ground. The book of Hebrews also gives a vivid description of the Lord's agony:

> *In the days of his flesh, Jesus offered up prayers and supplications, with loud cries and tears, to him who was able to save him from death, and he was heard for his godly fear. Although he was a Son, he learned obedience through what he suffered; and being made perfect he became the source of eternal salvation to all who obey him.* (HEBREWS 5:7–9 RSV)

That is what it meant for the Shepherd to be struck in the Garden of Gethsemane. As the book of Hebrews tells us, "For we do not have a high priest who is unable to sympathize with our weaknesses, but we have one who has been tempted in every way, just as we are—yet was without sin" (Hebrews 4:15). If He had never felt that divergence of His will from the Father's, that unwillingness to do what He ought to do because the Father willed it, then He could never have sympathized with you and me. We don't face the intense dread that He experienced. We can't even begin to fathom that. But we face the same divergence between our will and the Father's. Again and again, we face situations where we know that our will and His are not the same. Yet Jesus is our example. He has shown us what the heart of obedience looks like in a time of crisis: "Not what I will, but what you will."

How did Jesus submit to the Father and accomplish His mission? The same way you and I must. He did so by casting Himself on the Father's enabling strength. That is what His intense, anguished prayers in Gethsemane mean. There is a deep mystery here. I can go no further into it than that. Yet I see tremendous help here for those of us who struggle with the will of God.

I once knew a young couple who separated from each other early in their marriage. They had a baby, yet the father chose to leave his wife and child, intending never to return. So many bitter, angry words had been exchanged between them that he said he hated his wife, and she hated him. I sat down with this young man in my study, and we talked. I opened the Bible and told him he had a responsibility as a Christian to his wife and child. He rejected my counsel and stormed out of my office.

But over the next few days, the Spirit of God worked on his heart. He became aware that he could not expect God's blessing on his life if he deliberately refused to obey God's will. He knew he could never be happy while he was in a state of rebellion and disobedience. So, with every fiber of his being shrieking out against it, he made a decision to obey God and return to his wife and baby.

When he returned home, he found that God had done a similar work in his wife's heart. They came back together with a greater degree of humility, a recognition of their wrongs and sins, and a willingness to work out their differences. Gradually God restored the home and this couple's love for one another. Years have passed since then, and these two Christians have built a beautiful, durable marriage.

But it never would have happened if they had not said to God, "Not what I will, but what you will." Their hearts were not in it. Their emotions were not in it. The only thing this couple had going for them was that they had chosen to submit their wills to God, although doing so was contrary to every natural impulse within them.

That is the example that Jesus modeled for us in Gethsemane. That is our goal as followers of Christ, to bring our wills under submission to His. For there will inevitably come a time when, no matter what the Word of God says, you will not want to obey. But, just as Jesus has shown us by His example, we know that the only answer is to cast ourselves on God's mercy and grace, seeking His strength to do His will. If God does not go with us and work through us, it won't happen, because we do not have the strength. But God has the strength, and He makes it available to us through prayer.

The Betrayer Comes

Next Mark records the ease with which Peter's fierce resolve is overcome.

> Then [Jesus] returned to his disciples and found them sleeping. "Simon," he said to Peter, "are you asleep? Could you not keep watch for one hour? Watch and pray so that you will not fall into temptation. The spirit is willing, but the body is weak."
>
> Once more he went away and prayed the same thing. When he came back, he again found them sleeping, because their eyes were heavy. They did not know what to say to him.
>
> Returning the third time, he said to them, "Are you still sleeping and resting? Enough! The hour has come. Look, the Son of Man is betrayed into the hands of sinners. Rise! Let us go! Here comes my betrayer!" (MARK 14:37–42)

Satan does not have to work hard to overcome Peter. He collapses Peter's resolve by the simple expedient of making him too sleepy to pray. Peter is as weak as a newborn kitten when the moment of crisis arrives. Why? Because he lacks the strengthening power of prayer. The devil only had to make him sleepy—and I am convinced that this was a satanic attack. The sword that

Jehovah wielded against the Shepherd also affected the disciples. Satan came on them as a stealthy sandman, dropping sleep into their eyes. So they fell asleep instead of praying.

Jesus comes and finds them, and He says, "Peter, couldn't you watch even one hour? Where is all that bravado you boasted of just a short time ago? You said, 'Even if I have to die with you, I will never disown you.' Yet now you can't even stay awake and pray with me! I know you love me. Your spirit is perfectly willing. But, Peter, you relied on your flesh, and, my friend, the flesh is weak."

We have all felt this, haven't we? We have been asked to do something, and we say, "The spirit is willing, but the flesh is ready for the weekend." Yes, the flesh is tragically weak. The key is prayer. If Peter, like Jesus, feeling sleepy and weak, had cast himself on the Father and had told Him the problem, the Father would have carried him through. And had Peter relied on the strength of the Father to carry him through, he would not have denied his Lord.

Our problem is that we see our strength as our security and our weakness as our failing. The truth is that our weakness is our security, while relying on our strength produces failure. Just like Peter, I have learned from my sad experience (as well as the testimony of Scripture) that in the hour of testing, self-confidence invariably washes away. Only God-confidence will stand. And there is no room for God-confidence and self-confidence to coexist. One or the other must go.

I know that great things are about to happen whenever I hear a Christian say, "I'm scared. I don't think I can do this, but I'm going to try, because God has told me to. I'm going to rely on Him to strengthen me and work through me, because I can't do this in my own strength." I know that the person who approaches life with that sense of his or her inadequacy, coupled with an obedience to the will of God and a trust in the infinite power of God, will be used in a mighty way in God's eternal plan.

Prayer is a simple act, but what transforming power it brings into our lives. Sometimes we think it is impossible for us to do God's will. The task is too daunting or the temptation we face is too enticing to resist. But prayer makes all things possible. Prayer is our extension cord, plugging us directly into the same source of power that created time and space, energy and matter. That is the strength Jesus drew on in Gethsemane, when His strength failed, when sweat fell from His brow like drops of blood. Through prayer, Jesus stood firm and did the will of the Father.

In contrast to Jesus, we see Peter—Peter who was so bold and confident, Peter who slept. When the moment of betrayal arrives, Peter is woefully weak and unprepared.

> *Just as he was speaking, Judas, one of the Twelve, appeared. With him was a crowd armed with swords and clubs, sent from the chief priests, the teachers of the law, and the elders.*
>
> *Now the betrayer had arranged a signal with them: "The one I kiss is the man; arrest him and lead him away under guard." Going at once to Jesus, Judas said, "Rabbi!" and kissed him. The men seized Jesus and arrested him. Then one of those standing near drew his sword and struck the servant of the high priest, cutting off his ear.*
>
> *"Am I leading a rebellion," said Jesus, "that you have come out with swords and clubs to capture me? Every day I was with you, teaching in the temple courts, and you did not arrest me. But the Scriptures must be fulfilled." Then everyone deserted him and fled.* (MARK 14:43–50)

Three actions are emphasized in this paragraph. The first emphasis is the kiss of Judas. Mark uses the normal word for "kiss," which means "to love," in telling of the arrangement Judas had made with the chief priests. They were to seize the one whom Judas kissed. But in the moment when Judas carries this out, Mark uses an emphasized form of that word, a word that means a prolonged kiss, a lover's kiss. I do not think anything in all the annals of treachery was more contemptuous than this kiss of Judas—a deliberate, prolonged, cold-blooded act of counterfeit love for the Master.

The second emphasis is Peter's blundering defense. Mark writes, "Then one of those standing near drew his sword and struck the servant of the high priest, cutting off his ear." Mark does not identify the man with the sword, but John 18:10 tells us, "Then Simon Peter, who had a sword, drew it and struck the high priest's servant, cutting off his right ear. (The servant's name was Malchus.)" Peter is still trying to make a show of bravado. He grabs a sword, and, as the priests and soldiers move in on Jesus, he slashes away. But so poor is his aim that all he does is lop off the ear of the high priest's servant—a prime example of the flesh at work. Peter's sword doesn't wound any of the truly evil leaders of this plot, only poor, innocent Malchus, one of the high priest's unwitting underlings.

This is so typical of our misguided, fleshly attempts to defend the Lord by our strength. And all we accomplish by our pitiful flailings is to hurt the innocent. Looking back over my years of pastoral ministry, I wince at all the lopped-off ears I have left in my wake. So many wounded people, so many attempts to do what I thought was right, by my human wisdom, in my human strength. Luke 22:51 tells us that Jesus reached out and touched the servant and healed his ear. I am so grateful that God has placed His healing touch on the many ears I have wounded in my foolishness and impulsiveness.

The third emphasis is the fleeing of the disciples. They all forsook Jesus. After more than three years of walking with Him, seeing the miracles and healings He had performed, after witnessing the stilling of the storm, the miraculous feedings, and every other great work, they suddenly regard Him as nothing more than a condemned man. His willingness to give Himself over without resistance, His refusal to defend Himself, seems to be a renunciation of His messiahship. Anyone caught with Him, they fear, will share His fate, so it is every man for himself.

The Shepherd has been struck. Now the sheep are scattered, stumbling through the darkened olive grove of Gethsemane, fleeing for their lives.

Mark's Personal Postscript

Mark adds a postscript to this story that we do not want to miss. I believe that this is a personal postscript.

> *A young man, wearing nothing but a linen garment, was following Jesus. When they seized him, he fled naked, leaving his garment behind.* (MARK 14:51–52)

Bible scholars agree that this young man is Mark. This is Mark's way of saying, "I was there." I believe Mark tells us two things in this postscript.

First, I believe Mark gives us the conclusion of the story of the rich young ruler. You'll recall that a rich young aristocrat came to Jesus and asked the way to eternal life (Mark 10:17–22). Jesus told him to sell everything he had and follow Him. The young man went away sad, unable to part with his many possessions. As we saw, there is some evidence that this young man was Mark. The evidence is not conclusive, but it is intriguing and persuasive. So I believe that this incident in Gethsemane is Mark's way of saying, "Although I walked away from Jesus at first, I considered His words, and I knew He was right. So I did what He said; I sold all that I had and gave it to the poor. All I had left was a linen robe, and before the night was over, I lost even that! But the important thing is that I followed Jesus into the darkness of Gethsemane. I was there when they arrested Him."

Second, I believe this story is also Mark's way of explaining to us how we received the account about Gethsemane. None of the disciples could have given it. Eight of them were in a part of the garden some distance from Jesus. Three of them were close to Him, but they were sound asleep and could not have heard His anguished prayers. But somebody was watching as Jesus prayed—a once-rich young man who gave away everything to follow Jesus. He recorded this story so that you and I might find strength and hope in our hour of Gethsemane.

twenty-seven

Jesus and the Priests

➤ **Mark 14:53–72**

Take your morning newspaper and spread it out. Look at the headlines. What do you see? The bond markets are rising and the stock market is falling, or vice versa. The press is hounding the White House about this or that issue. Somewhere a plane has crashed. In Africa, people die in a brushfire war. An earthquake here, a flood there. A Democrat on trial for corruption. And in the Middle East, people talk endlessly in search of peace.

Next look up a newspaper from ten, twenty, or thirty years ago. What headlines will you find? The economy is making some people rich, while it is ruining others. The press is hounding the White House about this or that issue. Somewhere a train has derailed. In Asia, people die in a brushfire war. A tornado here, a volcano eruption there. A Republican on trial for corruption. And in the Middle East, people talk endlessly in search of peace.

Sometimes we get so caught up with the headlines of the moment, with the images that flicker on the nightly news or on CNN, that we lose sight of what is truly, eternally important. Events that once held us in a grip of fascination and obsession—the assassination of JFK, the first men on the moon, Watergate, the capture of Patty Hearst, the Iranian hostage crisis, the Marine barracks bombing in Lebanon, the *Challenger* space shuttle explosion, the Persian Gulf war—now seem faded in our memories, like events from ancient history. These events capture our attention for days or weeks, but they eventually fade from memory.

But when we look back two thousand years to the last event-packed week of our Lord, just before the cross and the resurrection, we are looking at an event of eternal importance. It continues to affect our lives in a mighty way, day after day. The events surrounding the death of Jesus are the most significant events in all of history. If we truly believe the testimony of Scripture, then we know that the events of that week are the focal point of time and space, not merely on earth but also in every galaxy, star, solar system, and planet throughout the vast reaches of space. That is why it is crucial that we study and understand the events of that week.

The Trial of Jesus

As we pick up Mark's narrative, Jesus has been arrested in Gethsemane, and the disciples have scattered and fled. Now Jesus faces trial. Later He will be brought before the secular authorities of Rome, but first He will be tried by the Jewish religious authorities. The Jewish leaders have made up their minds to kill Him. Mark does not record for us the Lord's appearance before Annas, the father-in-law of the high priest (for those events, see John 18). Instead, Mark takes us directly to the courtyard of Caiaphas, the reigning high priest.

> *They took Jesus to the high priest, and all the chief priests, elders and teachers of the law came together. Peter followed him at a distance, right into the courtyard of the*

high priest. There he sat with the guards and warmed himself at the fire. (MARK 14:53–54)

Notice how carefully Mark sets this scene for us. Jesus was in the inner room with the Sanhedrin. This assembly consisted of the high priest, all the chief priests, the scribes (teachers of the law), and the elders (seventy members of the Sanhedrin, plus their helpers and advisors). So a considerable crowd had gathered in the residence of Caiaphas, the high priest. There was Jesus in the midst of them. Not far away, in the outer courtyard, Peter sat with the guards around the fire. It was a chilly spring night in Jerusalem, and Peter was warming himself while straining to see and hear all that was going on within. These two scenes occurred side by side.

Mark contrasts these two scenes for a reason, and that reason will become apparent as we examine this account. The trial before the priest proceeds in two stages. First, there is the testimony of the witnesses.

> *The chief priests and the whole Sanhedrin were looking for evidence against Jesus so that they could put him to death, but they did not find any. Many testified falsely against him, but their statements did not agree.*
>
> *Then some stood up and gave this false testimony against him: "We heard him say, 'I will destroy this man-made temple and in three days will build another, not made by man.' " Yet even then their testimony did not agree.*
> (MARK 14:55–59)

The outcome of this trial was determined long before it was convened, for Mark records that the chief priests were looking for testimony because they were determined to put Him to death. This is reminiscent of justice in the wild West, where vigilante judges assured their victims that they would get a fair trial before they were taken out and hanged. The trial of Jesus was an illegal farce from the outset, and for several reasons.

First, it was held at night, and Jewish law insisted that all criminal trials before the priests be held in the daytime.

Second, it met in the wrong place. The Sanhedrin was to meet only in the hall set aside for that purpose, and only meetings held in that hall were valid. This meeting was convened in the residence of the high priest.

Third, the Sanhedrin was prohibited by law from reaching a verdict on the same day that the trial was held. Yet this verdict was reached instantly, or more accurately, the verdict was determined before the trial began.

Despite all the contrived, perjurious testimony, things did not go well for the priests. The problem with putting liars on the witness stand is that it is hard to get them to agree. As these witnesses paraded by, perjuring themselves one after the other, the discrepancies began to accumulate. The more they talked, the more obvious it became that something was seriously wrong with the evidence against Jesus.

Finally, Matthew tells us, two men managed to get their stories more or less synchronized.

> *Finally two came forward and declared, "This fellow said, 'I am able to destroy the temple of God and rebuild it in three days.' "* (MATTHEW 26:60–61)

That was the closest any of these witnesses had come to telling a coherent story. It was the strongest point in the case against Jesus, for there was an element of truth in what they claimed. Early in Jesus' ministry, when He first cleansed the temple, three and a half years before these events, Jesus had said, "Destroy this temple, and I will raise it again in three days" (John 2:19). But as John 2:21 adds, "the temple he had spoken of was his body," not a temple of stone. These witnesses had supplied enough factual detail to build some semblance of a case, but as Mark points out, "even then their testimony did not agree." So the case against Jesus was falling apart. The priests felt frustrated at this point, for it seemed they could not find a legal ground by which to rid themselves of Jesus.

"Are You the Christ?"

At this point, the high priest, Caiaphas, stepped in and saved their case by doing something illegal. He put Jesus on the spot and tried to force Him to incriminate Himself.

> *The high priest stood up before them and asked Jesus, "Are you not going to answer? What is this testimony that these men are bringing against you?" But Jesus remained silent and gave no answer.* (MARK 14:60–61)

Isaiah had prophesied, "He was oppressed and afflicted, yet he did not open his mouth; he was led like a lamb to the slaughter, and as a sheep before her shearers is silent, so he did not open his mouth" (Isaiah 53:7). Jesus understood that the testimony against Him was so weak it required no answer. He made no effort to defend Himself or to answer the obvious lies of the witnesses. The high priest was infuriated by Jesus' silence, so he put Jesus under oath and demanded that Jesus testify against Himself. We see this in Matthew's account.

> *But Jesus remained silent. The high priest said to him, "I charge you under oath by the living God: Tell us if you are the Christ, the Son of God."* (MATTHEW 26:63)

This was an intensely solemn oath. In response to this oath, Jesus broke His silence.

> *Again the high priest asked him, "Are you the Christ, the Son of the Blessed One?"*
>
> *"I am," said Jesus. "And you will see the Son of Man sitting at the right hand of the Mighty One and coming on the clouds of heaven."*
>
> *The high priest tore his clothes. "Why do we need any more witnesses?" he asked. "You have heard the blasphemy. What do you think?"*
>
> *They all condemned him as worthy of death. Then some began to spit at him; they blindfolded him, struck him with their fists, and said, "Prophesy!" And the guards took him and beat him.* (MARK 14:61–65)

The high priest asked Jesus if He was the Messiah, the Son of the Blessed One, that is, the Son of God, whose coming was foretold in the Hebrew Scriptures. The Lord's answer was: "I am." That is as clear an affirmation as it is humanly possible to make.

Many critics of the New Testament and liberal scholars insist that Jesus never claimed to be the Messiah or the Son of God. They tell us that these claims were made about Him by His disciples. If anyone ever says that to you, turn to this passage of Scripture. In other places Jesus also claims to be the Messiah and the Son of God, but this one is the clearest, because He was under solemn oath to tell the truth, and He simply and clearly states, "I am the Messiah. I am the Son of God." There is no doubt or ambiguity about it.

The rest of Jesus' reply is directed personally and pointedly to the high priest: "And you will see the Son of Man sitting at the right hand of the Mighty One and coming on the clouds of heaven." With these words, Jesus prophesies the destiny that awaits Caiaphas at his death. From the Scriptures and from anecdotal accounts, we know that when people die, they step out of time and into eternity. This is true whether they are believers or unbelievers. Events that are distant in time are suddenly present in eternity. As believers, we await the coming of the Lord with thousands of His saints to claim His own. I believe this explains why, when believers die, there is often a moment when they smile and a look of wonder and expectation comes into their eyes. Sometimes they even say that they see the Lord coming for them.

But unbelievers, like Caiaphas, also step out of time into eternity when they die. They see what Jesus describes here: "You will see the Son of Man sitting at the right hand of the Mighty One and coming on the clouds of heaven." That is a description of Jesus coming not as the Savior but as a judge, for that is how unbelievers will see Him. They will see the great white throne, the impressive scene described in Revelation 20 when all the dead are gathered together, the books are opened, and humanity stands before the Judge of all the earth.

To this high priest in his arrogant unbelief, Jesus says, "For now, you are the judge; I am the prisoner. But one day, I will be the judge, and you will be the prisoner. You will have to answer for what you are doing now." With this response, Jesus answers the blasphemous unbelief of the high priest. The high priest knows what Jesus means. In a hypocritical gesture of righteous indignation, Caiaphas tears his garments when he hears Jesus' claim to be the Messiah. By this gesture, Caiaphas accuses Jesus of blasphemy. Caiaphas knew that if he could coax Jesus into making that claim in the presence of the Sanhedrin, Jesus' doom would be sealed. So the sanctimonious priest makes his gesture of outrage and demands the verdict that he has sought all along. The men of the Sanhedrin respond as planned and immediately pass sentence: Jesus must die.

Evil Unleashed

Then a truly strange thing happens. Mark tells us that the moment the verdict has been reached, the forces of restraint that have held back the hatred of the priests, scribes, and elders is suddenly lifted. Their incredible hatred and sadistic cruelty spills forth. Everything they now do is a gross violation of Jewish law, yet nothing restrains them. They vent their hatred on Jesus and pour out all the poison of their pent-up jealousy and hatred. They spit on Him, one of the vilest of all insults. They beat Him, taking out their rage with their bare fists. They cover His face with a garment, then strike Him and demand, "Prophesy! Tell us who hit you." Some 750 years earlier, Isaiah had written:

> *I offered my back to those who beat me,*
> *my cheeks to those who pulled out my beard;*
> *I did not hide my face*
> *from mocking and spitting.* (ISAIAH 50:6)

From the courtyard outside, Peter was watching and listening to all of this, and he never forgot it. In his first letter, he tells us that we are to remember that scene and follow Christ's example.

> *When they hurled their insults at him, he did not retaliate; when he suffered, he made no threats. Instead, he entrusted himself to him who judges justly.* (1 PETER 2:23)

That is how Christians are to respond when we are abused and falsely accused. Instead of defending ourselves, justifying ourselves, or avenging ourselves, we are to return good for evil and entrust ourselves to Him who judges all things justly: God.

The Denials of Peter

Next Mark takes us back to the courtyard where Peter warms himself by the fire. We have already seen how Peter's bravado had led him to vow that he would never deny the Lord. In the Garden of Gethsemane, it was Peter who drew his sword in an attempt to defend Jesus. Yes, he fled the garden with the other sheep the moment the Shepherd was arrested. But now Peter has returned. He knows he failed Jesus in the garden, but now he is determined to redeem himself. So he has followed Jesus to the courtyard of the high priest, and he is warming his hands by the fire with the guards who had arrested Jesus. This was a brave and dangerous thing Peter did. He placed himself in the midst of the enemies of Jesus. Now his proud bravado will be tested, but it will fail the test.

> *While Peter was below in the courtyard, one of the servant girls of the high priest came by. When she saw Peter warming himself, she looked closely at him.*
> *"You also were with that Nazarene, Jesus," she said. But he denied it. "I don't know or understand what you're talking about," he said, and went out into the entryway.*

> *When the servant girl saw him there, she said again to those standing around, "This fellow is one of them." Again he denied it.*
>
> *After a little while, those standing near said to Peter, "Surely you are one of them, for you are a Galilean."*
>
> *He began to call down curses on himself, and he swore to them, "I don't know this man you're talking about."*
>
> *Immediately the rooster crowed the second time. Then Peter remembered the word Jesus had spoken to him: "Before the rooster crows twice you will disown me three times." And he broke down and wept.* (MARK 14:66–72)

The young woman who had let him in the door, a servant girl of the high priest, recognized him and said, "You also were with that Nazarene, Jesus." John, writing years later, tells us that there was another disciple present. Many of the commentators think it was John, but I think it was Mark. If, as I have already suggested, Mark was the rich young ruler, he would fit John's description of a disciple who was known to the high priest and who had spoken to this servant girl to let Peter into the courtyard. Mark was not one of the Twelve, but if my theory about him is correct, then he was a disciple. So the servant girl noticed this man, saw that one of Jesus' disciples had let him into the courtyard, and surmised that he was one of the disciples. So she accused him.

Where is Peter's bravado now? It has disappeared. Peter responds immediately, "I don't know or understand what you're talking about," and he walks away from her, hoping her inquisitive mind will turn elsewhere. But she's in no mood to leave him alone. She follows Peter and pursues the subject. This time, she says to the people standing around, "This fellow is one of them."

At this point, Peter would have gladly throttled the pesky servant girl who was making him so conspicuous. All he wanted was to melt into the crowd, but she wouldn't let him. What's worse, when Peter uttered his first two denials, the people who heard him noticed his accent. He was like a Texan at Oxford; his Galilean accent made him conspicuous. So the people around him said, "Surely you are one of them, for you are a Galilean." Again Peter denied it. Mark says, "He began to call down curses on himself, and he swore to them, 'I don't know this man you're talking about.' " This doesn't mean that Peter blasphemed or used foul language. It means that he bound his denials with a curse on himself. He said, in effect, "May God curse me if what I say is not the truth." He added a solemn oath to his denials to convince his accusers.

Mark carefully points out the contrast between Jesus speaking under oath in the courtroom of Caiaphas and Peter's oath in the courtyard. Jesus solemnly stated under oath that He was the Messiah, the Son of God. Peter bound a lying denial with an oath. The instant Peter made that denial, says Mark, "the rooster crowed the second time." And Peter's conscience was shattered. He knew what he had done, and he had failed Jesus precisely as Jesus had prophesied. Peter went out, broke down, and wept bitterly. That is the phrase Mark uses: "he broke down." The word for "broke down" in Greek is a powerful term. It means that Peter literally went out and threw himself on the ground in agony and tears.

Now, perhaps, we can see why Mark has so closely woven the threads of this story together. It is fascinating, not only in this account, but in all four gospels, to see how carefully the writers of Scripture select various incidents and place them in sequence or side by side. Mark has chosen his narrative elements in such a way as to heighten the contrasts between love and hate.

The hatred of the religious leaders is like an oily cloud of evil. We see how easily and eagerly they set aside law and tradition, justice and righteousness, in order to rid themselves of Jesus. He is an innocent man and they know it; yet they haven't an ounce of conscience or hesitation about sending this innocent man to His death. We see the venom and jealousy of their darkened hearts, for it all comes out of them in the form of spitting and physical assault, mocking and derision. These are evil, cruel men, as wicked in their own way as any street thug or common killer.

In contrast, we see a man, Peter, who truly loves the Lord, is determined with all his heart to defend Jesus to the end, yet who lacks the faith and character to stand firm in the time of crisis. After failing his Lord, Peter goes out and weeps. He has denied with an oath the one he swore to defend to the death.

The Failure of the Flesh

Why does Mark place these two scenes side by side? I think he does it so that we might understand that both of these storylines manifest one theme: the deceptive nature of what the Bible calls "the flesh." Although these priests and scribes were outwardly men of God, men of deep religious devotion, the reality is that they were merely men of the flesh, with fleshly ambitions for money, prestige, and power. They thought as the world thinks and operated by the world's rules: Take what you want by any means you can, and destroy anyone who stands in your way. When Jesus got in their way, they lashed out at Him with lies, slander, perjury, mockery, insult, injury, and violence. That is the flesh at work.

Yet Mark makes it clear that the love of Peter was no better than the hatred of the religious leaders. Peter's love, like the hate of the scribes and priests, arose from and depended on the flesh, on human resources. In the hour of crisis, the love of a friend was of no more help to Jesus than the hatred and scorn of His enemies. Love and loyalty mean nothing when they rest on the shaky foundation of a fleshly will.

I am often appalled at how much we in the Christian church have come to rely on what the Bible calls the flesh. We have adopted worldly, human wisdom and methods to conduct church business, to develop evangelistic and missionary strategies, to engineer church growth, and on and on and on. Churches hire consultants, just as worldly corporations do. Churches and parachurch organizations construct complex organizational structures and management hierarchies, just as worldly organizations do. Churches employ worldly strategies and techniques to create marketing programs and advertising campaigns. Instead of building the church on a biblical model, we use the world's model and tack on Bible verses here and there to Christianize our worldly, fleshly organization.

Many Christian leaders and organizations—some on the right, some on the left—have adopted the political ideologies of the world. We see Christian groups flexing their political muscle, pushing their legislative agendas, and laying plans to "take back our nation." We have traded servanthood and the power of God for activism and direct-mail campaigns. Christians on both sides try to change the world by winning ideological battles; they forget that God called us to win the world with love.

I learned long ago that when our Christian efforts become complex and unwieldy, when you need well-orchestrated organizations and hundreds of people to carry them out, then you have missed God's plan for His church. God's work is characterized by simplicity. As Paul wrote in 2 Corinthians 11:3 (KJV),

"But I fear, lest by any means, as the serpent beguiled Eve through his subtlety, so your minds should be corrupted from the simplicity that is in Christ."

The only way the kingdom of God advances is by human weakness resting on the power and wisdom of God. That power can accomplish anything. The power of the flesh accomplishes nothing. The power of money accomplishes nothing. The power of human wisdom and strategy accomplishes nothing. When anything good is accomplished, it is accomplished *only* by His strength operating in our weakness.

I believe that is the most powerful lesson that Peter learned from his failure on that terrible night. And I believe the moment he truly learned that lesson was when he threw himself down on the ground and wept those anguished tears. The priests didn't weep; they showed no remorse or conscience. There is no record that Judas wept, although he did display a kind of despairing remorse. But Peter, when he had denied his Lord three times, threw himself down and wept. There is great beauty and wisdom in these lines by the Scottish poet Charles Mackay (1814–1889):

> Oh, you tears,
> I'm thankful that you run.
> Though you trickle in the darkness,
> You shall glitter in the sun.
> The rainbow could not shine
> If the rain refused to fall;
> And the eyes that cannot weep
> Are the saddest eyes of all.

Or, as evangelist Charles H. Spurgeon (1834–1892) once observed, "May we never take a dry-eyed look at sin." When

Peter wept, he wept over his sin: the sin of abandoning and denying his Lord, the sin of trusting in his own unreliable flesh. Peter had failed, but failure was not the end of Peter's story. As we shall see, Peter's tears point ahead to a day that is yet to come, when the Lord will restore him. Through this terrible experience, Peter has learned the lesson that was proclaimed by the apostle Paul: Christians are those "who worship by the Spirit of God, who glory in Christ Jesus, and who put no confidence in the flesh" (Philippians 3:3).

It was a powerful lesson for Peter to learn, and it cost him unbelievable pain and sorrow to learn it. But as someone has said, God never wastes pain. God used Peter's pain to mold him and shape him and equip him for service. God used Peter's pain to teach him to rely not on his flesh but on the power of Almighty God.

The power of God created a universe of time and space, stars and planets. If we don't have faith in that power, we don't have faith. As we leave the story of Peter's failure, may the Lord truly teach us the unreliability of the flesh and of the certain triumph that comes from resting in the Spirit.

twenty-eight

Jesus and the Rulers

➤ **Mark 15:1–20**

In A.D. 26, the Roman emperor Tiberias Caesar appointed Pontius Pilate governor of the Roman province of Judea. At that time, the world had not yet heard of Jesus of Nazareth, who was then an unknown carpenter quietly plying His trade in Galilee. But within a few years, the lives of Jesus and Pilate would collide, and history would be forever changed.

The Jewish people in the province of Judea hated the Romans in general and Pontius Pilate in particular. From the beginning of his tenure as governor, Pilate had shown nothing but contempt for the Jews and their religion. One early incident is mentioned in Luke 13:1. There we see the casual brutality of Pilate, who ordered the slaughter of Galilean Jews who had gone to offer sacrifices at the temple in Jerusalem. To add blasphemy to butchery, Pilate had the blood of the Galileans mingled with the blood of the animal sacrifices on the temple altar.

Although Pilate was in Jerusalem at the time of Jesus' trial, he normally resided in Caesarea along the Mediterranean coast. He went to Jerusalem only on important occasions, such as Passover, to personally ensure that order was maintained. On one occasion, soon after he became governor, he sent a message from Caesarea to his troops in Jerusalem, ordering that flags bearing the image of Tiberius Caesar be raised throughout Jerusalem in the middle of the night. Pilate's intent was to honor Caesar, but such images were forbidden by the law of Moses, and the people of Jerusalem were outraged.

A huge mob of Jews trekked from Jerusalem to the coast. They came to Caesarea and surrounded the house of Pilate, demanding that the flags be removed. Pilate refused. So the Jews all went face down on the ground around Pilate's house and lay motionless for five days and nights. Finally Pilate sent the word to the crowd that they would receive their answer in the great stadium at Caesarea.

Once the crowd was assembled on the grassy field at the center of the stadium, Pilate gave the word, and a contingent of Roman soldiers in full armor surrounded the Jews. Pilate declared, "You will all be cut to pieces unless you accept the images of Caesar in your city." Then he nodded to his soldiers, and the soldiers drew their swords.

Instantly every one of the Jews dropped to the ground, face down. Each one bared his neck, inviting and daring the Roman swords. Several of the Jews shouted up to Pilate, "If you are going to kill us, then be done with it! We would rather die than see our city defiled by the image of your Caesar!"

Pilate was dumbfounded. He had expected either a fight or abject cowardice—but this! To bare their necks and invite the sword! The Roman governor quickly calculated his options. With a single word, Pilate could unleash a torrent of blood. Rome never hesitated to use deadly force to accomplish its aims, but a bloodbath over a few flags? Such a massacre could produce a provincial rebellion. A governor's job was to maintain order, and failure to do so would cost him favor with Rome.

After a few moments' consideration, Pilate turned to one of his aides and said, "Send an order to Jerusalem over my seal. The flags are to be removed immediately."

Pontius Pilate could be cold-blooded and cruel to achieve his ends, but this was a day to be pragmatic, not cruel. Above all, Pilate was a practical man, and if yielding to popular pressure would advance his interests, then he would gladly yield.

This practical, go-along-to-get-along side of the cruel Roman governor will become even more evident within a few years, during one of the Jews' religious festivals. At that time, an itinerant Galilean preacher, Jesus of Nazareth, will be brought to him for judgment. A mob of Jews will demand the preacher's execution. Pilate will examine the Galilean and find Him innocent and undeserving of execution under Roman law. Pilate will even make a serious effort to release Him. But when the mob demands, "Crucify Him!" and threatens to riot, Pilate will yield to popular pressure.

A practical man knows he must look first to his interests. And Pontius Pilate was, above all, a practical man.

The Story Behind the Story

We are nearing the close of Mark's account of the life of the Ruler who serves. Mark 15 tells about our Lord's appearance before the Roman governor, Pilate. The events around the cross are more than simple narratives told by the gospel writers. You may read them that way if you wish, and see nothing more than the tragic story of a good man who died for a cause. Such a storyline is easily found on the surface of this narrative. But if you read carefully and ponder deeply, you will discover strange and marvelous forces at work beneath the surface of this story. In the words of the hymn, "God moves in a mysterious way, His wonders to perform."

The story of the cross is a simple tale, yet what it does to us is radical, wonderful, and revolutionary. It is a story of strangely transforming power.

In 1 Corinthians 2:7–8, the apostle Paul says that he proclaims "God's secret wisdom, a wisdom that has been hidden and that God destined for our glory before time began. None of the rulers of this age understood it, for if they had, they would not have crucified the Lord of glory." Something profound is going on behind the scenes in this account, and we can catch glimpses of it as we carefully read this account.

In our previous study, we saw Jesus on trial before the Jewish religious leaders. Now we find Him appearing before a Gentile judge, the Roman governor. Yet the question that hovers over this Gentile hall of judgment is a profoundly Jewish question: Is Jesus the king of the Jews? The strange happenstance that this question would so occupy the mind of a Roman governor indicates that something much deeper is going on, something of mystery, embedded among the plot threads of this story.

As we move through this account together, I would ask you to be thinking of four key questions about this story:

Why did Pilate marvel at the silence of Jesus?
Why did the crowd choose Barabbas instead of Jesus?
Why did Pilate have Jesus flogged before His crucifixion?
Why did the Roman soldiers mock Jesus with such cruelty?

As we seek to answer those four questions, we will discover the story behind the story.

The Silence of Jesus

We find the first question raised in the first five verses of Mark 15. Here Mark records:

> *Very early in the morning, the chief priests, with the eld-*
> *ers, the teachers of the law and the whole Sanhedrin,*
> *reached a decision. They bound Jesus, led him away and*
> *handed him over to Pilate.*
>
> *"Are you the king of the Jews?" asked Pilate.*
>
> *"Yes, it is as you say," Jesus replied.*
>
> *The chief priests accused him of many things. So again*
> *Pilate asked him, "Aren't you going to answer? See how*
> *many things they are accusing you of."*
>
> *But Jesus still made no reply, and Pilate was amazed.*
>
> (MARK 15:1–5)

We do not know if Jesus was permitted any sleep that night. But we do know that in the early morning hours, He was brought before the Jewish religious leaders, and the priests held a consultation with the Sanhedrin. Their meeting at night was illegal, so to justify their actions, they had to have a second meeting during daytime hours. As soon as it was light, they gathered again.

The reason they consulted was that they knew the charge on which they had condemned Jesus would never stand before the Roman governor. They had convicted Jesus of blasphemy for claiming to be God, so He was worthy of death under Jewish laws. But the Romans would pay no attention to that charge. The Jewish leaders needed to accuse Him of a crime under Roman law. So, in the parallel account in Luke, we find that they levied three charges against Him. He was charged with perverting the nation, that is, arousing troublemakers and creating riots and dissension. He was charged with forbidding the payment of tribute to Rome, instructing the people not to pay their taxes. And He was charged with attempting to make Himself king instead of Caesar. Pilate seized on the third charge as the only issue of importance.

If you have ever been to Jerusalem, you have probably visited the Tower of Antonia, overlooking the temple area. This fortress had been built by Herod the Great in honor of the renowned Roman general Mark Antony. It was probably to this fortress that Jesus was taken to appear before Pilate, and Pilate seized the occasion to ask Him, "Are you the king of the Jews?"

Jesus' answer has puzzled many people over the years. He did not say, as He had previously said to the priests, "I am." He said, "It is as you say," or, more accurately, "You have said so," or, "So you say." In the Greek, Jesus' reply is neither an affirmation nor a denial but more along the lines of, "That is what you say. Am I the king of the Jews? According to your way of thinking, you would call me king of the Jews."

Why didn't Jesus answer the question definitively? We find an explanation in the expanded account in John's gospel.

> Jesus said, "My kingdom is not of this world. If it were, my servants would fight to prevent my arrest by the Jews. But now my kingdom is from another place."
>
> "You are a king, then!" said Pilate.
>
> Jesus answered, "You are right in saying I am a king. In fact, for this reason I was born, and for this I came into the world, to testify to the truth. Everyone on the side of truth listens to me." (JOHN 18:36–37)

From this answer, Pilate could tell that the kingship of which Jesus spoke was not a threat to Rome. Whatever kind of king Jesus might be, He was not a revolutionary bent on overthrowing the empire. I think Pilate understood what Jesus said and was relieved of any fear that the accusations of the Jewish leaders were true.

If we read between the lines, we can imagine what the Jewish religious leaders were thinking at this point. They could see that Pilate was satisfied with the answer of Jesus and that their case against Him was crumbling. Now it becomes clear why they became so angry, as Mark tells us, and why they began to accuse Jesus of everything they could think of. They needed to convince Pilate that Jesus was a dangerous criminal, or Pilate would release Him. Later in this passage, we see that Pilate perceptively understood that "it was out of envy that the chief priests had handed Jesus over to him" (Mark 15:10).

Pilate was no fool. He was cruel and callous, but he was no fool. He saw through the empty charges the priests had brought against Jesus, and he knew what was in their minds. These men envied Jesus. To envy someone means that you want what that person has. You are jealous, and if you cannot have what you want, you at least want to make sure the other person doesn't have it either. What did Jesus have that the priests envied? His persuasive power and His authority with the people. As the temple guards had said of Jesus, "No one ever spoke the way this man does" (John 7:46). Again and again, the priests had tried to trap Jesus with His words, but they could never catch Him. He always had a simple answer that demolished their schemes. This amazing ability of His made them angry and envious to the point of murder.

As the religious leaders heaped more and more charges on Him, Jesus remained silent. Pilate was amazed at this, and he encouraged Jesus to defend Himself: "Aren't you going to answer? See how many things they are accusing you of." Still Jesus made no reply. He did not reply even to Pilate, much less to the conflicting and increasingly absurd charges of His accusers. Pilate marveled that our Lord remained silent. What was there about the silence of Jesus that so impressed the Roman governor?

Later, as Jesus is being crucified, the chief priests and scribes will mock Him, saying, "He saved others, but he can't save himself!" (Mark 15:31). They are wrong, of course. Jesus could have saved Himself at any time, and I don't mean that, as God, He could have called ten thousand angels to His aid. I mean that in a quite natural and normal way, He could have easily persuaded Pilate to release Him. Pilate knew Jesus was innocent, and he was looking for a way to release Jesus. Pilate's sympathy was with Jesus, not with the priests. If Jesus had replied to Pilate in any way, if the Lord had given the Roman governor any pretext or word of self-defense, Pilate would have gladly used it to dismiss the charge and free Jesus immediately.

But Jesus would not cooperate with Pilate. He refused to give Pilate any grounds on which to free Him. The silence of Jesus effectively exposed the hatred of the priests. It ripped the mask from their faces, exposing the hypocrisy and evil within them. It stripped away their disguise, so that they had to openly reveal their jealousy.

Yet His silence also left Him defenseless against the cross.

"Give Us Barabbas!"

The first question has been answered: Why did Pilate marvel at the silence of Jesus? Because Jesus easily could have saved Himself at any time, yet He chose to go to the cross. That fact should leave us as awestruck as Pilate, for truly His choice to die in our place is the most amazing truth the mind can contemplate. As in the words of the hymn by Charles Wesley (set to a melody by Thomas Campbell):

> He left his Father's throne above
> (so free, so infinite his grace!)
> emptied himself of all but love,
> and bled for Adam's helpless race. . . .

And as Wesley says in a chorus within this hymn,

> Amazing love! How can it be
> that thou, my God, shouldst die for me?

The second question is this: Why did the crowd choose Barabbas instead of Jesus? The second movement of this story surrounds the question of this criminal, Barabbas. The account in Luke's gospel tells us that at this point Pilate sent Jesus to King Herod, who had the legal title of king of the Jews. Luke records:

> *When Herod saw Jesus, he was greatly pleased, because for a long time he had been wanting to see him. From what he had heard about him, he hoped to see him perform some miracle. He plied him with many questions, but Jesus gave him no answer. The chief priests and the teachers of the law were standing there, vehemently accusing him. Then Herod and his soldiers ridiculed and mocked him.* (LUKE 23:8–11)

This was Herod Antipas, who had executed John the Baptist. He was a satrap, or petty king, who answered to Rome (his father, Herod the Great, had built the temple in Jerusalem). Herod questioned Jesus, urged Him to perform a miracle, and finally mocked Him. You may remember what King Herod thought when he first heard the rumors of Jesus and the miracles He performed.

> *But when Herod heard this, he said, "John, the man I beheaded, has been raised from the dead!"* (MARK 6:16)

Now, as Jesus finally stood in the Herod's court, the king probably felt a little foolish for having feared this Galilean and His supposed miraculous powers. Looking at Jesus, Herod could see that He was not the resurrected John the Baptist. And if Jesus could work miracles, as the rumors about Him claimed, why didn't He do so now and set Himself free?

Herod was a rationalist who did not believe in miracles or in the resurrection from the dead. In his guilt over having murdered John the Baptist, Herod had lost his grip on his rationalist world-view for a time. But by this time, he had managed to push his conscience away, and his old rationalist skepticism was back in full force. He looked at Jesus and saw nothing but an ordinary man. A powerless man. A doomed man. Herod had his laugh at Jesus, and Jesus remained silent. When he finally grew weary of mocking Jesus, Herod sent Him back to Pilate.

Mark did not record the incident with Herod; instead, Mark picks up the story at the point where Jesus has returned from Herod and is back in the hands of Pontius Pilate.

> *Now it was the custom at the Feast to release a prisoner whom the people requested. A man called Barabbas was in prison with the insurrectionists who had committed murder in the uprising. The crowd came up and asked Pilate to do for them what he usually did.*
>
> *"Do you want me to release to you the king of the Jews?" asked Pilate, knowing it was out of envy that the chief priests had handed Jesus over to him. But the chief priests stirred up the crowd to have Pilate release Barabbas instead.*
>
> *"What shall I do, then, with the one you call the king of the Jews?" Pilate asked them.*
>
> *"Crucify him!" they shouted.*
>
> *"Why? What crime has he committed?" asked Pilate.*
>
> *But they shouted all the louder, "Crucify him!"*

> *Wanting to satisfy the crowd, Pilate released Barabbas*
> *to them. He had Jesus flogged, and handed him over to be*
> *crucified.* (MARK 15:6–15)

All four gospels tell us of Barabbas. He was a bloodthirsty revolutionary who had committed murder during an insurrection against the occupation forces of Rome. The gospels tell us nothing of the life of Barabbas before or after these events.

One of the most interesting facts about Barabbas is his name, which means "son of the father." In a dramatic historic coincidence, we find that there is some evidence that his full name was Jesus Barabbas, that is, Jesus, son of the Father (this information comes down to us from the early biblical scholar Origen). It seems that this is yet another example of how God teaches us through subtle symbolism. The crowd was confronted by a stark choice between Jesus Barabbas, "son of the father," who is ruled by hate, who accomplishes his aims by force, who sacrifices anyone who gets in his way; and Jesus, the Son of God the Father, who is ruled by love, who accomplishes His aims by servanthood, who sacrifices Himself for the sake of others. The crowd chose the man of hate over the man of love.

So we have to ask why. Why did they choose Barabbas? The answer seems to be that they were disappointed with Jesus. This was only days after the Lord's triumphal entry into Jerusalem, when He was acclaimed as the Messiah. Jesus had awakened within the people the hope that He was indeed the Messiah, the one they thought would deliver them from Roman oppression. Their concept of messiahship centered around political liberation. When the people saw Jesus standing helpless before the Roman governor, either unwilling or unable to defend Himself, their loyalty to Him collapsed. In anger and disappointment, they turned away from Him and chose a different Jesus—an insurrectionist Jesus, a political liberationist Jesus, a murderous Jesus.

They had the opportunity to choose the true Messiah, the Son of God, the Ruler who serves. Instead, they shouted, "No, not him! Give us Barabbas!" (John 18:40).

We face the same choice this Jewish crowd faced: Jesus or Barabbas? Have you ever been disappointed in Jesus? Have you ever expected Him to act in a certain way, but He didn't? You thought you understood Him and knew how He should respond, but He seemed to let you down. Has that ever happened to you? It has to me. There have been times in my life when I have been angry and disappointed with God. I have accused Him of failing in His promises.

We think we know what God ought to do, even though He has told us again and again, " 'For my thoughts are not your thoughts, neither are your ways my ways,' declares the LORD. 'As the heavens are higher than the earth, so are my ways higher than your ways and my thoughts than your thoughts' " (Isaiah 55:8–9). We can't figure God out. He will be true to Himself, He will never lie, He will never deceive us. But He is more than we can grasp, more than we can comprehend. Like this crowd, when we get angry with God, when we become disappointed with Jesus, we all too easily turn from Him to some other Jesus. And there is always another Jesus.

For example, a group of scholars and theologians, the Jesus Seminar, has as its goal to clear away everything its members consider a myth surrounding the real facts of the historical Jesus. What do the scholars of the Jesus Seminar consider to be a myth? Like King Herod and the Sadducees, they exclude anything miraculous, such as the Virgin Birth, the healings, the calming of the storm, and the resurrection. After they have excluded everything they consider mythical about Jesus, they are left with a Jesus who was a radical social activist (which should not surprise us, since the members of the Jesus Seminar are mostly liberal social activists). These scholars and professors do not conduct archaeological or historical research to come to their conclusions. They simply meet and vote.

When the Jesus Seminar convenes, each member is given a colored marble with which to cast his or her vote. A question is put to the group: Did Jesus say such-and-such? Did Jesus perform this miracle? Did Jesus rise from the dead? And each scholar votes. A black marble if the scholar is convinced the event never happened. Gray if it probably never happened. Pink if it might have happened. Red if the scholar is certain it did happen. By such votes, the Jesus Seminar has determined the Christmas story and the Easter story are fables. What's more, the Jesus Seminar has decided that only 18 percent of the recorded sayings of Jesus are authentic. In fact, in the gospel of Mark, which we are studying, these scholars have decided that Jesus uttered only one of the many statements that Mark records. (They voted for Mark 12:17: "Give to Caesar what is Caesar's and to God what is God's.")

I submit that the Jesus of the Jesus Seminar is nothing but a Jesus Barabbas. They are not satisfied with the Jesus of the gospels, so they demand a Jesus that is to their liking, their taste—a Jesus who will affirm their political and social agenda. That is what the Jews demanded when they cried, "Give us Barabbas!"

Many Jesuses are available to you, if the real Jesus is not to your liking. There have always been plenty of Jesuses to go around. The ancient cultists had a Gnostic Jesus and a Manichaean Jesus. There are Buddhist and Muslim Jesuses. There is a New Age Jesus. There is the Jesus of liberation theology. And every one of these Jesuses is a Barabbas.

There is only one Jesus the Lord, the Jesus of the New Testament, the Jesus who, as the Apostles' Creed states, was conceived by the Holy Spirit, born of the Virgin Mary, suffered under Pontius Pilate, was crucified, dead, and buried, and who is raised and alive today. That is the Jesus you must accept or reject. And if you cannot accept this Jesus, then the only Jesus that is left to you is a Barabbas.

The Flogging of Jesus

So the second question has been answered: Why did the crowd choose Barabbas instead of Jesus? Because the authentic Jesus disappointed them. They wanted a political and social Messiah who would free them from Roman oppression.

The third movement of this story deals with: Why did Pilate have Jesus flogged before His crucifixion? Pilate knew that the crowd wanted him to release Barabbas and not Jesus. He asked them, "What shall I do with the one you call the king of the Jews?" And they said, "Crucify him!"

I think that Pilate must have been horrified at this point. He had tried to shift responsibility to Herod, but to no avail. There was no basis in Roman law for Jesus to be crucified, yet the crowd demanded it. Pilate, the consummate politician, knew that his power depended on giving the people what they want. Pilate was a people pleaser. But this situation threatened to substitute mob rule in place of Roman law. Surely, Pilate thought, there had to be some way out of this dilemma.

And then an idea occurred to Pilate. He could have Jesus flogged.

It was not normal practice to flog or scourge a prisoner before crucifying him. There is no evidence that the other thieves who were crucified with Jesus were flogged before they went to the cross. But Pilate ordered this horrible punishment to be imposed on Jesus—a man Pilate considered to be innocent. It is impossible to fully convey to you the horrors of a Roman flogging. It was carried out with a whip made of long leather cords, into which were imbedded bits of metal and bone. As the leather cords struck the victim's back, those pieces of metal and bone would cut and flay his flesh, leaving it a bloody mass.

If Pilate believed that Jesus was innocent and was trying to avoid sending Him to the cross, why did he subject Jesus to the excruciating horrors of a flogging? The only conceivable conclusion: Pilate flogged Jesus in a failed attempt to save His life. This was Pilate's last-ditch attempt to spare Jesus. He hoped that by lashing Jesus and leaving Him bloodied and mutilated, he would so horrify the crowd that they would say, "He's been punished enough." But Pilate was wrong.

In John's gospel, we read that after the scourging of Jesus, Pilate led Him before the crowd and announced, "Behold the man!" (John 19:5 KJV). But the chief priests and scribes would accept nothing less than death for Jesus. So they stirred up the crowd to cry, "Crucify Him! Crucify Him!"

John 19:8 tells us that Pilate was afraid: afraid of the crisis that was unfolding, afraid of the crowd, and afraid of Jesus. His fear of Jesus was so great that he took Jesus back into the palace, away from the clamoring mob, and asked Him, "Where do you come from?" (John 19:9). Still Jesus gave him no answer.

Pilate was a man of doubtful character, trapped in a dilemma. People of strong character always know what to do in a dilemma, because they make decisions based on principles of right and wrong. But people of doubtful character, who base their decisions on what is expedient, easily get impaled on the horns of a dilemma. Pilate knew the right thing to do in this situation; he

246 PART TWO: The Ruler Who Serves

knew it was illegal and immoral to execute an innocent man. But those are principles, and Pilate was an unprincipled man. He had built his career not on principles but on pleasing people and grasping power. Caught between two opposing powers, his lack of character was starkly revealed.

Pontius Pilate was afraid, and he was a coward. He dithered between justice and expediency, unable to make up his mind to do what he knew was right. In his fumbling attempt to let Jesus go free, Pilate succeeded only in multiplying Jesus' pain on His way to the cross. If Pilate had any conscience, it must have troubled him deeply that his bungling had only served to compound the torture and suffering he had tried to avert.

So Pilate, in his moral cowardice, has called down on himself the condemnation of history. In the one great test of his character, Pontius Pilate failed bitterly. He yielded to the people and became an accomplice in the crime of crimes, the murder of the Son of God.

Here again we see that the cross is at work behind the scenes, exposing the dark recess of the human heart, bringing hidden guilt out into the open.

"Hail, King of the Jews!"

The third question has been asked and answered: Why did Pilate have Jesus flogged before His crucifixion? It was a failed attempt to avoid making the right and courageous moral choice.

So now we come to the fourth question: Why did the Roman soldiers mock Jesus with such cruelty? Mark's account continues:

The soldiers led Jesus away into the palace (that is, the Praetorium) and called together the whole company of soldiers. They put a purple robe on him, then twisted together a crown of thorns and set it on him. And they began to call out to him, "Hail, king of the Jews!" Again and again they struck him on the head with a staff and spit on him. Falling on their knees, they paid homage to him. And when they had mocked him, they took off the purple robe and put his own clothes on him. Then they led him out to crucify him.

(MARK 15:16–20)

This mockery was a strange thing. Roman soldiers were disciplined professionals who did not usually indulge in gratuitous cruelty to their prisoners. They were callous men, accustomed to carrying out grisly orders. They could casually nail a man to a cross and then go to breakfast. But these soldiers seem to derive a sadistic enjoyment from tormenting Jesus.

The soldiers in charge of Jesus called the whole company together, all the soldiers who were off-duty or standing around, so they joined in this sport. They made the crown of thorns and forced it down on the Lord's head. They put a reed in His hand as a scepter and bowed before Him. They spit on Him and struck Him. Again: why?

I think the answer is revealed in what they said to Him: "Hail, king of the Jews!" Surely they were not angry with Jesus. They had never seen Him before and knew little about Him. But they were angry with the Jews.

The Jews were difficult for the Romans to govern, because they were a proud and freedom-loving people. The Jews were fiercely devoted to their religion and their God. And they were continually chafing under Roman rule, often to the point of rebellion and insurrection.

So when this Jew fell into their hands—a man who, it was said, aspired to become "the king of the Jews"—these soldiers lost control. All the pent-up hatred and resentment against the Jewish people poured out and found its object in this one lonely Jew. Jesus became the focus of their bigotry and racial hatred. Once again we see how the cross unveils what is hidden.

Now the fourth question has been asked and answered: Why did the Roman soldiers mock Jesus with such cruelty? Because of unreasoning, racist hatred against the Lord's chosen people, the nation of Israel.

As human history moves inexorably toward a close, toward the return of the Lord Jesus Christ, we can expect to see a rise of unreasoning hatred toward God's people, the people of His church, we Christians, and the people of the nation of Israel. Satan seeks to destroy God's eternal plan by the persecution of the church and the destruction of the Jewish people. One of the most visible expressions of Satan's violence against the Jews was the Holocaust.

As Christians, we need to remember what the Holocaust means to the Jewish people. Jews call it *Shoah,* a word that has no exact English equivalent but that suggests a great disaster, an unthinkable destruction, drenched in blood and tears. That event remains the dominant reality in many, if not most, Jewish lives. It has scarred the Jewish soul and shaken the Jewish faith in God and humankind. It has left a residue of anger, fear, and disillusionment that refuses to go away. One-third of the world's Jewish population vanished in the Holocaust, including 1.5 million Jewish children and 90 percent of all European Jews. Eighty percent of the world's Jewish scholars, teachers, rabbis, and students were fed to the Holocaust by Nazi Germany.

I don't believe this was an aberration of history. The Holocaust was part of the satanic plan, a hellish stratagem to thwart the plan of God. Satan has vowed to destroy God's people, Israel, and God's church. We can see the ugly inspiration of Satan in the mockery and torture of Jesus, in the persecution of the Jews, and in the persecution of the church. These are not separate and isolated events but different fronts by which the enemy wages war against God. If we truly love the Lord Jesus Christ, then our hearts are surely moved with sorrow to see Him flogged and beaten, mocked and spat on. And if our hearts are so moved, then we should love and pray for His people, the people of His church around the world, many of whom face persecution daily, and His special people, the Jews.

We have asked and answered four crucial questions surrounding the suffering of Jesus before He went to the cross. But there is one final question to be asked, and only you can answer it.

What will *you* do with Jesus?

We have seen what others have done with Jesus.

Judas traded Jesus for money. You say you could never do what Judas did, but if your career, your income, your possessions, your status mean more to you than Jesus does, then you have already traded Jesus for money. What will *you* do with Jesus?

The scribes and priests saw that Jesus exposed their corruption and hypocrisy, so they tried to shut Him up and put Him out of their lives. You say you could never do to Jesus what they did, but if you are living a double life, pretending to be religious while hiding your sin, then you have already done what the scribes and priests did. What will *you* do with Jesus?

The crowd wanted a messiah, but not a messiah like Jesus. He was a bitter disappointment to them. So they rejected Him and demanded a different Jesus, a Jesus Barabbas. You say you could never do what that crowd did, but if you want only a Jesus who will serve your wants and meet your expectations, if you want Him to be your servant but not your king, then all you really want is Barabbas. What will *you* do with Jesus?

Pilate tried to strike a compromise between Jesus and His accusers. He tried to spare Jesus while maintaining friendship with the world. In the end, Pilate not only crucified Jesus but flogged Him as well. You say you could never do what Pilate did, but have you compromised with the world? Have you forgotten that friendship with the world is enmity against God? What will *you* do with Jesus?

King Herod was fascinated by the miracles of Jesus. He demanded to see Jesus perform for him. When Jesus would not perform, Herod sent Jesus away. You say you could never do what Herod did, but are you only interested in what Jesus can do for you? If Jesus doesn't perform mighty works at your command, do you lose interest and send Him away? What will *you* do with Jesus?

The cross is close now. As we move deeper into its shadow, we find that it has a strange and marvelous way of penetrating beneath the surface of our lives, bringing out the hidden wisdom of God and wrenching forth our hidden sin and shame. In the shadow of the cross, everyone stands naked before God. He sees your heart and mine with crystal clarity. And He asks you a question that you must answer.

What will *you* do with Jesus?

twenty-nine

The Awful Penalty

➤ **Mark 15:21–47**

In the heart of the Hawaiian Islands is the island of Molokai. Today that island is a paradise, but during the 1800s it was an island of horrors. In 1848, an outbreak of leprosy (Hansen's disease) occurred in Hawaii, probably brought to the island chain from China. By the 1860s, the outbreak had become a terrifying epidemic; at that time there was no cure, as there is today. The Hawaiian government rounded up everyone infected with the disease, often tearing fathers or mothers or children away from their families, and quarantined them on the island of Molokai.

The leper colony was located on Kalaupapa Peninsula, which was cut off from the rest of Molokai by a sixteen-hundred-foot cliff. Kalaupapa was hell on earth. There was no dock or harbor, so the ships would drop anchor offshore, and the lepers would be made to jump overboard and swim to the rocky shore. Some died in the water. More died of exposure within days. The government did not provide shelter, drinking water, or amenities. Those who survived found what shelter they could in caves or rude shacks made of leaves and branches. Occasionally supply ships would toss crates of food into the water; if the currents were favorable, the crates would reach the jagged shore, where the lepers could retrieve them.

The lepers huddled together to help each other survive. Their former lives and families became a distant memory. They were condemned and without hope.

The Kalaupapa leprosy colony existed for seven years before Father Damien arrived. Father Damien de Veuster was a Belgian priest who volunteered for service among the lepers at Kalaupapa. He was a young man, just thirty-three, when he arrived in 1873. His skills ranged from carpentry (for building houses and churches and caskets) to medicine (for treating wounds, bandaging sores, and amputating rotting limbs). For years he lived among the lepers. He taught his skills to them, constructed buildings, cared for the living, buried the dead, encouraged them through his prayers and preaching.

One evening, Father Damien filled a basin with boiling water, preparing to wash his feet. At his elbow, he had a pitcher of cold water. It was his custom to mix the hot and cold water to a bearable temperature before putting his feet in the basin. This night, he forgot the cold water, but when he put his feet in the boiled water, he felt no pain. Leprosy is a disease that destroys the nerves and robs the victim of pain.

That was in 1885. After twelve years living among the lepers, Father Damien had taken their disease into himself. The following Sunday, he stood before his congregation in the simple wooden church he had built, and he began his sermon with the words "We lepers." Four years later, he was dead at the age of forty-nine.

The life of Father Damien reminds us of the one who came among us while we were isolated and condemned by sin, castaways without any hope. He came as a carpenter, a healer, and a teacher. He encouraged us with His prayers and preaching. And in the end, He took our disease into Himself, giving His life for us. He was the one of whom Isaiah prophesied:

> *Surely he took up our infirmities*
> > *and carried our sorrows,*
> *yet we considered him stricken by God,*
> > *smitten by him, and afflicted.*
> *But he was pierced for our transgressions,*
> > *he was crushed for our iniquities;*
> *the punishment that brought us peace was upon him,*
> > *and by his wounds we are healed.*
> *We all, like sheep, have gone astray,*
> > *each of us has turned to his own way;*
> *and the* LORD *has laid on him*
> > *the iniquity of us all.* (ISAIAH 53:4–6)

We come now to the moment that Isaiah spoke of, when Jesus was pierced for us, when He was crushed for us, when our sin, was laid on Him as He hung on the cross. May we approach this portion of Mark with a special sense of awe and reverence, because of the sacredness of the sacrifice Jesus made for us. May we approach it prayerfully, asking God to imprint this scene on our hearts and minds. As we glimpse something of the awful penalty that Jesus paid on our behalf, may we understand that we are not merely witnessing the tragic martyrdom of a religious idealist. We are watching as a ransom payment is made for our souls.

"And They Crucified Him"

We begin by observing that Mark's account of the crucifixion is different in tone and detail from that of the other three gospels.

Mark leaves out a number of details that other gospel writers include. For example, Mark includes only one sentence spoken by Jesus (in all, the four gospels record seven statements of Jesus on the cross, the well-known seven words of the cross). The description of Jesus' actions and words that Mark records are limited to three short passages. Here is the first passage:

> *They brought Jesus to the place called Golgotha (which means The Place of the Skull). Then they offered him wine mixed with myrrh, but he did not take it. And they crucified him.* (MARK 15:22–24)

If you go to Jerusalem, you will find, just outside the Damascus gate of the northern wall of the old city, a mound that looks like a skull. Many scholars believe this is the place where Jesus was crucified.

Before the crucifixion began, one of the soldiers offered Jesus wine mingled with myrrh (Greek *smurnizo*). Matthew 27:34 says they offered Him "wine to drink, mixed with gall" (Greek *chole*). "Gall" or *chole* is a general term referring to any bitter substance. Mark tells us specifically that the gall was myrrh, a bitter gum resin that was believed to have a narcotic effect. The Romans commonly drugged crucifixion victims to make it easier to drive the nails through their hands and feet. Jesus probably refused the drink because He had no intention of struggling or making the task difficult for His executioners. This is one more way we see how willingly Jesus accepted our penalty and laid down His life for us.

Then Mark makes a powerful statement in four short words: "And they crucified him."

The gospel writers demonstrate reserve when describing the crucifixion. They do not describe the driving of the nails or the agony Jesus endured. All of the incomprehensible horror of the cross is compressed into those four stark words: "And they crucified him."

Mark passes over almost all of the first three hours on the cross. In his second passage describing the words and actions of Jesus on the cross, Mark takes us to the dark abyss of the Lord's loneliness:

> *At the sixth hour darkness came over the whole land until the ninth hour. And at the ninth hour Jesus cried out in a loud voice, "Eloi, Eloi, lama sabachthani?"—which means, "My God, my God, why have you forsaken me?"*
> (MARK 15:33–34)

Then there is Mark's third and final passage describing the Lord's words and actions on the cross. In that passage Mark takes us to the final moment of His earthly life.

> *With a loud cry, Jesus breathed his last.*
> *The curtain of the temple was torn in two from top to bottom.* (MARK 15:37–38)

Mark's account of the crucifixion—of the moments when Jesus hung on the cross and gave His life for us—is simple and concise. I think that is because Mark's focus is not on what the people in the crowd see as they gaze at the cross but what Jesus sees as He looks out on the crowd. We will next examine that perspective.

The View from the Cross

Gathered around the foot of the cross were a great number of individuals or groups of individuals. Mark focuses on each of them so that we might witness their reactions to the crucifixion of our Lord. Mark intended this account to contrast the mysterious workings of God and the ways and the thinking of humanity. The writer wants us to see that this event is truly timeless.

If Jesus were crucified in your hometown today, you would find these same people gathered around the cross. The cast of characters would remain unchanged. Oh, the faces would be different, but the characterizations, the personality types, the attitudes, the actions, the words would all be displayed in our time and place as they were on that day, outside of Jerusalem.

Now let's go back to the beginning of these events, to a point immediately following the Lord's trial before Pilate. There we find the first of these character sketches drawn by Mark. It involves an incident that occurred as Jesus was on His way to the cross. The Roman soldiers are taking Jesus out to crucify Him. As they pass through the streets of Jerusalem, Jesus stumbles and falls. So the Roman soldiers grab a stranger from the crowd and force him to carry the cross of Jesus.

> *A certain man from Cyrene, Simon, the father of Alexander and Rufus, was passing by on his way in from the country, and they forced him to carry the cross.* (MARK 15:21)

Imagine the thoughts and feelings of this man, Simon. He is from the country of Cyrene in North Africa and has come to Jerusalem to celebrate the Passover. He has left his lodgings outside the city and has no idea that this momentous event, the crucifixion, is about to take place. Suddenly his plans for the day are interrupted by a strange procession winding through the narrow streets of the city. Simon steps aside to let the Roman soldiers pass, and then he sees a beaten, bleeding man stagger and fall beneath the heavy burden of a wooden cross. Before he knows what is happening, Simon is grabbed by the rough hands of the soldiers and is pushed out into the street. The cross is placed on Simon's back, and he is ordered to carry it outside the city.

It is likely that Simon was angered by this interruption and resentful over being forced to shoulder this burden. I think we can identify with this man, because we can recall many times when we have felt this way whenever we have felt that God was calling us to shoulder a cross. We resent it when God sends something into our lives that interrupts our schedules and upsets our plans. We resent it when circumstances create a burden in our lives or bring pain and suffering to our souls. I have felt this way, and, I'm sure, so have you. This, I believe, must have been what Simon of Cyrene felt as he was forced to bear the cross of Jesus.

There is evidence in Scripture that this event had a tremendous effect on Simon's life. There is a hint in Acts that Simon of Cyrene was there on Pentecost (see Acts 2:10). Mark makes clear that Simon was the father of Alexander and Rufus, who are well known to the Gentile believers to whom Mark is writing. Paul, in Romans 16:13, mentions a Rufus with whom he was closely associated and whose mother had been kind to Paul. It is probably the same Rufus. So it is likely that Simon of Cyrene became a Christian as a result of this interruption of his plans. If so, then one of the Lord's statements probably had a special meaning for him throughout his life: "If anyone would come after me, he must deny himself and take up his cross and follow me."

Soldiers and Robbers

The Roman soldiers who crucified Jesus gathered around the foot of the cross. This was a time of great popular unrest and rebellion in Palestine, and crucifixions were common. Historians tell us that following one of these insurrections, which took place some years before the crucifixion of Christ, two thousand Jewish dissidents were rounded up and crucified. So these Roman soldiers had a lot of experience with crucifixion. That is why they seem so callous. Immediately after they nailed Jesus to the cross and hoisted the cross into place, these hardened soldiers got down on the ground, took out a pair of dice, and began to gamble as Jesus hung dying.

Such casual indifference to human suffering and death seems unthinkable to us. These men were more interested in the pleasure of a game and making money than they were in the death and blood of Jesus. I think these men symbolize for all time a kind of person we all know, the person who is interested only in money and entertainment and who can't be bothered with the deeper issues of life, especially the issue of the cross. Talk to such people about Jesus, and they will shrug with indifference. Talk to them about the fate of their eternal souls, and they will laugh and turn away. The only way you can get their attention is by talking to them about money or pleasure. They are focused only on the immediate and give no thought to what is eternal.

Mark next introduces us to the two robbers who were crucified with Jesus.

> *They crucified two robbers with him, one on his right and one on his left. (Mark 15:27)*

Later Mark adds:

> *Those crucified with him also heaped insults on him. (Mark 15:32)*

These two men were revolutionaries or terrorists who had been arrested in a violent insurrection. They were angry young men who were committed to the unlikely, quixotic goal of overthrowing

Roman rule in Palestine. In the process of carrying out their acts of murder and terror, they took what they wanted and didn't care who might get hurt in the process. They must have heard of Jesus and known of His claims of messiahship, and like the rest of the populace, they mistakenly understood that the promised Messiah would be a political and military deliverer. So now they hung on either side of the man who, a few days earlier, had been cheered by the crowds on His way into Jerusalem. He had proved a bitter disappointment as a revolutionary, so these two revolutionaries now reviled Him, heaping all their frustrations on Him, because He was of no help to them. He was dying on a Roman cross, just as they were.

Many people in our world operate by the same philosophy as these robbers: "I take what I want, and I don't care who gets hurt in the process. What's mine is mine, and what's yours is mine." If living by that philosophy gets them into trouble (and it inevitably does), they feel entitled to be excused. Oh, they might be interested in Jesus if He could help them escape the consequences of their actions. But on discovering that they must accept the fate they have designed for themselves, they will turn on Jesus and mock Him, just as these robbers did.

Mark's gospel doesn't tell us the full story of these two robbers. But by comparing this account with the parallel account in Luke, we find that one of these robbers eventually repents of his abuse toward Jesus. Luke records:

> *One of the criminals who hung there hurled insults at him: "Aren't you the Christ? Save yourself and us!"*
>
> *But the other criminal rebuked him. "Don't you fear God," he said, "since you are under the same sentence? We are punished justly, for we are getting what our deeds deserve. But this man has done nothing wrong."*

> *Then he said, "Jesus, remember me when you come into your kingdom."*
>
> *Jesus answered him, "I tell you the truth, today you will be with me in paradise."* (LUKE 23:39–43)

One of the most beautiful things about the story of the crucifixion is that one of these dying men realizes the truth. This crucified Jesus is in fact a king who is about to enter a kingdom where He will have full authority and power. How did this man know that? What did he see as he watched Jesus die? What was it about Jesus that changed this man's heart and convinced him of who Jesus was? We are not told, but we know that there was something about the way Jesus faced death that had great power to change a man's heart. So this man was convinced. No, more than convinced, he was converted as he hung dying alongside the Messiah. His dying words were a plea for mercy: "Jesus, remember me when you come into your kingdom." And Jesus answered him with a word of beautiful assurance: "I tell you the truth, today you will be with me in paradise."

Mockers, Priests, and a Curiosity Seeker

Mark also tells us that there were certain passersby at the foot of the cross.

> *Those who passed by hurled insults at him, shaking their heads and saying, "So! You who are going to destroy the temple and build it in three days, come down from the cross and save yourself!"* (MARK 15:29–30)

These were just bystanders, but when they saw Jesus hanging on the cross, they remembered that He was the one who had made such great claims. So they taunted Him: "You made those ridiculous claims! You said you were going to destroy the temple and raise it up again! Well, you don't look so powerful now!" Mark illustrates the derision by telling us that they were "shaking their heads" at Him.

The irony is that He was in the process of fulfilling the words they flung back at Him. The temple He promised to destroy was the temple of His body, and that destruction was taking place before their eyes. He had willingly placed Himself there, and with every ounce of blood that drained from His veins, His temple was being destroyed. Little did they know that on the third day, the rest of His prophecy would be fulfilled.

Many people in the world are like those bystanders. If Jesus would only stick to teaching harmless religious ideals, they would have no problem with Him. But when He makes extravagant promises and claims to supernatural power, when He says, "I am the Son of God," or, "No one comes to the Father except through me," they reject Him. They want nothing to do with such absurd and irrational notions. They shake their heads with derision.

Next Mark portrays the priests and scribes, the men who plotted the death of Jesus, as they stand at the foot of the cross.

> *In the same way the chief priests and the teachers of the law mocked him among themselves. "He saved others," they said, "but he can't save himself! Let this Christ, this King of Israel, come down now from the cross, that we may see and believe."* (MARK 15:31–32)

These priests had been frightened and jealous of Jesus before. They had seen Him teach and bless the crowds in ways they could never do. But they had plotted against Him, and now they had Him where they wanted Him, or so it seemed. Although He had willingly placed Himself in their hands, they thought they had beaten Him. So this was their moment of triumph, and they reveled in it. They taunted Him: "He saved others, but he can't save himself! Let this Christ, this King of Israel, come down now from the cross, that we may see and believe."

I see a powerful symbolism in those words, and a profound parallelism to our times. These religious leaders say to Jesus, "Come down now from the cross, that we may see and believe." In other words, "Separate yourself from the cross, Jesus! Abandon the cross! The only Christianity we will believe in is a crossless Christianity!" Does that sound familiar? Many people call themselves Christian but cannot accept the cross. They accept the sayings of Jesus, or most of them. They accept the works of Jesus, as they interpret them. But the cross? "Oh, no! That's too negative, too disturbing. We want only nice, happy, positive thoughts in our Christianity."

So if you ever hear a gospel preached that doesn't have at its core the cross of Jesus Christ, then you are listening to what Paul called "a different gospel," which is an abomination to God (see Galatians 1:6–9). Those who think the cross of Christ and the blood of Christ are negative or disturbing do not understand the Christian gospel. The bad news of the cross is at the very heart of the Good News of Jesus Christ.

Mark tells us about another fellow at the cross who was interested in all the proceedings. His name is not given to us, but he enters the picture when Jesus calls out to the Father, moments before Jesus dies.

When some of those standing near heard this, they said, "Listen, he's calling Elijah."

One man ran, filled a sponge with wine vinegar, put it on a stick, and offered it to Jesus to drink. "Now leave him alone. Let's see if Elijah comes to take him down," he said. With a loud cry, Jesus breathed his last. (MARK 15:35–36)

Some people have mistaken this man's actions for compassion. The wine vinegar, they assume, is intended as an anesthetic to relieve the Lord's suffering. But close examination reveals that this is not the case. The man is jeering at Jesus, even laughing at Him, as he says, "Let's see if Elijah comes to take him down." He shoves the vinegar, which is spoiled wine, at Jesus to get a reaction from Him, like a wicked child who enjoys poking and torturing small animals. There is no compassion in this man. He is enjoying the crucifixion. He is a sick and disgusting curiosity seeker. This is human nature at its worst.

Such people are with us today. When a tragically depressed person crawls out on a high ledge, contemplating suicide, these people are on the street below, shouting, "Jump!" They rubberneck at traffic accidents, fascinated by scenes of tragedy and death. If the state sold tickets to an execution, they'd be first in line. They are curiosity seekers, thrill seekers, shriveled souls who delight in the suffering of others.

If you think this kind of person is unusual or rare, look at the content of movies and television shows. Look at all the ways Hollywood has come up with to torture, maim, mutilate, and kill people in the name of entertainment. And then there are the so-called reality shows that serve up videotape of real accidents, real fires, real crimes, real deaths—again, in the name of entertainment. Of all the incidents that surround the crucifixion of Jesus, I think the account of this sick-minded thrill seeker is by far the most characteristic of the great mass of people today.

The Centurion, the Women, and the Secret Disciple

At this point, Jesus calls out with a loud cry and breathes His last, but the story is not over. Mark has three more accounts to relate, three more individuals or groups of people to introduce to us. But these final three individuals or groups are of a different character from the ones we have met thus far. After the death of Jesus, there is no mention of anybody who abuses, mocks, or reviles Him. Those who hate Jesus seem to slink away, leaving only a small group of people who love Him.

The first person we meet after the death of Jesus is probably the last person we would expect to find among His admirers. It is the centurion who was in charge of soldiers who carried out the crucifixion.

> *And when the centurion, who stood there in front of Jesus, heard his cry and saw how he died, he said, "Surely this man was the Son of God!"* (MARK 15:39)

This Roman centurion was a pagan. Given the culture from which he came, he no doubt believed in many gods. Yet the cross brought him to a sobering awareness of ultimate reality. To the men in his command who had carried out the crucifixion, this event had been a job, even a joke. But to this centurion, this crucifixion was a ghastly mistake, the execution of a man not only innocent but also divine. There was something about the way Jesus died that the centurion had never seen before—a dignity, a nobility, a force of personality that transcended the merely human.

Notice that the centurion speaks in the past tense: "This man was the Son of God." There is no hope here, no glimmer of redemption or resurrection, only a sense of incalculable loss and grievous error. The centurion knows that a horrible injustice has been committed, and it can never be undone. And because of that, the centurion does not understand what this event means to his life, to his soul.

I think that is how many people today look at the story of the cross. They say, "Yes, Jesus was the Son of God." But they do not take it any further than that. They are impressed by the life and teaching of Jesus, but they never personalize His death and say, "He died for me." So they fail to lay hold of the meaning of His death for their lives. It is not enough to say, "Jesus was the Son of God." We must go further, make it personal, and say, "Jesus, please be the Lord and Savior of my life."

Next Mark introduces us to a group of women who have gathered around the cross of Jesus.

> *Some women were watching from a distance. Among them were Mary Magdalene, Mary the mother of James the younger and of Joses, and Salome. In Galilee these women had followed him and cared for his needs. Many other women who had come up with him to Jerusalem were also there.* (MARK 15:40–41)

Here are the women who loved Jesus, but where are the men? Where are the disciples who walked with Him? Where are the men who promised never to leave His side? Where is bold, blustering Peter at this hour? John's gospel tells us that John was at the cross with Mary, the mother of Jesus. In those first three hours, Jesus, despite His suffering, committed His mother to the care of the disciple John. But from this account in Mark it would seem that John and Mary are no longer present; perhaps John has led Mary away.

In any case, these women are the only ones who remain around the cross. These women loved Jesus to the end. Love, a love that doesn't end even with the death of the beloved—that is one of the truly beautiful characteristics of women. Although the men around Jesus had fled in terror, these women were not afraid to show their love for the Lord. This is a beautiful tribute to the strength of womanhood.

These women are not gathering around the cross in hope but in utter hopelessness. They do not expect a resurrection. They do not expect God to act in their hour of despair. Their love remains, but their hope and faith are gone. Sometimes, in the Christian life, we come to the end of ourselves. We still love God, but we have no hope, no faith, that He will deliver us. We see only darkness and despair. It will be helpful, in such times, to remember that a resurrection is coming soon.

There is one last person Mark wants us to meet. He is a faithful follower of the Lord, a secret disciple. His name is Joseph of Arimathea.

> *It was Preparation Day (that is, the day before the Sabbath). So as evening approached, Joseph of Arimathea, a prominent member of the Council, who was himself waiting for the kingdom of God, went boldly to Pilate and asked for Jesus' body. Pilate was surprised to hear that he was already dead. Summoning the centurion, he asked him if Jesus had already died. When he learned from the centurion that it was so, he gave the body to Joseph. So Joseph bought some linen cloth, took down the body, wrapped it in the linen, and placed it in a tomb cut out of rock. Then he rolled a stone against the entrance of the tomb. Mary Magdalene and Mary the mother of Joses saw where he was laid.* (MARK 15:42–47)

Joseph of Arimathea was a wealthy member of the Sanhedrin. He had believed in Jesus but was afraid to profess his belief openly. All through the record of the trial of Jesus, there is no mention of Joseph. He didn't raise his voice in the court when Jesus appeared before the Sanhedrin. He was afraid to openly voice his support of Jesus, afraid of what the others in the Sanhedrin would think or do. But after Jesus died, when His body hung lifeless on the tree, a transformation took place within Joseph. Something about the crucifixion stirred a newfound courage within this man. At long last, Joseph stood up to be counted.

A lot of us are like that. We are willing to go along with Christianity, as long as there is no price to pay. But it doesn't take much—a little ridicule, a raised eyebrow, a reproachful comment—and we hide our Christian beliefs. But for some of us, a moment comes when the chips are down, when a choice is thrust on us. Do we stand with Christ or not? Are we followers of Christ, or are we ashamed of Christ? If our faith is genuine, if our relationship with Christ is real, then we stand up and say, "Yes, I'm a Christian too." Thank God for Joseph of Arimathea, who at last found the courage to stand up for what he believed.

If We Will Come

At the close of Mark's account, the writer confronts us with three profound and cataclysmic events, three narrative threads that combine to form one strong cord of truth.

During the last three hours of Jesus' life, a mysterious and terrible darkness comes over the land. At the end of that darkness comes what has been called "Emmanuel's orphaned cry"—*"Eloi, Eloi, lama sabachthani?* My God, my God, why have you forsaken me?"

Almost immediately after that cry, Jesus dismisses His spirit. It is important to understand that He didn't simply die; He dismissed His spirit. He wasn't put to death. He gave up His life. His death was deliberate and voluntary. He wasn't a victim; He was a sacrifice.

A half-mile away, in the court of the temple, within the sacred enclosure of the holy place, something amazing happened. The great veil that enclosed the Holy of Holies was torn from top to bottom. That veil marked off a place where only the high priest was permitted to enter once a year. Now, as if by an invisible hand, that veil was split, and the Holy of Holies was exposed.

These three events are tied together to form one significant, meaningful truth. The orphan cry in the darkness of the cross, the dismissing of the spirit of Jesus, and the rending of the veil in the temple—Mark brings them all together so that we can understand their meaning.

When Jesus called out, "My God, my God, why have you forsaken me?" many of the bystanders must have recognized the opening words of Psalm 22. When you read through that psalm, it is as if you are reading Jesus' version of the crucifixion. There is no adequate explanation for Jesus' question except that which Paul gives in 2 Corinthians 5:21: "God made him who had no sin to be sin for us, so that in him we might become the righteousness of God."

I don't think it's possible for us to remotely understand the depths of separation and loneliness Jesus felt at the moment He became sin for us. We cannot grasp what it means. But we can know this. The awful sense of aloneness and darkness that wrenched such a cry from the throat of Christ is what lies ahead of us if He is not our Lord and Savior. He took on Himself the awful penalty that we have earned by our sin.

Then Jesus dismisses His spirit, and the veil of the temple is torn. Why? Why did the veil split in two?

It was God's dramatic way of saying for all time that the way into His heart is wide open. Anyone who wishes to be saved may come. The priests who plotted against Jesus, the Roman governor who signed His death warrant, the soldiers who drove the nails into His flesh, the bystanders who mocked and wagged their heads—all, all, all may come. That is what the torn veil means. The penalty has been paid for the hateful, the corrupt, the cruel, the selfish, the murderous. The price of sin has been paid in full.

Os Guinness tells the story of a Russian Jewish man, a dissident in the former Soviet Union. The Soviet authorities arrested him for antigovernment activities, and he was tried, convicted, and sentenced to fifteen years in the gulag, the Soviet system of forced labor camps. Yet God used the gulag in this man's life, because while he was imprisoned, a fellow prisoner shared the gospel with him, and he became a Christian.

The man had a four-year-old son at the time of his arrest. During his fifteen years in the gulag, under conditions approaching those of a Nazi death camp, only two things sustained him: his newfound faith in the Lord Jesus Christ and the hope of seeing his son again.

Finally, his fifteen-year sentence completed, the man was released. When he was reunited with his son, the man hardly recognized this big, strapping nineteen-year-old as the boy he remembered. With a thrill of excitement, he noticed that his son was wearing a cross around his neck. The father told his son about finding the Lord during his imprisonment. Then he asked the young man, "How did you come to know Jesus Christ?"

The young man seemed confused. "Father, I don't know what you mean," he replied. "I don't believe in Jesus. He's nothing but a myth."

The man's heart sank. "But—you're wearing a cross!"

The nineteen-year-old looked down and fingered the piece of jewelry that dangled from his neck. "Oh, you mean this? For my generation, a cross is just a fashion statement."

How tragic! For all too many people, the cross is nothing but a fashion statement. But for those who have had a life-changing encounter with the Lord of history, the cross is the most profound statement ever made. The apostle Paul tells us, "For the message of the cross is foolishness to those who are perishing, but to us who are being saved it is the power of God" (1 Corinthians 1:18). The cross, once an ugly instrument of torture and death, has become the beautiful, sacred instrument of our eternal life.

thirty

A Rumor of Hope

> ➤ **Mark 16:1–8**

The army of Napoleon Bonaparte had advanced to within six miles of the Austrian town of Feldkirch. The mountain village was undefended, and unless help arrived, it would fall without a struggle. As Napoleon made plans to attack the following morning, Christians gathered to pray together in the little church in the center of town.

It was the night before Easter Sunday, 1805.

At sunrise, the bells of the little church began to ring. The sound of those bells echoed among the mountains and reached the ears of Napoleon. It never occurred to Napoleon that this day was Easter Sunday. When he heard the bells ringing, he mistook them for bells of celebration. He thought that the people of the town were celebrating the arrival of the Austrian army.

Immediately Napoleon canceled the planned attack and moved his troops away from Feldkirch. The town was saved, because the enemy heard the sound of Easter joy and retreated.

As we approach the final chapter of Mark's gospel, the Easter bells are joyously ringing. Our ancient enemy, Death, is in full retreat.

From Despair to Ecstasy

The noted theologian Dr. Carl F. H. Henry once wrote about the resurrected Jesus: "He planted the only durable rumor of hope amid the widespread despair of a hopeless world." A rumor of hope! That is the keynote for our study in Mark 16.

Here, at the entrance to an empty tomb, we hear the first whisperings of that wonderful rumor: "He has risen!" Soon that rumor will begin echoing through the narrow stone-paved streets of Jerusalem: "He has risen!" Then it will be magnified and amplified across the province of Judea: "He has risen!" Ultimately it will shout, like a blast of thunder rolling across an awestruck world: "He has risen!"

But the rumor begins amid hopelessness and despair. Mark writes:

> *When the Sabbath was over, Mary Magdalene, Mary the mother of James, and Salome bought spices so that they might go to anoint Jesus' body. Very early on the first day of the week, just after sunrise, they were on their way to the tomb and they asked each other, "Who will roll the stone away from the entrance of the tomb?"*
>
> *But when they looked up, they saw that the stone, which was very large, had been rolled away. As they entered the tomb, they saw a young man dressed in a white robe sitting on the right side, and they were alarmed.*
>
> *"Don't be alarmed," he said. "You are looking for Jesus the Nazarene, who was crucified. He has risen! He is not here. See the place where they laid him. But go, tell his disciples and Peter, 'He is going ahead of you into Galilee. There you will see him, just as he told you.' "*

Trembling and bewildered, the women went out and fled from the tomb. They said nothing to anyone, because they were afraid. (MARK 16:1–8)

There Mark ends his story. (The earliest and most reliable Greek manuscripts do not contain verses 9 through 20, and it is almost certain that Mark did not write those verses. However, I believe that God intended us to have verses 9 through 20 as part of His Word, and we will see why as we examine those verses in the next and final chapter of this book.)

Mark's account of Jesus' resurrection opens with the words "when the Sabbath was over." The other gospels do not mention the Sabbath (Saturday), but Mark gives us this brief account of it. The Saturday before the resurrection must have been the darkest day these disciples had ever experienced—a day of shattered hopes, broken dreams, guilt, shame, desolation, and fear. It was a day in which the future looked like a blank wall, devoid of hope or possibility. Why go on? Why bother with living? The Lord was dead, and the disciples had abandoned Him and failed Him. All the once-bright dreams of a coming kingdom, with Jesus as King, were ended forever, or so it seemed.

Perhaps you have some inkling of what the followers of Jesus felt on that Saturday between the cross and the empty tomb. Perhaps you know the shame and guilt of having abandoned or denied your Lord. Perhaps you know the depression and hopelessness of seeing your goals set aside, your dreams shattered. It may be that someone you loved and had been building a future with has suddenly been snatched away from you. Now your future looks like a blank wall. You wonder, why go on? Life seems like a dreary, endless Saturday, and Sunday is never coming.

If that is how you feel, then this story is dedicated to you. You may not be able to see it now, but there is a resurrection in your future. I can't tell you what shape or form it will take. But God is in the business of turning dark Saturdays into glorious Sundays. Your open tomb is coming. Prepare to be amazed.

I think it is instructive, as we read the various gospel accounts of the resurrection, to observe that none of these accounts deal with the events of that terrible Saturday. Mark is the only one who mentions that day, and he does so in passing: "when the Sabbath was over." What does that tell us? It means that when the time came for the disciples to sit down and write their accounts, the memory of that dark Sabbath was so swallowed up by the joy of the resurrection that it was hardly worth mentioning.

Mark 16 begins with the darkest day in human history but ends with the discovery of the empty tomb. We see the women who found the empty tomb, and they are leaving that place full of such joy and explosive hope that they dare not breathe a word to anyone. Look closely at the last two sentences of this passage: "Trembling and bewildered [Greek *ekstasis*], the women went out and fled from the tomb. They said nothing to anyone, because they were afraid [Greek *phobeo*]." I have added the Greek words to these sentences so that we can see more clearly what Mark is telling us. It would be a mistake to read that last phrase, "they were afraid," in the conventional English sense that these women felt terrified, threatened, frightened, or scared.

It is true that the Greek word used here for "afraid," *phobeo,* is often used in the New Testament to mean "terrified, struck with fear or alarm." But that word is also commonly used to mean "struck with awe and amazement" and even "filled with reverence, worship, and pious obedience." And the previous sentence makes the meaning clear. The New International Version poorly translates the previous sentence, saying that the women were "trembling and bewildered," when a more accurate rendering would be "trembling and astonished." The Greek word that the New International Version translates as "bewildered" is *ekstasis*, from which we get our English word "ecstasy." *Ekstasis* means to be amazed, to be beside oneself with profound awe (especially religious awe), to be thrown into a state of mingled startlement and wonderment. So these women were not terrified or frightened, nor were they bewildered and confused. They were caught up in an ecstasy of wonder over the discovery they had made: Jesus is alive!

If you had just stumbled onto the proof of the resurrection, proof that the one you loved and thought dead was miraculously alive, what would you feel? Exactly what those women felt: trembling *ekstasis* and awestruck *phobeo*. So let's go back through this account and understand why this was true, why these women were so suddenly transported from the depths of despair to the trembling heights of ecstasy at the sight of an empty tomb.

The Tomb and the Grave Clothes

The first thing to be examined in Mark's account of the resurrection is the stone that had sealed the body of Jesus inside the tomb. Mark records:

> *When the Sabbath was over, Mary Magdalene, Mary the mother of James, and Salome bought spices so that they might go to anoint Jesus' body. Very early on the first day of the week, just after sunrise, they were on their way to the tomb and they asked each other, "Who will roll the stone away from the entrance of the tomb?"*

But when they looked up, they saw that the stone, which was very large, had been rolled away. (MARK 16:1–4)

The women came full of worry and concern over the stone that blocked the mouth of the tomb, but when they arrived, the stone was rolled away. You can visit the Garden Tomb in Jerusalem, which many scholars and historians believe was the tomb of Jesus. We can't know for certain that it is the actual tomb, but we do know that it fits the description of the gospel accounts. I believe it is the tomb of Jesus.

If you visit the Garden Tomb, you will find that the stone is no longer there. It was removed or destroyed sometime during the decades or centuries after Christ. But you can see a narrow groove carved in the stone in front of the empty tomb. The massive, disk-shaped stone was rolled in this groove to either seal or unseal the tomb. The entrance to the tomb is almost as tall as a man, so the stone used to cover that entrance must have weighed at least a thousand pounds. That's why these women were concerned about the stone. Unless someone moved the stone, they would not be able to anoint Jesus' body with spices and burial perfumes.

When the women arrived, they were shocked to find that the stone already had been rolled back. The tomb was open.

Matthew tells us that very early, long before daybreak, an angel had come and rolled back the stone. His face was like light-ning, brilliantly shining, so that he dazzled and dismayed the guards who were standing watch over the tomb. They fell to the ground as dead men. When they recovered their senses, they stumbled off in fear.

Later, when the women arrived, there was no sign of anyone outside the tomb, but the door of the tomb was open. This told them that something amazing had happened. So they crept closer, looked inside—and the body of Jesus was gone. That which they had come to anoint was no longer there.

The empty tomb has been the answer to skeptics for twenty centuries. No one has ever been able to explain it. Every generation has tried. For example, Hugh Schonfield's *The Passover Plot,* which is subtitled *A New Interpretation of the Life and Death of Jesus,* is the oldest interpretation of all. It attempts to explain away the resurrection by relying on the lie circulated in the first century by Roman soldiers: the body was stolen. No one, including Schonfield, has ever successfully explained how this could have happened. If the enemies of Christianity had stolen the body, they would have readily produced it to prove Jesus was dead. And it would have been impossible for Jesus' friends and followers to steal the body, for Roman guards were stationed at the tomb, which was sealed.

The most amazing fact of all—a fact that immediately confronted these women as they entered the tomb—was the presence of the grave clothes. The body was gone, but the grave clothes were left behind. In Luke 24:12 and John 20:6–8, we find a description of the grave clothes. The cloth that had been around the Lord's head was neatly folded and separated from the other grave clothes. The grave clothes, the strips of linen that had been wound around the body, had not been unwrapped or unwound. They were lying in the form of a person, as though the body had vanished from inside them.

The other gospels tell us that when these women left the tomb, they ran to the disciples and told them the news; then Peter and John came running to the tomb. When Peter and John saw the grave clothes, they were convinced that Jesus had risen. The presence of the grave clothes, together with the way they were arranged, has never been explained.

The power of the evidence, including the evidence of the empty tomb, was one of the reasons Christianity spread so quickly in the early days of the church. Hundreds of eyewitnesses could confirm every detail of the gospel story. There was even physical evidence of the resurrection. No one had to question whether the tomb was truly empty or not, because the tomb was there for anyone to inspect, just beyond the walls of the city. Anyone in Jerusalem could take a fifteen-minute walk to the tomb and see that the disciples were telling the truth.

That is why the Jewish historian Flavius Josephus, whose writings are considered authoritative because they are based on documentary evidence and interviews with eyewitnesses, records the story of Jesus and the resurrection without raising the slightest hint of doubt or uncertainty. In his *Antiquities of the Jews,* Josephus writes:

> Now, there was about this time, Jesus, a wise man, if it be lawful to call him a man, for he was a doer of wonderful works—a teacher of such men as receive the truth with pleasure. He drew over to himself many of the Jews, and many of the Gentiles. He was [the] Christ; and when Pilate, at the suggestion of the principal men amongst us, had condemned him to the cross, those that loved him at the first did not forsake him, for he appeared to them alive again the third day as the divine prophets had foretold these and ten thousand other wonderful things concerning him; and the tribe of Christians, so named from him, are not extinct at this day.[1]

Although skeptics and rationalists would like to dismiss the resurrection with a wave of the hand, the evidence does not allow it. The resurrection is not a legend. It is the central fact of human history.

The Message of the Angel

So Jesus is no longer in the tomb, but the tomb is not unoccupied. Mark records:

> *As they entered the tomb, they saw a young man dressed in a white robe sitting on the right side, and they were alarmed.*
>
> *"Don't be alarmed," he said. "You are looking for Jesus the Nazarene, who was crucified. He has risen! He is not here. See the place where they laid him. But go, tell his disciples and Peter, 'He is going ahead of you into Galilee. There you will see him, just as he told you.'"* (MARK 16:5–7)

The angel's message to these women contains the answer to twenty centuries of skepticism. The angel first says, "You are looking for Jesus the Nazarene, who was crucified." Many attempts have been made to explain away the resurrection. The women went to the wrong tomb. The disciples invented a second Jesus to impersonate the risen Lord when the resurrection failed to take place. Jesus wasn't dead when He was buried; He was unconscious, and the cold conditions in the tomb revived Him. All such theories run aground on the words spoken by the angel. He says that Jesus of Nazareth, the one who was crucified, has risen. The identity of the former occupant of that tomb is firmly established.

The angel also says, "He has risen! He is not here." The risen Jesus is not a disembodied spirit. The resurrection was not a spiritual resurrection but a bodily resurrection. The body of Jesus rose from the dead. Some cults and groups argue against a bodily resurrection, claiming that only the spirit of Jesus rose, and He now lives as a purely spiritual being. But the Bible does not allow such a theory.

Furthermore, the angel tells them, "But go, tell his disciples and Peter, 'He is going ahead of you into Galilee. There you will see him, just as he told you.' " The angel identifies a specific geographical spot on the face of the earth as the place where Jesus will be found: Galilee. This statement underscores the claim of Scripture that Jesus is alive, that He rose bodily, and that He appeared to people at a specific juncture of time and space.

Notice also the gentle, compassionate touch in those words. The angel tells the women to give a special message of hope to Peter. The last time we saw Peter in this account, he was standing in the courtyard of the high priest during the trial of Jesus. A servant girl was following him around, accusing him of being one of Jesus' disciples, and he was avoiding her, running from her, denying the truth, trembling in fear. But angel says, "Tell his disciples and Peter."

By this statement, we see that Jesus is available to individuals, not just to groups or organizations or movements or churches or to the world. The Lord is interested in Peter, in individuals, in me and in you. His personal concern for individuals has been the hallmark of Christianity ever since. Each of us can know Him personally and intimately, not just as a figure of history, or as a coming king, or as a great religious figure, but in one-to-one communion and intimate fellowship.

The angel also said, "He is going ahead of you into Galilee. There you will see him, just as he told you." Just as He told you. The angel is affirming the trustworthiness of the Lord's promises. The words of Jesus are faithful words. The resurrection should not have taken His followers by surprise, because He had already said He would be crucified, rise on the third day, and meet them. The angel's message is not a new message but a repetition of what they had already heard from the Lord's lips. Everything He said will be fulfilled.

The Rumor Spreads

The empty tomb, the empty grave clothes, and the message of the angel had a profound effect on these women. It filled them with hope, with joy, with excitement. In an instant, they were transported from the depths of despair to an ecstasy beyond our imagining. So they went out with gladness to begin spreading this rumor of hope, just as the angel had told them—the only durable rumor of hope the world has ever known.

This glorious rumor was hastened along by the appearances of Jesus before witness after witness. The first appearance was to Mary Magdalene. John's gospel tells us that after the other women left the tomb, Mary Magdalene lingered. There, in the early morning light, Jesus appeared to her. At first she thought He was the gardener, but when He spoke her name, she knew who He was. He showed Himself alive first of all to Mary. She went running with the news, and Peter and John came to the tomb, saw the grave clothes, and were convinced.

In Luke's gospel we read that later in the afternoon, Jesus also appeared to two disciples on the road to Emmaus. In that strange encounter, He walked with them and taught them from the Scriptures about Himself. Yet for some mysterious reason, they did not recognize Him until that evening, when He broke bread and gave it to them. At the moment He gave them the bread, their eyes were opened—and Jesus vanished from their sight. The two disciples said to each other, "Were not our hearts burning within us while he talked with us on the road and opened the Scriptures to us?" (Luke 24:32).

John 20:19–25 tells us that on the evening of the first Easter Sunday, in the Upper Room, the disciples were gathered. Suddenly Jesus appeared among them and showed Himself alive to them. A week later, Jesus returned to that same room. That time He presented His wounded hands and side to doubting Thomas, so that Thomas would be convinced and believe.

And what about the angel's message to the women? "He is going ahead of you into Galilee. There you will see him, just as he told you." I believe this is a reference to that intimate account we find in John 21. There, Peter has returned to the Sea of Galilee, and he goes out to fish. Perhaps, having failed and denied his Lord, Peter feels he is fit only to return to his former life as a fisherman. He still does not understand the future Jesus has planned for him.

So Peter goes out in the boat with six other disciples. Jesus stands on the shore, but just as the disciples on the Emmaus road didn't recognize Him, neither do Peter and his companions. When Peter is unable to catch any fish, Jesus calls out to them and tells them to cast their nets on the other side of the boat. The result is a vast catch that strains their nets almost to the breaking point.

Returning to shore, Peter and the others find Jesus broiling fish over a fire, and He also has some bread. At this point, they know they are in the presence of the resurrected Lord.

There, on the beach of the Sea of Galilee, a beautiful scene takes place. Jesus says to Peter, "Peter, do you love me?" And Peter replies, "You know I do, Lord." Three times Jesus asks, three times Peter answers, and the third time Peter says, "Lord, you know all things; you know that I love you." Then Jesus gave Peter his commission: "Feed my sheep." With that, Peter was fully reinstated, and he had a new job description. He was no longer to be a fisherman but a shepherd—a pastor to the flock of God. That became Peter's lifelong mission. And that is why the angel had the women at the tomb convey a personal word to Peter.

That was not the last appearance of the resurrected Lord. Paul tells us that Jesus later appeared to more than five hundred people at one time, on a mountain in Galilee.

Still later, in the village of Bethany, not far from Jerusalem, Jesus showed Himself for the last time. He led His disciples from Bethany to the Mount of Olives. From the top of that mountain, He was taken from them and disappeared behind a cloud, and they saw Him no longer.

Believing Is Seeing

One of the powerful impressions left by Mark's account of the resurrection is this: the women believed, although they did not see. They saw an empty tomb. They saw empty grave clothes. But they did not see the Lord. Nevertheless they believed. They were filled with ecstatic awe, because they believed.

Of course, Mary Magdalene stayed behind and had a personal encounter with the Lord, but the other women believed without seeing. Later, some of these same women might have been in the Upper Room and saw the Lord appear. But seeing Him did not make them believe. They believed before they saw Him, so for them, believing was seeing.

How wonderful it must have been to have seen the risen Lord! All those who did so were regarded with unusual respect and awe in the early Christian community. Of course, not all were privileged to do that.

When Jesus appeared to Thomas and invited him to touch His wounds, Jesus told Thomas, "Because you have seen me, you have believed; blessed are those who have not seen and yet have believed" (John 20:29). In other words, "Thomas, you think seeing is believing. You're mistaken, my friend. Believing is seeing. Happy are those who, having not seen, still believe." With those words, Jesus is looking down the long tunnel of ages to come, including our age. He is seeing millions of believers, including you and me, and He is affirming that we love Him and believe in Him, even though we have never seen Him.

Although Peter is one of those who walked with Jesus, talked with Him, and knew Him intimately, Peter also wants us to know that believing is seeing. He writes:

> *Though you have not seen him, you love him; and even though you do not see him now, you believe in him and are filled with an inexpressible and glorious joy.* (1 PETER 1:8)

That has been the experience of millions of believers, beginning with that first Easter morning and continuing to this day. We have not seen the risen Lord, for He departed this realm of visible things many centuries ago. But we have the testimony. We have the evidence. As Luke writes in Acts 1:3, "he showed himself to these men and gave many convincing proofs that he was alive." These convincing proofs are persuasive to the intellect and encouraging to the soul. They awaken hope within us, just as those women found their hope awakened by the empty tomb and the word of the angel.

Out of that hope, a rumor was born. It is the only durable rumor of hope the world has ever known. For those who have not yet heard this wonderful rumor, the world is still a dark place, as empty of hope as that terrible Saturday between the cross and the resurrection. But we have this rumor to share with the world. It is like a brilliant light at midnight. It is like food in a land of famine. It is the good news, the greatest rumor ever told. And if we do not go out and spread it, who will?

Some years ago, I was in Mexico, where I had the privilege of visiting with Eunice Pike. She and her brother, Dr. Kenneth Pike, were accomplished linguists with Wycliffe Bible translators. Miss Pike told me about the early days of Wycliffe Bible translators in Mexico. Cameron Townsend, the founder of the organization, had gone to Mexico to obtain permission from the Mexican government to translate the Scriptures into the languages of the Indian tribes. The government officials opposed this work, because they believed that if the Indians had the Bible in their languages, it would cause unrest. I'm not sure what the rationale behind this thinking was, but that was what they claimed. Townsend did everything he knew, talked to every official he could find, and had all of his Christian friends praying that God would open this door. But the officials of the Mexican government refused to budge.

Finally Townsend decided to stop pressing the issue. Instead, he and his wife would go live in an obscure Indian village, learn the language, minister to the people as best they could, and wait for God to move. They lived in a tiny trailer in the village, and it was not long before he noticed that the fountain in the center of the plaza produced beautiful, clear spring water. But the water from the fountain ran down the hill and was wasted. He suggested that the Indians plant something in the watered area and make use of it. Soon they were growing twice as much food as before, and their economy blossomed. The Indians were grateful.

Townsend wrote the story and sent it to a Mexican newspaper. After the story was published, it was passed along to the president of Mexico, Lazaro Cardenas. The Mexican president was amazed that an American would take such a deep interest in the people of an obscure Indian village. "I must meet this man!" he said. So he got into his limousine and was driven out to the village. Townsend happened to be standing in the plaza when the president's car pulled up. Told that the man in the car was the president of Mexico, Townsend seized the opportunity, approached the limousine, and introduced himself to the president.

"You're the man I've come here to see!" said the president. Townsend explained his desire to translate the Scriptures into the Indian languages. At that moment, Cameron Townsend forged a lifelong friendship with President Cardenas. God used that friendship to open many doors for the gospel.

Cameron Townsend spread the rumor of hope by going into the world, living among the people, and making a difference in their lives. That is something we can all do in our neighborhoods, our apartment buildings, our workplaces, the schools where we study or teach, the gyms where we work out, and every other place we spend time and encounter people. We have a wonderful rumor of hope, so let's spread it wherever we go.

thirty-one

Alive Forever!

➤ **Mark 16:9–20**

One of those who sailed aboard the ill-fated *Titanic* in 1912 was Scottish evangelist John Harper. Accompanied by his six-year-old daughter, Nana, Harper was sailing to America as the newly called pastor of Chicago's Moody Church. After the ship struck an iceberg and began sinking, Harper put his daughter into a lifeboat, then called out to the people on the tilting deck, "Women, children, and unsaved into the lifeboats!" He was ready for eternity, but his love for others was so great that he wanted any who were unsaved to have every opportunity to live and find Jesus.

When the lifeboats were gone, Harper preached the message of salvation to those who, awaiting death, remained huddled on the deck of the *Titanic*. He gave his lifejacket to another man and then jumped into the water, where he clung to a piece of wreckage.

The dread numbness of hypothermia seized Harper as he clung to life in the icy sea. After just a few minutes in the water, his heartbeat was slowing and his muscles were becoming rigid. He could feel his consciousness ebbing away, but then he saw a man floating nearby. With teeth chattering uncontrollably, Harper called out, "Man! Are you saved?"

"No," the stranger answered, "I am not!"

Harper explained the gospel to the man, then said, "Do you believe?"

"Yes!" the stranger answered. And there, in the middle of the icy North Atlantic, this stranger gave his heart to Jesus Christ. A short time later, this new believer was pulled from the water by a passing lifeboat, but Harper was never found. For years afterward, that survivor—John Harper's last convert—told the story of the evangelist's last words. Those words gave a lost soul the power to believe and live forever.

The Theme: Believe!

We come at last to the closing verses of the gospel of Mark. The key to this passage is the word "believe." This emphasis on belief caps the thrust of Mark's gospel, because it is clear from our study of Mark that he does not present the Christian story as merely an account of the life of a crucified martyr. Mark underscores the fact that the death and resurrection of Jesus Christ is something to be believed. It is intended to change our lives.

The primary emphasis in these closing verses is on the belief of the apostles whom Jesus was to send out into the world with the story of His death and resurrection. This passage can be divided into three parts:

Part 1: The Basis of Apostolic Belief (Mark 16:9–14)
Part 2: The Call to Apostolic Preaching (Mark 16:15–16)
Part 3: The Apostolic Witness Confirmed (Mark 16:17–20)

As we have noted, Mark 16:9–20 is not found in the oldest and most reliable Greek manuscripts. Because of this fact, some Bible scholars question whether these verses belong to the gospel of Mark. I would point out that while this is true, it is also true that the overwhelming majority of the Greek manuscripts do contain these verses. Also, two of the earliest church fathers, writing from the beginning of the second century, quote from this passage. From the beginning, the church has accepted these twelve verses as God's inspired Word, even though they may not have come from the hand of Mark.

In this passage you will note one immediate change from the rest of Mark's gospel: it is not in narrative form. Up to this point, Mark has been narrating in sequence the events as they happened to Jesus, bringing us to the crucifixion and resurrection. This last section, however, does not narrate events. It briefly summarizes events that occurred over a period of about forty days. This change to summary form perhaps indicates that someone other than Mark wrote this passage.

We must remember, however, that the human authorship of this passage does not matter. If God is the author of Mark 16:9–20, then it is God's Word for us, regardless of whose hand held the pen.

Part 1: The Basis of Apostolic Belief

Let's delve into the first section of this passage and examine the basis of apostolic belief.

> *When Jesus rose early on the first day of the week, he appeared first to Mary Magdalene, out of whom he had driven seven demons. She went and told those who had been with him and who were mourning and weeping. When they heard that Jesus was alive and that she had seen him, they did not believe it.* (MARK 16:9–11)

Immediately the writer underscores the fact that these disciples, when they heard of Mary's experience with Jesus, did not believe it. You remember how the women had come to the tomb early in the morning, at the first light of dawn, and found the stone rolled away and saw the angel. The angel told them that Jesus had risen, as He had promised He would. But the women did not see Jesus then.

Mary Magdalene, according to John's account, went ahead of the other women, saw the empty tomb, then ran to tell Peter and John. While she went to tell those two disciples, evidently the other women were with the angel at the tomb, so Mary Magdalene did not hear the angel's explanation.

Peter and John ran to the tomb. Peter went inside and saw the grave clothes lying there still wrapped as though they were around a body, along with the cloth that had been around Jesus' head, now neatly folded and placed aside. This convinced Peter and John that Jesus was risen, but they still had not seen him.

Meanwhile, Mary Magdalene returned more slowly to the tomb. John tells us that she was in the garden, weeping. There she saw a man she mistook for the gardener. She asked the man where they had taken the body of Jesus. At that moment, He spoke her name, and she knew the man was Jesus. She fell at His feet and worshiped Him. This was the first appearance of the risen Lord to one of His followers. Mark agrees with John that Jesus came first to Mary Magdalene.

Mary Magdalene ran and told the other disciples. But Mark tells us that when Mary told them that Jesus was alive and that she had seen Him, they would not believe her.

Mark's gospel next records the Lord's appearance to two disciples. This is the same appearance that Luke records in Luke 24:13–31, the appearance on the road to Emmaus. Here is the summary of that event as recorded in Mark:

> *Afterward Jesus appeared in a different form to two of them while they were walking in the country. These returned and reported it to the rest; but they did not believe them either.* (Mark 16:12–13)

It was a journey of some eleven miles from Jerusalem to the little village of Emmaus. As these two disciples (one, says Luke, was named Cleopas) were walking on that road, Mark says that Jesus "appeared in a different form" so that they didn't recognize Him. The three of them carried on a long conversation, during which Jesus began with Moses and the prophets and showed them all the many Old Testament passages that referred to Messiah. Although Jesus had told His disciples many times that He would be crucified and raised again, it was only at this time, as Jesus led them through all the messianic prophecies of the Old Testament, that they began to understand.

At the end of their journey, as they sat at table with Him, He broke the bread and blessed it. They suddenly recognized Him. Perhaps they saw the nail prints in His hands as He held out the bread. Perhaps there was something in the way He blessed the bread and broke it that they had seen before, at one of the great feeding miracles, perhaps, or in the Upper Room. In any case, their eyes were opened, they recognized Him—and instantly He disappeared.

These two disciples returned to Jerusalem and told the eleven apostles what they had seen, but again, the apostles did not believe them. So Jesus took an even more direct approach.

> *Later Jesus appeared to the Eleven as they were eating; he rebuked them for their lack of faith and their stubborn refusal to believe those who had seen him after he had risen.*
> (Mark 16:14)

The writer of these lines, whether Mark or a co-author, wants us to understand the climate of persistent and stubborn unbelief that prevailed among the apostles after the resurrection. Despite the many prophecies and predictions Jesus made of His death and resurrection, the Eleven found it difficult to accept that Jesus was now risen and living among them.

The significant thing is that Jesus expected the Eleven to believe, even though they had not seen Him. He wanted and expected them to believe the reports of the eyewitnesses who had seen Him. They were trustworthy persons and were reporting what they had experienced. After all the wonders they had seen Jesus perform, after all He had taught them, these reports should have been enough to convince the disciples that Jesus was raised from the dead. He is so concerned about their unbelief that He rebukes them, much as He often had to rebuke them for unbelief in the years He ministered among them.

When Jesus takes them to task for their refusal to believe the eyewitnesses, you see the importance He attaches to the eyewitnesses and their credibility. This same importance is underscored in His confrontation with Thomas. The doubting disciple had heard the eyewitness reports and refused to believe. He demanded physical proof.

But Jesus knows that the Christian faith and the Christian church will never be built on a basis of physical evidence. It will be based on belief—not blind belief, but belief in credible reports by reliable eyewitnesses. Jesus is telling the Eleven, and He is telling you and me, "When trustworthy witnesses report what they have seen— and especially when they only report what I already told you to expect—don't be so stubborn and skeptical. Respond with belief."

These Eleven were granted a great privilege. They saw the risen Lord with their own eyes. The moment could have been made even more joyful if the Lord could have appeared to them and commended them for their faith instead of rebuking their unbelief. The good news for you and me is that our faith rests on a solid foundation. Even though we have not seen Him face to face, we have reliable eyewitness accounts, and we have this special word of approval from the Lord: "Blessed are those who have not seen and yet have believed" (John 20:29).

Part 2: The Call to Apostolic Preaching

After rebuking the disciples for their unbelief, Jesus gives them a command, which we know today as the Great Commission.

> *He said to them, "Go into all the world and preach the good news to all creation. Whoever believes and is baptized will be saved, but whoever does not believe will be condemned."* (Mark 16:15–16)

Translators and Bible teachers tend to emphasize one word as the primary imperative of the Great Commission, and that word is the verb "go." That, I believe, is a mistaken emphasis. The central command in the Great Commission is not "go" but "preach." The Lord's words should more accurately be rendered, "As you go into all the world, preach the good news to all creation." The verb "go" is not a command; it's a given. Our Lord takes it for granted that as the church grows and develops, the good news will spread. He expects His church to be on the go. His command relates to what we are to do as we go, and His command is that we are to preach the gospel.

In making this point, I am not diminishing the emphasis on missions, for the fact that the church will be a missionary enterprise, a going enterprise, is an accepted fact. The question is, when we go, what are we to do? The answer: preach the good news. And what is the good news? That Jesus died and rose again. Nothing could be clearer than that.

The good news is not a lofty, complicated theological principle that requires years of study to understand. The good news is the cross and the empty tomb. That's all, and that's enough.

The good news transforms lives. The good news restores broken families. The good news is the solution to human evil. The good news rescues us from sin and despair and makes us alive forever.

I should point out that some people get confused as to what the good news is. Some people think that the good news is that heaven awaits us after we die, or that God is love, or some other wonderful thing. This is true, and it is good, but it is not the good news that Jesus commissioned us to preach. It is not the good news of the cross and the resurrection. Heaven is not the good news; it is merely a result of the good news.

The good news is that the power of evil and sin has been shattered by the cross, and the power of death has been broken by the empty tomb. The Lord is alive, and He lives in us and through us, giving us the power to truly live. This is the good news that we should be preaching as we go.

I once went to a Christian conference where a number of speakers talked about how the Christian faith influences family issues. Some of the speakers were insightful and clear, but others seemed to garble the gospel message in an appalling way. One speaker gave an outline of Christian history that went like this. The disciples gathered around Jesus, and He taught them how to love one another. The disciples then taught this same lesson to the early church; as the early Christians taught others how to love, the Christian cause spread throughout the world. Our task is to continue teaching more and more people to love one another, so that the world can become a vast loving community.

Well, that sounds very nice, doesn't it? Who would claim that people should *not* love one another? Jesus taught that we should. But that is not the gospel. That is not the good news we are to preach as we go. Nowhere in this speaker's presentation was there any mention of the death and resurrection of Jesus Christ. Here was Christianity without any good news. And Christianity without the good news is not Christianity; it is hogwash.

Some people try to have Christianity without the cross, because the cross is bloody and offensive. Others try to have Christianity without the resurrection, because the resurrection is mysterious and supernatural and can't be scientifically explained. It violates our rationalist sensibilities, and surely no educated person believes in such things anymore.

But the fact is that Christianity without a cross and an empty tomb is not Christianity. It is mere pabulum dispensed in the vain hope that we will all become better people. It is mere moral teaching. The problem with mere moral teaching is that it is impossible to live by. People don't need to be told what to do and how to live. We all know that we should be honest, kind, loving, sexually pure, and so forth, but we lack the power to live as we should.

What we need is not moral teaching but transformation. We need to be changed at the core of our being so that we can do what we already know is right. That is what the Bible calls salvation. That is why Jesus said, "Whoever believes [this good news] and is baptized will be saved, but whoever does not believe will be condemned."

Some people may quibble over the word "baptism." Some take baptism to an unwarranted extreme and say it is necessary not only to believe but also to be baptized. They say that if you believe and are not baptized, you will never be saved. This view is unsupported by the rest of Scripture. What Jesus means is that belief ought to be real, and the reality of that inward belief is demonstrated by the outward action of baptism. Only belief that changes us within and alters our outward lifestyle is real belief. The way we demonstrate this change is by being baptized.

Baptism does not add anything to what the belief alone has accomplished; it only demonstrates it. If for some reason you cannot be baptized, that does not affect salvation—a truth that is affirmed by the Lord's promise to the repentant thief on the cross: "I tell you the truth, today you will be with me in paradise" (Luke 23:43). The thief died unbaptized but saved.

God knows and reads the heart. Ordinarily, belief is to be translated into action by the sacrament of baptism, which visibly expresses the fact that we go down into death with Christ and we rise again with Christ to walk with Him in newness of life. But it is not baptism that saves. We are saved by grace through faith in Christ.

Some people feel uncomfortable with that word "saved." They associate it with the kind of person who rushes up to you, grabs you by the lapels, and demands to know, "Are you saved?" This kind of buttonhole evangelism has given genuine evangelism a bad name. However, I think those who struggle against the word "saved" have not understood the hopelessness of humanity.

When you truly understand the depths of your sin and you cast yourself on the mercy of God to save you, then you finally know that only one possible word fits. Jesus Christ didn't die to improve us, or make us nicer people, or give us a bit of an assist. Jesus died to save us. As an unknown poet observed,

> Your best resolutions must wholly be waived,
> Your highest ambitions be crossed;

You need never think that you'll ever be saved,
Until you've learned that you're lost.

The reality is that we are like drowning men and women, lost far out at sea, helpless and without hope—unless someone comes to save us. This is not a mere metaphor or analogy. This is cold, hard, spiritual fact: Jesus saves. And the good news is that if we believe in the Lord Jesus Christ, in His death and resurrection, we will be saved.

Part 3: The Apostolic Witness Confirmed

This supernatural event, the resurrection, is under intense attack in our day. But this should not surprise us, because the resurrection was under equally intense attack in the first century. Jesus knew that pressure would be brought against the apostles in an effort to force them to deny the reality of the resurrection. So the Lord's next word to them was a promise to confer on the apostles certain signs that would accompany them and encourage them in preaching the gospel.

> *"And these signs will accompany those who believe: In my name they will drive out demons; they will speak in new tongues; they will pick up snakes with their hands; and when they drink deadly poison, it will not hurt them at all; they will place their hands on sick people, and they will get well."* (MARK 16:17–18)

This passage raises a controversial question with regard to the gifts of the Holy Spirit. Probably no greater debate divides the church than the issue of the charismatic movement. I frankly do not like to use the word "charismatic" to describe a movement that stresses one or two gifts of the Spirit, for all the gifts of the Spirit are charismatic. "Charismatic" comes from the Greek word *charis*, meaning "gift." In 1 Corinthians 12 the apostle says that every Christian has one or more charismatic gifts.

It might be better to call the charismatic movement by a different name, such as the glossolalia movement. The term "glossolalia" comes from the Greek *glossa* ("tongue") and *lalia* ("to speak"), and this is a more accurate term for a movement that stresses speaking in tongues. This movement relies heavily on the closing verses of Mark's gospel for biblical support of its views.

> *"And these signs will accompany those who believe: In my name they will drive out demons; they will speak in new tongues; they will pick up snakes with their hands; and when they drink deadly poison, it will not hurt them at all; they will place their hands on sick people, and they will get well."*
> (MARK 16:17–18)

One can easily interpret these verses as though Jesus is saying that such signs will accompany everyone who believes. The text makes it seem this way, and this is how many interpreters have understood this passage. The biggest problem with this view is that for twenty centuries, millions of people have been converted and have believed the gospel, without evidencing any of these signs.

Some people have claimed to manifest these signs in certain instances, but if this is to be understood as the norm, then these signs would be everywhere. Every time a person became a Christian, some of these signs would be manifested. Therefore these miraculous signs ought to be the most frequent occurrence in all Christendom, but they are extremely rare.

What does this tell us? For one thing, it tells us that we have misunderstood this passage if we read it that way. Such an interpretation doesn't square with what God is doing in the world.

I think there is a rather simple solution to the problem. If we put the passage back in its context—the unbelief of the apostles when they were told about the resurrection—then we can see that Jesus is addressing these words to the apostles themselves. When Jesus says to them, "These signs will accompany those who believe," He is speaking about the apostles. I think we can even insert two words without violating the text: "These signs will accompany those *among you* who believe."

Jesus is saying to the apostles, "Now go and preach the gospel in all creation. And to encourage you for those times when you face hostility, I will give you certain gifts or signs. These signs— miraculous acts that only God could perform—will accompany you as you preach the gospel." Let's look at each of these signs in the order Jesus gave them.

"In my name they will drive out demons." The apostles would be given power to deliver people from demons, power to set people free from demonic influence.

"They will speak in new tongues." That is, the apostles would be given power to praise God in a new language. The term "new tongues" means speaking in a language that hasn't been learned. Paul writes, "For anyone who speaks in a tongue does not speak to men but to God. Indeed, no one understands him; he utters mysteries with his spirit" (1 Corinthians 14:2). I don't know why it is hard for many Christians to accept the plain sense of Scripture on this matter. In most quarters of the glossolalia movement, people consider tongues a means of speaking to people, of preaching the gospel, or of conveying messages or prophesying events. Yet Paul states that tongues are for speaking to God, not people. Paul also says that speaking in tongues is an act of praise and thanksgiving to God for His magnificent works, as a sign to unbelievers. Tongues are not given as a sign to believers, but to unbelievers. The apostles were sent out with this sign, and I believe others besides the apostles received this gift as well.

"They will pick up snakes with their hands; when they drink deadly poison, it will not hurt them at all." The apostles would have power to survive physical attacks on their lives. Bitten by a poisonous serpent or administered a poison, they would not die. They would have power to survive such attacks so that the gospel might go out. This would be one of the authenticating signs given to them.

You may have heard that certain backwoods preachers and faith healers will sometimes handle rattlesnakes and drink strychnine as evidence of their faith. These performances usually involve a great deal of showmanship and hoopla. Periodically one of these snake handlers will make news by dying during a public performance. The promise of these apostolic signs was never intended to be used as a publicity stunt or turned into a carnival sideshow.

"They will place their hands on sick people, and they will get well." This sign is the power to heal by the laying on of hands. One of the evidences of this sign is that it would invariably work. The apostles would lay hands on the sick and 100 percent of them would recover. Again, this is a far cry from the hit-or-miss track record of many faith healers today.

It is important to note that the apostle Paul exhibited all of these signs. Paul cast out demons in the name of the Lord Jesus, spoke in tongues to God (he evidently practiced this gift in the synagogue), was bitten by a poisonous snake without being harmed (Acts 28:5), and had power to lay hands on the sick, so that they were healed. He did these things again and again. This is why he once wrote to the Christians in Corinth, "The things that mark an apostle—signs, wonders and miracles—were done among you with great perseverance" (2 Corinthians 12:12).

These, then, are the signs of an apostle. They were authenticating signs to accompany those who first went out with the gospel into an unbelieving and hostile world. This interpretation of these verses is confirmed, I think, by the final paragraph:

> *After the Lord Jesus had spoken to them, he was taken up into heaven and he sat at the right hand of God. Then the disciples went out and preached everywhere, and the Lord worked with them and confirmed his word by the signs that accompanied it.* (MARK 16:19–20)

Thus God's seal of authentication was given to their ministry, and encouragement was added to their faith. We have another reference to these apostolic signs in the letter to the Hebrews.

> *How shall we escape if we ignore such a great salvation? This salvation, which was first announced by the Lord, was confirmed to us by those who heard him. God also testified to it by signs, wonders and various miracles, and gifts of the Holy Spirit distributed according to his will.* (HEBREWS 2:3–4)

So Mark's gospel closes with the Lord in heaven—not "the heavens" far off in space, but the heavenly realms, the invisible dimensions of life here among us. Jesus is not out there somewhere. He is here, living as Lord in the midst of His church, directing its events, planning its strategy, carrying it unto the farthest reaches of the world. In obedience to His command, the apostles scattered throughout the world and preached this good news. Their witness was continually confirmed by these great signs.

And so the foundation was laid for this great building that Paul calls the church, the body of Christ. In Ephesians 2, Paul says that the foundation was laid by the apostles and the prophets, Christ Jesus being the chief cornerstone, on which the whole building grows. This building, made not of bricks and mortar but of the lives of Christian believers, has become a beautiful place of habitation for God.

May God grant that our work will rest on this great foundation that has already been laid and that no person can lay a second time. May we proclaim the good news of Jesus Christ, the good news of the cross, the good news of the resurrection, the good news that all who believe in Him are alive forever.

A pastor in Glasgow, Scotland, told this true story to Billy Graham. A woman in this pastor's parish was in financial difficulty and behind in her rent. So the church took up a collection to help her pay her back rent. The pastor then went to her home to give the money to her. He knocked and knocked at the door, but no one answered. Finally the pastor went away.

Later he saw this woman at the market. He told her he had been to her house, and he told her the purpose of his visit. "I was so disappointed that you weren't home," he said.

The woman's eyes widened. "Oh, was that you?" she said. "I thought it was the landlord, and I was afraid to open the door!"

The good news of Mark's gospel is that Jesus has paid our debt on the cross. Now He is alive forever, and He brings us the gift of eternal life. Jesus stands at the door of our lives, and He knocks. All of His riches are ours for the taking, if we will believe and open the door.

Listen! He's knocking!

What will your answer be?

Notes

Chapter 15: The Way of the Cross

1. C. S. Lewis, *Mere Christianity,* from *The Best of C. S. Lewis* (Washington, D.C.: Canon, 1969), 450.

Chapter 30: The Rumor of Hope

1. Josephus, *The Antiquities of the Jews* 18.3.3, from *The Works of Josephus,* trans. William Whiston (Peabody, Mass.: Hendrickson, 1987).

Note to Reader

The publisher invites you to share your response to the message of this book by writing Discovery House Publishers, Box 3566, Grand Rapids, MI 49501, USA. For information about other Discovery House books, music, or videos, contact us at the same address or call 1-800-653-8333. Find us on the Internet at http://www.dhp.org/ or send e-mail to books@dhp.org.